Christ Our Life

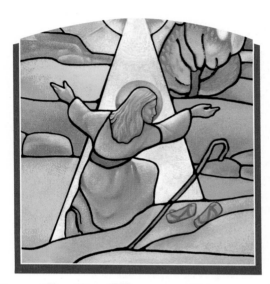

God Calls a People

Authors

Sisters of Notre Dame
Chardon, Ohio

Reviewers

Sister Mary Judith Bucco, S.N.D.

Sister Margaret Mary Friel, S.N.D.

Sister Mary Jean Hoelke, S.N.D.

Sister Mary Cordell Kopec, S.N.D.

Sister Mary Charlotte Manzo, S.N.D.

Sister Ann Mary McLaughlin, S.N.D.

Sister Mary Donnalee Resar, S.N.D.

Sister Katherine Mary Skrabec, S.N.D.

Sister Eileen Marie Skutt, S.N.D.

Sister Mary Jane Vovk, S.N.D.

LOYOLAPRESS.
A JESUIT MINISTRY
Chicago

Nihil Obstat
Reverend John G. Lodge, S.S.L., S.T.D.
Censor Deputatus
May 22, 2007

Imprimatur
Reverend John F. Canary, S.T.L., D.Min.
Vicar General, Archdiocese of Chicago
May 25, 2007

Christ Our Life
found to be in conformity

The Ad Hoc Committee to Oversee the
Use of the Catechism, United States
Conference of Catholic Bishops, has found
the doctrinal content of this catechetical
series, copyright 2009, to be in conformity
with the *Catechism of the Catholic Church.*

The *Nihil Obstat* and *Imprimatur* are official declarations that a book is free of doctrinal and
moral error. No implication is contained therein that those who have granted the *Nihil Obstat* and
Imprimatur agree with the content, opinions, or statements expressed. Nor do they assume any legal
responsibility associated with publication.

Acknowledgments

Excerpts from the *New American Bible* with Revised New
Testament and Psalms Copyright © 1991, 1986, 1970
Confraternity of Christian Doctrine, Inc., Washington, DC.
All rights reserved. No portion of the *New American Bible*
may be reprinted without permission in writing from the
copyright holder.

Excerpts from the English translation of *The Roman Missal* © 2010,
International Commission on English in the Liturgy Corporation
(ICEL); excerpts from the English translation of *Rite of Penance* © 1974,
ICEL; excerpts from the English translation of *A Book of Prayers* ©
1982, ICEL; excerpts from the English translation of *Book of Blessings* ©
1988, ICEL. All rights reserved.

English translation of Canticle of Zechariah by the International
Consultation on English Texts.

Grail translation of Psalm 100 taken from *The Psalms: A New
Translation* © 1963 by Wm. Collins Sons & Co. Ltd. and published by
Harper Collins Ltd. Used by permission of A. P. Watt Ltd., London,
on behalf of The Grail, England.

Excerpt from *Anne Frank: The Diary of a Young Girl* by Anne Frank,
copyright 1952 by Otto H. Frank. Used by permission of Doubleday,
a division of Random House, Inc.

Excerpt from *Good Parents, Tough Times* by Charlene C. Giannetti and
Margaret Sagarese. Copyright © 2005, 2001 by Giannetti & Sagarese.
Loyola Press. All rights reserved.

Excerpt from *Raising Faith-Filled Kids* by Tom McGrath. Copyright ©
2000 by Tom McGrath. Loyola Press. All rights reserved.

Loyola Press has made every effort to locate the copyright holders
for the cited works used in this publication and to make full
acknowledgment for their use. In the case of any omissions, the
publisher will be pleased to make suitable acknowledgments in
future editions.

Cover art: Lori Lohstoeter
Cover design: Loyola Press and Think Design Group
Interior design: Think Design Group and
Will Capellaro, Loyola Press

ISBN 13: 978-0-8294-2419-5, ISBN 10: 0-8294-2419-9

© 2009 Loyola Press and
Sisters of Notre Dame, Chardon, Ohio

For more information related to the English
translation of the *Roman Missal, Third Edition,*
see www.loyolapress.com/romanmissal.

*Dedicated to St. Julie Billiart, foundress of the Sisters of Notre Dame,
in gratitude for her inspiration and example*

LOYOLAPRESS.
A JESUIT MINISTRY

3441 N. Ashland Avenue
Chicago, Illinois 60657
(800) 621-1008
www.loyolapress.com

14 15 16 Web 10 9 8 7

Contents

Especially for Families

A Note to Families begins on page v. There is a Getting Started page at the beginning of each unit. At the end of each unit, you will find a Family Feature that explores ways to nurture faith at home.

(continued next page)

(continued from previous page)

Note to Families

Goal of This Year's Program

This year your child will study the Old Testament and its meaning for Catholics. Study of the Old Testament guides your child to see in Jesus the fulfillment of all the Father has promised, as well as the perfect response to his love. Your child is encouraged to respond to God's call to enter into a loving relationship with God and with the Church. This response manifests itself in love and care for all people.

A Family Program

Your faith makes a profound impact on your child. Mindful of this fact, the *Christ Our Life* series provides Family Features in each unit. These features give you an opportunity to share the faith experience as a family. They also help you and your child better understand the message of each unit.

Family Pages

At the beginning of each unit, you will receive a Letter to Parents. It informs you about the scriptural concepts your child is studying, allows you to ponder the Word of God in your own life, and offers suggestions for family prayer and activities related to the topic of the unit.

Family Celebrations

At the end of each unit, you will receive a family celebration, which combines knowledge, good works, and prayer. The celebration gives your child a chance to take a leadership role and to share what he or she has learned. It may be carried out as part of a family night or before dessert at a family meal, or incorporated into your family prayer time.

Other Means for Family Involvement

At the end of each chapter is a section called Things to Do at Home, which includes stories and activities for your family members to read and do together to enrich your faith life.

You can also help your child memorize What Catholics Should Know, which begins on page 205 of the student book. Your child should also master the contents under the We Remember section at the end of each chapter.

Note to Families

Ten Principles to Nurture Your Child's Faith

1. Listen with your heart as well as with your head.

2. Encourage wonder and curiosity in your child.

3. Coach your child in empathy. It is a building block for morality.

4. Display religious artwork in your home. This will serve as a steady witness that faith is an important part of life.

5. Gently guide your child to a life of honesty.

6. Whenever appropriate, model for your child how to say "I'm sorry."

7. Eat meals together regularly as a family. It will be an anchor for your child in days to come.

8. Pray together in good times and bad. Worship regularly together as a family.

9. Be generous to those who need help. Make helping others an important focus of your life as a family.

10. See your child for the wonder that God made. Communicate your conviction that your child was created for a noble purpose—to serve God and others in this life and to be happy with God forever in the next.

Visit **www.christourlife.org/family** for more family resources.

God Reveals a Plan of Love

For I know the plans I have for you, says the LORD, plans for welfare and not for evil, to give you a future and a hope.

Jeremiah 29:11

How to Read the Bible as a Catholic

CATHOLICS BELIEVE that everything in the Bible is true. So, then, is it a fact that

- God created the world in seven days?
- Adam lived to be 930 years old?
- Noah built an ark?
- Jonah was swallowed by a large fish?

If everything in the Bible is true, does this mean that Catholics have to choose between science and the Bible?

The key to understanding how to read the Bible as a Catholic is to understand the difference between truth and fact. Simply put, something can be truthful without being factual. For example, if you are trying to download a large file onto your computer and it is taking a long time, you might say that it is "taking a million years." You would be speaking the truth: the file is taking a long time to download. However, the information is not factual: the file is not taking a million years to download. Figurative language such as this communicates truth without relying totally on facts.

We say that as Catholics, we believe that everything in the Bible is true. What we mean is that the Bible teaches us, without error, the truth about God. Although the Bible does contain historical information, the authors of the Bible were not primarily concerned with historical or scientific facts. Their goal was to teach the truth about God.

With this in mind, we can say that the first creation story in the Book of Genesis is true, although it does not attempt to teach scientific facts. It teaches us truths about God and his relationship with creation, such as

- God is the author of all creation.
- God brings order out of chaos.
- Human beings are created in God's image.
- Everything God created is good.

As Catholics, we can learn from what scientists are teaching us about creation and, at the same time, learn from the Book of Genesis about the religious truth of Creation.

Likewise, when the Bible says that Adam lived to be 930 years old, it is teaching the religious truth that he lived a long life, which is a sign of God's blessing.

The story of Noah's Ark is also true: we drown in sin and only those who obey God's voice are saved.

Finally, the story of Jonah is true: when you say no to God's will, you will find yourself in darkness.

When reading Old Testament stories, don't be overly concerned with historical and scientific facts. The important thing is to search for the religious truth being taught in each story. Remember, everything in the Bible is true. After all, God has given us his Word!

The Bible Reveals God's Saving Love

Invited by God

How do you feel when you are invited to a party or to a friend's house? Every time you receive an invitation, you have been chosen to take part in something. You must decide how you will respond. If you say yes, you can enjoy all that has been planned. You can deepen your friendship with the person who invited you and with all the other guests.

Name two places you would like to be invited.

_____

_____

This year God invites you to go on a journey with his Chosen People through a study of the **Old Testament**. As you journey, you will see how much God loves his people, especially those who are poor and vulnerable. You will see how God is calling you to love his people. You will learn how God's people responded to that love. You will see that their journey is much like your own journey to God's kingdom.

Who is this God who invites you? God is the all-powerful, all-knowing, all-loving one who is perfect in every way. God always was and

always will be. God is so great and so far beyond our understanding that we can never completely grasp who God is. Fortunately, God helps us to know him. God reveals himself to us as Father, Son, and Holy Spirit—three divine and inseparable persons in one God.

All of creation reveals how good and how great God is. The Scriptures tell us more. They tell how God made himself known to the Hebrews. They reveal God's plan to save all people by sending his Son Jesus to earth. Jesus, by his death and Resurrection, fulfilled God's plan. What's more, Jesus reveals what God is like more clearly than creation and Scripture do. He is the perfect revelation of God. The Church, the community of faith, helps us understand God's revelation.

God's message on the next page reveals his attitude toward you. Read it and write your

name on the line. Take some time to tell God how you feel about this message.

> **Fear not, _____,**
> **for I have redeemed you;**
> **I have called you**
> **by name:**
> **you are mine**
>
> *Isaiah 43:1*

Why Study the Old Testament?

Here are seven good reasons to study the Old Testament. Check the three that are most convincing to you.

- ○ The history of the Jewish people is our history too.

- ○ Jesus read, studied, and prayed the Hebrew Scriptures.

- ✓ The Old Testament is God's Word.

- ✓ Educated people are expected to know Bible stories.

- ✓ The Old Testament helps us to understand Jesus.

- ○ God speaks to us personally in the Bible.

- ○ Reading the Old Testament helps us to understand our Jewish brothers and sisters.

A story in Luke's gospel tells how Jesus used Scripture to teach about himself. On Easter Sunday, Cleopas and a companion, who were disciples of Jesus, were on their way from Jerusalem to Emmaus. As they walked, they talked about Jesus' death and the rumors of his Resurrection. The risen Jesus joined them on the road, but they did not recognize him. When Jesus asked what they were discussing, the disciples told him how disappointed and confused they were. They had hoped that Jesus was their Messiah, the Savior. Jesus listened to their story. Then he explained how the Hebrew Scriptures foretold the events in Jerusalem. He pointed out how passages about the Messiah referred to Jesus. The disciples were filled with joy as their fellow traveler spoke.

By evening they were near Emmaus. The two disciples invited Jesus to stay with them. While they were eating supper, Jesus took bread and said the blessing. Then he broke the bread and gave it to them. With that, Cleopas and his friend recognized Jesus. Then Jesus disappeared. The disciples said to each other, "Weren't our hearts burning within us as he spoke to us and opened the Scriptures to us?" Excitedly they returned to Jerusalem. There they spread the news that Jesus was risen. They told others what he had taught them.

Jesus also helps us to know him and understand his teachings through Scripture. The persons and events in the Bible reveal to us the greatness of God's love.

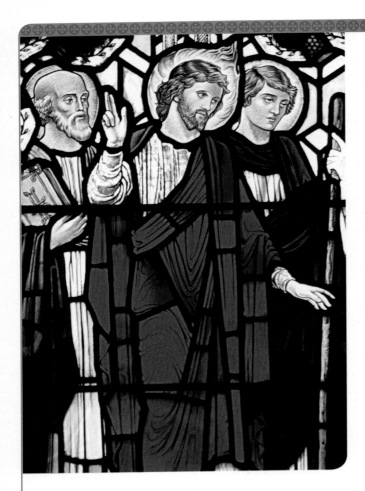

A Sacred Deposit

When you get your allowance or you receive money for your birthday or other special occasions, you might put some of the money in a bank. When you put money in a bank for safekeeping, it is called "making a deposit." A deposit is something that is entrusted to someone or something else for safekeeping.

Jesus gave to the Apostles a "sacred deposit"— his Word. Under the guidance of the Holy Spirit, the Apostles shared Jesus' message and used it to bring God's Word to the people. Today, the Sacred Scripture, along with Sacred Tradition, is entrusted to the Church for safekeeping. The Church's bishops continue to safeguard and share this Sacred Deposit with the help of priests, religious men and women, and catechists. With the help of the bishops, and under the guidance of the Holy Spirit, we can understand what God, who is the author of the Sacred Scripture, is saying to us today.

Jesus helped the two disciples on the road to Emmaus to understand his teachings through Scripture. Take a moment to ask Jesus to help you this year to come to know him and his teachings through Scripture. Ask Jesus to fill you with his Holy Spirit so that you can recognize God's presence in the words of the Bible and in the people you meet each day.

Jesus Fulfilled Old Testament Promises

Match each Old Testament reference with its New Testament fulfillment. Print the correct letter on the line.

___C___ The Messiah will be born in Bethlehem. (Micah 5:1)

___D___ The Messiah will surrender himself to death and let himself be regarded as a sinner for the sake of sinners. (Isaiah 53:12)

___B___ Jerusalem's king will come victorious and humble, riding on a donkey. (Zechariah 9:9)

___A___ The eyes of the blind will be opened; the ears of the deaf will be unsealed. (Isaiah 35:5)

A. Jesus healed many people.

B. Jesus rode into Jerusalem on a donkey while the people waved palm branches.

C. Jesus was born in Bethlehem.

D. Jesus suffered and died on the cross.

We Remember

How does God reveal himself to us?

God reveals himself to us through creation, through Scripture, and through Jesus.

What are some good reasons for reading the Old Testament?

- The history of the Jewish people is our history too.
- Jesus read, studied, and prayed the Hebrew Scriptures.
- The Old Testament is God's Word.
- The Old Testament helps us to understand Jesus.
- God speaks to us personally in the Bible.
- Reading the Old Testament helps us to understand our Jewish brothers and sisters.

What does it mean to refer to Sacred Scripture as a single sacred deposit of God's Word?

God's Word is entrusted to the Church for safekeeping.

We Respond

The promises of the Lord I will sing forever, proclaim your loyalty through all ages.

Psalm 89:2

Word to Know

Old Testament

Things to Do at Home

1. Ask five people, including members of your family, why they think it is important to read the Bible. Report their answers to your class.

2. Read Psalm 91. Use it as a model to write a prayer telling God how you feel about his promises to protect you.

3. Read Jeremiah 7:23. Write a summary of what God tells us we must do to enjoy life with him.

4. Every night for a week, read a short passage from the Bible before you go to bed.

5. Discuss with your family what this Sunday's readings tell you about God.

6. Find out whether your family has a special Bible. If so, look through it together. Talk about why the Bible is special, and where it can be placed in your home to honor its important role in your lives. If your family does not have a Bible, make arrangements to purchase a family Catholic Bible and display it in a place of honor in your home.

Visit **www.christourlife.org/family** for more family resources.

Studying the Old Testament Unscramble the words below to complete each sentence.

God's Chosen People were the ___Hebrews___.
sbwrehe

We call the scriptures of the Hebrew people the ___Old testament___.
dol ansetttem

God reveals himself in ___Creation___.
ntrociea

The Old Testament tells about God's ___love___ for the Chosen People.
vole

The Old Testament tells how the Hebrews ___responded___ to God's love.
dnrdosepe

The Old Testament reveals God's plan to ___save___ all people.
vsea

On the way to Emmaus, Jesus used Hebrew Scriptures to teach about ___himself___.
meihslf

Jesus studied and ___prayed___ the Hebrew Scriptures.
ypeadr

The Old Testament helps us understand ___Jesus___.
sejsu

Some verses of the Old Testament foreshadow ___events___ in Jesus' life.
nevest

A Bible Ad Complete this ad for the Bible.

Take and Read

● Journey with the Chosen People by reading the ___Old testament___.

● Come to know about God's great ___love___.

● Find out about God's plan to ___save___ you.

● Learn more about your journey to God's ___Kingdom___.

● Discover how to meet God and listen to God through his Word in the ___scripture / bible___.

● ___Jesus___, the Son of God, will help you.

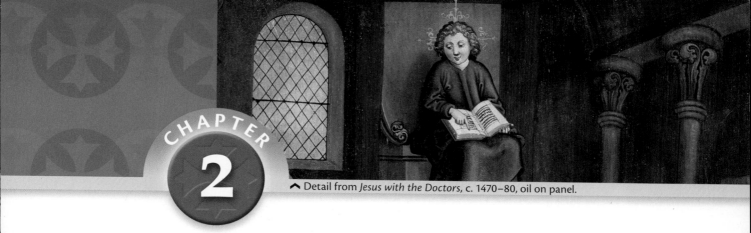

^ Detail from *Jesus with the Doctors*, c. 1470–80, oil on panel.

Scripture Is God's Saving Word

What a Revelation!

Ms. Ruiz asked each of her students to write three sentences telling about one of his or her parents.

Ms. Ruiz found there were two kinds of papers. Look at the descriptions on the right. Some students told facts about their parents. Put a ✓ beside those paragraphs. Some children told about the love of their parents. Put an ✗ beside those paragraphs.

Describing God

We can also describe God in two ways. We can list the facts we know about him or we can tell about the love between God and us.

Tell one fact about God.

_____

Write one sentence about the love between God and you.

_____

The Hebrew people often spoke of God's love for them and their response to God. Love was the way God revealed himself to them.

Sarah wrote this about her dad:

○
> My dad died last year, but I remember how he took care of me when I was hurt in a car accident. He lay down on the road beside me so that I wouldn't be afraid. Mom and I miss Dad.

Luis wrote about his dad:

○
> My dad is a lawyer. He graduated from Harvard Law School. He likes to play golf.

Jake told about his mother:

○
> My mom is great! Even though she works every day, she still has time to come to soccer games with Jim and me. She makes us feel good even if we lose.

Maria told about her mother:

○
> My mom is a bank president. She wears expensive clothes and likes to go shopping for new ones. She is tall and pretty.

Self-Taught Bible Facts

The following boxes contain information about the Bible. You can teach yourself about the Bible using the boxes and a sheet of paper. When you finish this activity, you will be on your way to becoming a Bible expert!

- First, cover the page with the sheet of paper. Read and study one box at a time. On the right of each box there is a question. Answer the question silently.
- When you move the paper down to reveal the next box, you will see the answer to the previous question on the right.

All that God has taught about himself and his will for his people is called **revelation.** Revelation is contained in Scripture and Tradition, which form a single deposit of God's Word.

What do we call all that God has taught about himself and his will for his people?

revelation

Tradition refers to beliefs and practices that have been passed down throughout the ages and that have become a part of the Church's teaching. Tradition is found in the prayers and practices of God's people.

What are the beliefs and practices passed down throughout the ages and made a part of the Church's teaching?

Tradition

Sometimes different people told the stories and the details were changed. But God guarded the stories so that they still revealed the message he wanted his people to have. He inspired the people who told these stories. This means God is the primary author of the Bible and that he guided the thoughts and words of its human authors to tell others of his love and care.

Where is revelation found in addition to Tradition?

Scripture

After these stories had been repeated for hundreds of years, they were written down. God inspired the writers to write what he wanted his people to know. But he left the writers free to express the message in their own way. God also inspired the editors who gathered the writings together. Through inspiration God is the primary author of the Bible.

Who is the primary author of the Bible?

God

The collection of writings through which God revealed himself to the Jewish people was completed about one hundred years before Jesus was born. Jewish and Christian people consider the Old Testament sacred. The word *old* in the Old Testament refers to God's original Law. The Old Testament is a preparation for the Gospel, which fulfills God's Law.

What does the Old Testament refer to?

God's original Law

Christians believe that God revealed himself fully through his Son Jesus, whose name means "*God saves.*" After Jesus' death and Resurrection, the Holy Spirit inspired, or guided, certain people to write about Jesus. Their writings are called the **New Testament.** In the New Testament, the Gospels are important because Jesus is at their center. The last book of the New Testament was written about A.D. 100.

What does inspired *mean?*

guided by the Holy Spirit

Together the Old Testament and the New Testament make up the Bible, or Sacred Scripture. It took over a thousand years to write and collect the entire Bible.

What makes up the Bible, or Sacred Scripture?

the Old Testament and the New Testament

God speaks to us in the Scriptures, and the Holy Spirit helps us to interpret, or understand, God's Word. **Interpretation** is the key to understanding what God says to us in the Bible. The Church also helps by teaching us the meaning of the Bible so that we can learn to care for God's creation and for one another.

What is the key to understanding the Bible?

interpretation

How else does God speak to us? _____

A Bible Message in Code

Work out the rebus to find out what one psalm writer thought about God's Word.

A [lamp] **2** *my* [feet] *is* **U + R** word ,

a [light] **2** *my* [path] . **Oh Lord, give me**

lie + **F** [accordion] – *on* + *ng* **2 U + R** word .

A Sacred Library

The word *Bible* comes from the Greek word for book, *biblios.* But the Bible is really a collection of books, a minilibrary. The writers of the Bible wrote God's message in different kinds of books. They wrote in a way that people of their time would understand.

The **Law** is the first five books of the Bible. It is usually called the **Pentateuch,** which means "five scrolls." These were not the first books written, but they tell stories about the beginnings of God's people. They tell the story of the Creation and the Covenant. They also tell how God cared for his people on their journey to the Promised Land and called them to live by his Law. These books are also called the **Torah.**

The historical books tell how God cared for his people during their history. These books show that God is the Lord of history—that God oversees the events of history. They are not always complete or scientifically and historically accurate. Their purpose is to remind the Hebrew people that God has been with them during all the events of their lives.

Wisdom literature tells people how to live wisely. These books showed the Israelites how to act as God's people and how to pray. They contain psalms, poems, prayers, sermons, proverbs, riddles, and parables.

The prophetic books tell about the prophets and their messages to God's people. When the people had turned away from God, the prophets reminded them of God's love. They called the people to be faithful to God and to their covenant with him. The prophets also told the people to be just to one another.

Taking Inventory

Count the books in each section of the Old Testament. List your answers below.

The Law	————
The historical books	————
Wisdom Literature	————
The prophetic books	————
Total books in the Old Testament	————
Total books in the New Testament	27
Total books in the Bible	————

It is important to know that the Catholic Church accepts and venerates 73 books in the Bible, while the Protestant Bible includes only 66. The Catholic Bible includes 7 Old Testament books that are not in the Jewish Scriptures or the Protestant Bible. As you study, it is important to make sure that you are using a Catholic Bible.

To what category do each of the following books belong? Use **L** for Law, **H** for historical books, **W** for Wisdom Literature, **P** for prophetic books.

————	**1.**	Genesis
————	**2.**	Judith
————	**3.**	Psalms
————	**4.**	Jonah
————	**5.**	Wisdom
————	**6.**	Ruth
————	**7.**	Exodus
————	**8.**	Isaiah
————	**9.**	Job
————	**10.**	Ezekiel

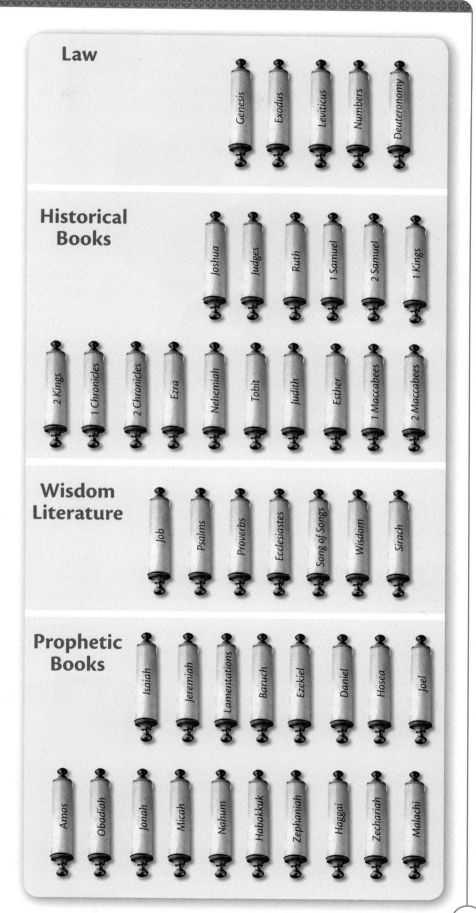

Law: Genesis, Exodus, Leviticus, Numbers, Deuteronomy

Historical Books: Joshua, Judges, Ruth, 1 Samuel, 2 Samuel, 1 Kings, 2 Kings, 1 Chronicles, 2 Chronicles, Ezra, Nehemiah, Tobit, Judith, Esther, 1 Maccabees, 2 Maccabees

Wisdom Literature: Job, Psalms, Proverbs, Ecclesiastes, Song of Songs, Wisdom, Sirach

Prophetic Books: Isaiah, Jeremiah, Lamentations, Baruch, Ezekiel, Daniel, Hosea, Joel, Amos, Obadiah, Jonah, Micah, Nahum, Habakkuk, Zephaniah, Haggai, Zechariah, Malachi

Locating Scripture Passages

Each book of the Bible is divided into chapters. Each chapter is divided into verses. Biblical references are listed in the following manner:

- First the book, such as Exodus, is listed.
- Then the chapter number, such as 15, is given.
- Finally the verse or verses are given.

Find the Emmaus story in Luke 24:13–35.

A Moment with Jesus

God speaks to us at every Mass as his Word is proclaimed. He speaks to us whenever we read the Bible. It is a good practice to read the Bible every day. Take a moment now to ask the Holy Spirit to help you read the Bible more often and to understand the message. Thank Jesus for speaking to you through the Bible.

A Lucky Throw

In 1947, near the ancient Qumran settlement in Israel, a young shepherd made an amazing discovery. While searching for a lost goat, the shepherd tossed a stone into a cave, hoping to frighten the goat out of hiding. Instead, he heard the shatter of pottery. Inside the cave was an ancient library of scrolls hidden inside clay jars and wrapped in linen. The shepherd had found the first of what came to be known as the Dead Sea Scrolls, which are among the only surviving Biblical documents written before A.D. 100. Between 1947 and 1956, local settlers and teams of scientists would uncover around 600 scrolls and scroll fragments in 11 different caves. The scrolls included almost every book of the Hebrew Bible. The Dead Sea Scrolls are considered among the most important religious documents that we have today.

The caves at Qumran in Israel, where the Dead Sea Scrolls were found in 1947.

Summary

We Remember

What are the four parts of the Old Testament?

The Law (Pentateuch), the historical books, Wisdom Literature, and the prophetic books.

What is revelation?

Revelation is all that God has taught us about himself and his will for his people.

What is inspiration?

Inspiration is God's action in guiding the human authors of the Bible. God guided their thoughts and desires to pass on truths that he wanted to teach, but left the authors free to express the truths in their own ways.

❮ A Russian icon depicting Saint John writing his Gospel.

We Respond

Read Psalm 136:1–7. Write two things God has done for you. After each one write, "God's love endures forever."

_____

_____

_____

_____

_____

_____

Words to Know

Law	revelation
interpretation	Torah
Pentateuch	tradition

Things to Do at Home

1. The original Sacred Scriptures were written in Hebrew or Greek. There are many English translations of the Bible done by different groups. Each group gives its version a name. The New American Bible (NAB) is the official Catholic translation of the Bible. It is the Bible translation we hear proclaimed in the readings at Mass. See which Bible you have at home. If you do not have a family Bible, talk with your family about getting one. Your teacher or parish priest can help you.

2. If you have a family Bible, take time to note some of its special features. Family Bibles are often very old, because they are passed on from one generation to the next. Look at the copyright date. How old is your Bible? Many family Bibles have a family tree or pages to record the births and deaths of family members. They may also have a table of contents, an index, a list of abbreviations, and a Bible dictionary. Does your Bible have special family pages? Does it have maps, interesting art, or special prayer pages? Talk with your family about what makes your family Bible unique.

3. Plan to keep the Bible where you can read from it and honor it as the Word of God.

4. With members of your family, play a game of 20 Questions. Have one person secretly choose the identity of a celebrity. Then have other players ask yes or no questions until they determine the name of the celebrity, or until 20 questions have been asked. When you have finished playing, talk with your family about how this game involves revelation—the revealing of information that leads to discovery. Talk about how God reveals himself to us in the Bible.

Visit **www.christourlife.org/family** for more family resources.

We Review

Words About the Word   Match each term with its definition. Not all terms will be used.

____ 1. God guiding the thoughts of biblical authors and editors

____ 2. Sacred writings from the time before Jesus that tell about God

____ 3. First five books of the Bible, Torah

____ 4. All that God has taught about himself and his love for his people

____ 5. When the Bible was completed

____ 6. Beliefs and practices passed down throughout the ages and made a part of the Church's teaching

____ 7. Early Scripture manuscripts found between 1947 and 1956

____ 8. Word that means "books"

____ 9. Person of the Trinity who helps us understand the Bible

____ 10. Title given to God because he inspired the Bible

A. revelation

B. Pentateuch

C. Dead Sea Scrolls

D. inspiration

E. about 100 B.C.

F. about A.D. 100

G. Tradition

H. Holy Spirit

I. primary author

J. Bible

K. Old Testament

Getting Some Practice

Find the following Old Testament passages in your Bible. Write each passage in the space provided.

Exodus 3:10 _____

1 Samuel 17:32 _____

_____

Psalm 100:1 _____

Jeremiah 1:6 _____

Categories   Name the type of biblical books described.

1. Books that call the people to be faithful to God and to be just.

2. Books that tell about the beginnings of God's relationship with his people.

3. Books that tell how to live wisely.

4. Books that tell how God cared for his people in the events of history.

_____   _____   _____   _____

Everything God Created Is Good

Creation: A Sign of God's Love

People have always told stories of how the earth was formed and how human life began. A lot of these stories have many different gods, both good and evil. The universe is often created from something that already exists. For example, in one story from ancient Babylon, the god Marduk kills a sea monster who is also a goddess. He then makes the heavens and earth out of her body.

The Israelites did not believe that creation came from violence. They knew from experience that the one true God was loving and caring. They were inspired by God to write creation stories based on this faith. These stories are found in the Book of Genesis.

The story of Creation in Genesis reflects what people understood about the universe when the first creation story was composed. Most people thought that the earth was flat and held up by columns. The sky was like a dome over the earth. There was water below and around the

earth, and water above the dome. When gates in the dome were opened, it rained or snowed. It is this view of the universe that is described in the first chapter of Genesis.

We come to recognize God's existence through the beauty of his creation. Creation is a sign of God's wisdom, power, and glory. It is most of all a sign of God's love. God's marvelous creation is like an announcement about his loving plan for us, which reaches its goal in Jesus Christ. Think of all the people who love you and all the love that you have for others. All of this love combined is not even a drop compared to the ocean of God's love. Through God's creation we learn that God loves us and wants to be loved in return. Although we speak of the Father as Creator, the Son and the Spirit are united with him as one creating God.

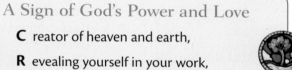
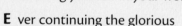
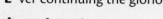

A Sign of God's Power and Love

C reator of heaven and earth,

R evealing yourself in your work,

E ver continuing the glorious

A ct of creation!

T hank you for created beauty, for my

I mmortal soul, my wonderful body, for

O ther gifts of your love!

N ever will I forget your goodness.

The First Story of Creation

The first story of creation in the first chapter of the Book of Genesis sounds like a poem. The rhythm of its words makes it enjoyable to hear. Here is part of the story to read aloud.

Solo 1: In the beginning,

All: when God created the heavens and the earth,

Solo 1: the earth was a formless wasteland,

Solo 2: and darkness covered the abyss,

All: while a mighty wind swept over the waters.

Solo 1: Then God said,

All: "Let there be light,"

Solo 1: and there was light. God saw how good the light was. God then separated the light from the darkness.

Solo 2: God called the light "day," and the darkness he called "night."

All: Thus evening came, and morning followed—the first day.

Solo 2: Then God said, "Let there be a dome in the middle of the waters, to separate one body of water from the other."

All: And so it happened:

Solo 1: God made the dome, and it separated the water above the dome from the water below it.

Solo 2: God called the dome "the sky."

All: Evening came, and morning followed—the second day.

Genesis 1:1–8

Michelangelo Buonarroti, detail from *The Creation of Adam*, 1511.

Two Stories—True Stories

In the Bible there are two stories about the creation of the first man and the first woman. Read Genesis 1:26–30 and then Genesis 2:7,18–23. How do these stories show that people are important creations of God?

Did God create the universe as we know it in just six days or over millions of years? Did God make the first people from earth or through evolution, a series of changes in different life forms? The fact is, the creation stories are not scientific reports. Rather, they are stories meant to teach religious truths. Some of these truths are given here.

- There is only one God.
- God created all things and takes care of creation.
- God is good, wise, powerful, orderly, and loving.
- Everything and everyone depends upon God.
- God created human beings in his image.
- Men and women have equal dignity.
- God made people masters and stewards of creation.
- Things of creation were made to help all people and to bring them joy.

God's First Gift

Our first gift from God was our human life. God made each of us special and unique, loving and lovable. God gave us the wonderful gifts of a body, united with a soul that makes us human, so that we could share in his truth, goodness, and beauty and give glory to him.

Like plants and animals, we grow, eat food, and reproduce. Like animals, we feel, sense, and move from place to place. But unlike any other creatures on earth, we have a soul that enables us to think, judge, choose, love, and live forever. It is through the special gifts of intellect and **free will** that we are like God, made in God's image and likeness. God shares with us his knowledge, freedom, and power. God gives us freedom and the right to exercise it, as well as dignity and the responsibility to protect it. Best of all, through love God reveals and gives himself to us and dwells within us.

A Moment with Jesus

The gift of human life is more precious than we can imagine. The variety and differences among persons make life more beautiful and enjoyable. The Psalms, which Jesus prayed, often express our appreciation for God's creation. Take a moment to quietly pray the following psalm. Then ask Jesus to help you recognize God's presence in all of creation.

I thank you for the wonder of my being,

wonderful are all your works!

adapted from Psalm 139:14

Giving Thanks

How can we show God that we are grateful to him for creating us and that we respect the gift of life in ourselves and others?

_____

_____

Name another of God's gifts.

_____

How might this gift be used for good?

_____

Doing God's Work

God wants to share another gift with us—his creative work. That is why God calls us to be stewards of the earth. Because of the **stewardship** we have been given, we first care for human life and protect it. We also care for and protect the gifts of the earth, such as water, air, minerals, trees, and land. Caring for creation means replacing what we have taken from the earth, repairing any damages, and disposing of wastes properly. If we care for creation, we also avoid using products that harm the earth.

God wants us to find new, creative ways to use his gifts in art, science, and labor. The earth belongs to everyone. God wants us to share the gifts and their products with others in the world. The Church encourages us to promote peace and justice among all peoples and nations. All work has dignity because it is participation in God's work of creation.

Name an occupation in which people are called to act as stewards of the world's resources:

_____

How do people in this line of work act as stewards of the world?

_____

How Can I Help?

Read these ways that you can be a steward for God's creation. If a sentence describes you, color the circle green.

- ⭕ I don't litter.
- ⭕ When I see litter on lawns or at school, I pick it up.
- ⭕ I do not waste water.
- ⭕ I do not waste food.
- ⭕ I help clean our house.
- ⭕ I donate time, money, or possessions to help the poor.
- ⭕ I recycle paper.
- ⭕ I recycle cans, glass, and plastic bottles.
- ⭕ I do not vandalize buildings or objects.
- ⭕ I am kind to animals.

No matter how many circles you colored, there are many more ways that you can do your part. You might start a recycling drive at school. You might organize a group to pick up trash in your neighborhood. Use a kid-friendly search engine to research online other ways that you can be a steward for God's creation.

We Remember

What do the stories of creation in the Book of Genesis teach us?

These stories teach us the religious truth about the creation of the world.

What did God create?

God created us and gave us gifts of body and soul. God created the earth and all its gifts to help us and give us joy.

How are human beings different from other creatures?

We have a soul that enables us to think, judge, choose, love, and live forever. We have an intellect and free will.

We Respond

Complete this prayer of adoration by filling in the names of creatures that reflect God's qualities.

I praise and thank you, God, for

your wisdom that I see in

_____,

your power that I see in

_____,

your gentleness that I see in

_____,

and your love that I see in

_____.

Words to Know

free will
stewardship

Things to Do at Home

1. With your family, read about creation in Psalm 104. Talk about the similarities and differences between Psalm 104 and the passages about creation that you read in Genesis 1:26–30 and Genesis 2:7,18–23.

2. Make a creation poster based on a poem like the one on page 17.

3. With members of your family, take a walk and name all the things you see that God created. List ways you can use these items properly or help to save and protect them.

4. Talk with your family about how you can all become stewards of God's creation. Think of things that your family can do together.

5. Talk to your parents about arranging a visit to a zoo, an aquarium, or a planetarium. Talk about the wonderful things God has made. Write a prayer about one thing that impressed you.

Visit **www.christourlife.org/family** for more family resources.

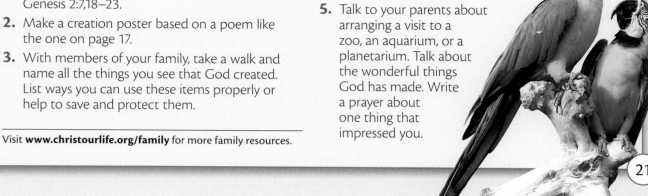

Beginnings   Identify what is described.

1.   The first book of the Bible: _____

2.   What God created everything out of: _____

3.   What God created on the first day: _____

4.   What we have in addition to a body: _____

6.   The stewards of the earth: _____

7.   Two gifts that make us like God: _____

The Master at Work

Check (✓) the sentences that are true descriptions of God's work of creation.

___ 1. Everything God created is good.

___ 2. God keeps everything in existence.

___ 3. God created evil things.

___ 4. God created some creatures that were like himself.

___ 5. Creation is a sign of God's love.

___ 6. God created the world for all people to share.

___ 7. The description of creation in the Bible is scientifically correct.

___ 8. God expects us to care for his creation.

Compare and Contrast

Compare and contrast the two stories of creation in the Book of Genesis (Genesis 1:1–2:4 and Genesis 2:4–25). Read the two stories and then describe three similarities and three differences.

Similarities:

1. _____

_____

2. _____

_____

3. _____

_____

Differences:

1. _____

_____

2. _____

_____

3. _____

_____

CHAPTER 4

^ Jan Brueghel the Elder, *The Garden of Eden*, c. 1600.

God Offers Love and Mercy

The Problem of Evil

Where did evil come from? How did **sin** enter our world? With so much suffering around us, how are we still able to hope and trust?

Throughout history, people of all ages, all over the world, have tried to answer these questions. The book of Genesis, under God's inspiration, addresses some of these mysteries. The writers of Genesis used stories to tell us about sin and God's faithful love and mercy. They told two different creation stories. In Genesis 1 we learn about how the first man and woman were created and given a beautiful garden to live in.

The Fall

God created all things good. The Adam and Eve story explains how sin came into the world. God created Adam and Eve to live close to him and to one another. He created them in his own image, and gave them the gifts of intellect and free will. They could freely find happiness in life and remain united with him.

God knew what could make people happy and be at peace with themselves, others, and the world. He asked Adam and Eve to obey. By trusting God's plan for them, they would know true happiness.

But by their own free choice, Adam and Eve disobeyed God. They were proud and refused to depend on God and his plan for them. They broke faith with God. They brought sin into the world and lost God's life in them: the gift of sanctifying grace. They became divided from God and from each other. Love unites, but sin divides.

This first sin changed everything. Because of this sin, human beings are born without grace and with a tendency to sin. This condition is called original sin. It is through Baptism that grace is restored, and we again become children of God. After the sin of the first man and woman, sin spread throughout the world, repeating its story of pain and separation.

Evil remains a mystery to us—we cannot fully understand it. However, through his death and Resurrection, Jesus overcame evil. By virtue of our baptism into the death and Resurrection of Jesus, we share in Jesus' mission to care for and protect those who are victims of evil, especially those who are poor and vulnerable.

"It's really a wonder that I haven't dropped all my ideals because they seem so absurd and impossible to carry out. Yet, I keep them, because in spite of everything I still believe that people are really good at heart."

Anne Frank: The Diary of a Young Girl

The Story of Adam and Eve

In the second story of creation, Genesis 2:4—3:24, we learn that when Adam and Eve lived in the garden of Eden, Paradise, God had given them only one rule. They were not to eat the fruit from the tree of knowledge of good and evil. If they did, they would die.

One day a serpent came to Eve and asked her why she didn't eat the fruit from this tree. The serpent told her that she and Adam would not die if they ate the fruit, but that they would have great knowledge and be like gods.

Eve ate the fruit and gave some to Adam, who also ate it. At that moment, Adam and Eve had knowledge of their sin. When they heard God calling them, they tried to hide from him.

But God knew they had disobeyed. When God questioned them, Adam blamed Eve, and Eve blamed the serpent. God then told how each would be punished. The serpent would have to crawl on the ground and be an outcast from all other animals. Eve would bear children with pain. Adam would work for food with much difficulty. God said to the serpent,

"I will put enmity between you and the
    woman,
    and between your offspring and hers;
He will strike at your head,
    while you strike at his heel."

Genesis 3:15

Then God made clothes for Adam and Eve and sent them away from the garden. They left with God's promise that someday he would send someone to overcome sin and restore life.

The savior would be Jesus, the new Adam, who would bring about the new creation. Mary, the mother of Jesus, would be the new Eve, the new mother of all the living. She would be the sinless one who always listened to God. Through her Son, evil would be conquered forever. By believing in Jesus Christ, we find new life in the Holy Spirit, who helps us to overcome evil.

A Moment with Jesus

We could not overcome evil if not for Jesus Christ, who sends his Holy Spirit to strengthen us. Take a moment now to ask Jesus to help you be open to his Spirit. Ask the Holy Spirit to help you overcome temptation. Thank Jesus for giving us the grace we need to obey the Father's law of love.

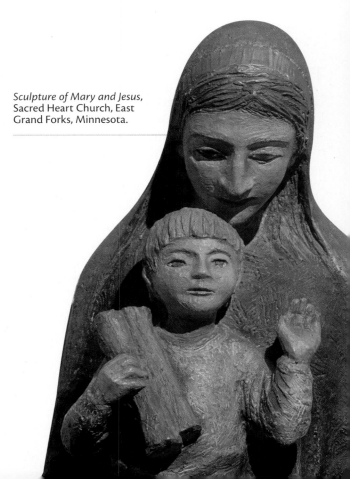

Sculpture of Mary and Jesus,
Sacred Heart Church, East
Grand Forks, Minnesota.

Triumph of Love and Mercy

God created us because he wanted to share his life and love with us. He wants us to be happy. When we sin, we look for happiness in the wrong places. We turn away from God's love. We direct our power to love toward ourselves, rather than toward God and others.

When this happens, sin spreads and divides. Soon everyone is affected. Many problems in the world today come from the evil of sin.

The effects of sin are separation from God, unhappiness, destruction, conflict, suffering, and death. These evils are with us, but God's love and mercy are also with us.

God's response again and again has been one of love and mercy. The message of Genesis is not only that people sin—it is also the message that God's love is faithful and total.

Nothing can prevent God from calling us to union with him. When Adam and Eve sinned, God promised to send a savior to redeem us and unite us with God. That savior was his only Son, Jesus.

No matter how much evil we may find in the world, or how hard things may become for us, we still hope, we still believe, we still love. Armed with this faith and strengthened by the Holy Spirit, we strive to protect the fundamental rights of all people who would otherwise suffer the effects of evil in our society.

How are we able to do this? Read 1 Peter 1:3–7. Spend a few moments thinking about God's message. Respond to God's message by writing your thoughts or your own prayer.

_____

_____

_____

Relationships in Conflict

The book of Genesis tells of the spread of sin in the world. The following three stories illustrate how sin weakens and destroys relationships with God and with others. They also show us God's merciful love.

The Story of Two Brothers

Genesis 4:1–16

Cain, the first son of Adam and Eve, was a farmer. The second son, Abel, was a herder. Each of them brought offerings to God from their labors. Cain brought the fruit of the land that he tilled. Abel brought one of the best animals in his flock. God accepted Abel's offering, but he did not accept Cain's.

Rather than asking God why his offering was unacceptable, Cain instead turned on his brother. He invited Abel to go out into the field with him. There Cain killed Abel. God called to Cain, "Where is your brother Abel?"

In Genesis 4:9 you can find Cain's reply. Write it here.

i dont know. Am I supposed to take care of my brother?

God punished Cain by sending him away from his land to wander the world as an outcast. But God still showed mercy. God loves sinners, too. He continually tries to save them. He protected Cain in a special way. Read Genesis 4:15. Write what God did for Cain.

He put a mark him so no one he met would kill him.

The Story of the Flood

Genesis 6–9

Like many people of long ago, the Hebrews had a flood story that they passed on from generation to generation. Their story is about how common sin had become, and how God was displeased with the people's wickedness.

God told Noah, who had remained faithful to him, to build a special boat called an ark. He directed Noah to take with him on the ark his family and one pair of every kind of animal.

When Noah had done this, the rains began. Soon the whole earth was covered with water. All living creatures, except those in the ark, were destroyed. For many days and nights the rain continued. When it stopped and the dry land appeared, God called Noah from the ark. Noah offered sacrifices to God. Then God made a covenant between himself and Noah and every living creature. He promised never to destroy the world by flood again.

> **God gave Noah a special sign of this everlasting covenant. Find it in Genesis 9:13 and draw it here.**

The Story of the Tower of Babel

Genesis 11:1–9

The flood story was not the end of sin. People continued to do wicked things. Some people used to build towers, called *ziggurats*, to honor their gods. In the story of the Tower of Babel, the people decided to build a tower for a different reason.

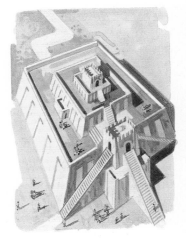

Read Genesis 11:4 and write why the people wanted to build their tower.

_____

_____

According to this story, people throughout the whole world used to speak the same language. The Lord saw that the people building the tower were very proud. Because they had forgotten him, God confused their language. The people could no longer understand each other and could not complete their tower. They could not even live together. They moved to various parts of the earth. Sin had divided them.

Reconciliation—A Return to God and an End to Conflict

Although people sinned, God did not abandon them. He constantly offered them ways to return to him. Every sin separates us from God and our neighbor. Every effort to turn from sin helps heal this separation. This return to God and our neighbor is called reconciliation. Through his Son, Jesus, whose name means "God saves," we have been shown the way to return to the Father. Through his Holy Spirit, we spread Jesus' message of reconciliation, helping all people to recognize that we are brothers and sisters.

Headlines

Newspapers often carry stories of sin and conflict. Think about how sin weakened or destroyed relationships in the Genesis stories. Then read the headlines below. Match each headline with the correct consequence of sin.

D Sin separates people from God.

B Sin separates people from each other.

C Sin even separates nation from nation.

A Sin destroys and leads to sadness and death.

Ⓐ **Flood Destroys Earth**

Man Kills His Own Brother Ⓑ ★★

TOWER CRUMBLES— World Divides Ⓒ

Ⓓ **Disobedience Leads to Downfall**

Making Choices

The stories of Adam and Eve, Cain and Abel, Noah's Ark, and the Tower of Babel teach us that we can choose between good and evil. God created us so that we can share in his wonderful creation. God placed a desire for happiness within each of us. However, in seeking happiness, sometimes we choose to do things that are against the law of God. Sometimes we choose to sin, like the people in the Book of Genesis.

With the help of the Holy Spirit, we can avoid sin and make good moral choices. When making a moral choice, we need to consider three things:

- what we have chosen to do,
- the intention behind our choice, and
- the circumstances surrounding the act.

The Church helps us to make good moral choices by helping us to develop our **conscience**. We can develop our consciences by learning from our mistakes and from the mistakes of others. We also develop our conscience by praying for guidance, reading and listening to Scripture, and learning about the teachings of the Church.

Psalm 100

Cry out with joy to the Lord, all the earth.
Serve the Lord with gladness.
Come before Him, singing for joy.

Know that He, the Lord, is God.
He made us, we belong to Him,
We are His people, the sheep of His pasture.

Go within His gates, giving thanks.
Enter His courts with songs of praise.
Give thanks to Him and bless His name

Indeed, how good is the Lord,
Eternal His merciful love.
He is faithful from age to age.

Grail Translation

A Forgiving Spirit

Read the following stories. How would you end each story? How might you act differently or what might you do to show forgiveness if you were in each situation?

1. Hannah's mom told her to wash the dishes. But Hannah had plans to meet her best friend after dinner. Besides, Hannah often did the dishes when her older sister, Taylor, went out with her friends. Hannah yelled, "I do everything around here! Why doesn't Taylor ever do anything?" Then Hannah ran out of the room.

_____

_____

_____

2. José saved all summer to buy a new baseball bat. One day José let his brother, Jorge, borrow his new bat. He asked only that Jorge be careful with it. While Jorge was using the bat, he heard a *crack!* It was hard to see the crack, but Jorge knew that the next time someone used it, the bat would splinter and break.

_____

_____

_____

3. Brandon was going to his friend's apartment next door. As he was leaving, his little sister Emily ran up and asked to go with him. Brandon said, "No, go away and leave me alone for once!" and stormed out of the apartment. When he got home later, he saw how sad Emily looked.

_____

_____

_____

4. Logan forgot to draw a map for his history homework. So he asked his friend Ryan if he could copy. Ryan let him. After the maps had been turned in, their teacher called both boys into the hall. He asked if one of them had copied.

_____

_____

_____

5. Amber's friends were talking about Mei, a new girl in their class. Although she didn't know Mei very well, Amber did not want to be left out. So she joined her friends in telling made-up stories about Mei to the other kids in class.

_____

_____

_____

_____

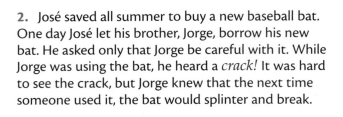

We Remember

What is sin?

Sin is a person's free choice to turn away from God. It is the source of all evil.

What are the effects of sin?

Sin weakens or destroys a person's relationship with God and others.

In the Book of Genesis, how did God respond to people when they sinned?

When people sinned, God responded with love and mercy.

We Respond

Thank you, Lord, for loving me so much.

Thank you, for always forgiving me.

When I trust you in all things, I learn true happiness.

Teach me to live a life filled with joy and hope.

Words to Know

conscience

sin

Pieter Brueghel the Elder, *The Tower of Babel*, 1563.

Things to Do at Home

1. Use a kid-friendly search engine to find online news stories that show the effects of sin and the people who are affected most by it. Talk with your family about these stories. Discuss the choices the people involved made and what they might have done differently as children of God. Then work with your family to make a list of intentions. Keep these intentions in your prayers.

2. You might read *Anne Frank: The Diary of a Young Girl*. It tells how Anne, a young Jewish girl, remained hopeful in a very difficult situation.

3. Think about how the Holy Spirit influences your life and the choices that you make each day. Thank God for sending the Holy Spirit to help you make good moral choices.

4. Pray Psalm 100 with a friend or a member of your family.

5. Read these stories from the Bible. Talk with your family about the choices the people in each story made and how their choices affected them and their society. Also talk about God's response to those choices.

   Adam and Eve: Genesis 3:1–24

   Cain and Abel: Genesis 4:1–16

   The Flood: Genesis 6:5–9:17

   The Tower of Babel: Genesis 11:1–9

6. Strive to be a minister of reconciliation at home and at school. Whenever possible, look for ways to be a peacemaker, helping others to resolve conflict.

7. Talk to your parents about making good moral choices. Ask them about the people who helped them to form their conscience.

Visit **www.christourlife.org/family** for more family resources.

Who's Who? Match the people with the description that best fits them.

A. Abel   **E.** People of Babel
B. Eve   **F.** Adam
C. Satan   **G.** Cain
D. Mary   **H.** Noah

____ **1.** Her son would be the savior of the human race

____ **2.** Offered the best of his flock to God

____ **3.** Good person who was saved in the worldwide flood

____ **4.** Killed his brother

____ **5.** Blamed his sin on his wife

____ **6.** First mother of the human race

____ **7.** Tried to build a tower in order to be famous

Word Challenge Choose a word from the box to answer each clue. Then use the circled letters to work out the sentence at the bottom.

1. Source of evil: __ __ __
   ₁

2. One effect of sin: __ __ __ __ __ __ __
   ₂   ₃

3. Another effect of sin: __ __ __ __ __ __ __
   ₄ ₅   ₆

4. Cain and Abel: __ __ __ __ __ __ __ __
   ₇ ₈   ₉

5. Sign of God's promise to Noah: __ __ __ __ __ __ __
   ₁₀

6. Creator of the world: __ __ __
   ₁₁   ₁₂

7. Was built in Babel to show power and pride: __ __ __ __ __
   ₁₃

8. God's response to sinners: __ __ __ __ __
   ₁₄

brothers
mercy
rainbow
tower
God
sin
conflict
separation

Reconciliation is the return to a __ __ __ __ __ and __ __ __ __ relationship with __ __ __
and __ __ __ __ __ __ __ __ after it has been __ __ __ k __ __ __ __ or destroyed by sin.

(9 6 5 5 14) (9 2 3 14) (11 2 12) (1 4 10 11 9 7 2 8) (13 4 6) (4 1 4 12)

Picture This! Draw a cartoon or comic strip of one of the sin stories described in this chapter.

People in the Bible

Read each person's statement. Circle the letter that describes the character whose name appears on the frame. Then write on the lines the names of the characters described in the two other columns.

a. I offered God the best things I had grown.

I was banished for killing my brother.

I was protected by God from having harm done to me.

_____

b. I was the first man.

My wife gave me forbidden fruit to eat.

I helped to bring original sin into the world.

_____

c. I asked Eve why she did not eat from the tree of knowledge.

I told Eve that she would not die if she ate the fruit.

I told Eve that eating the fruit would give great knowledge.

_____

ADAM

a. I was the second son born to Adam and Eve.

I offered to God the best of my flock.

I was killed by my older brother.

_____

b. I was sent to bring about the new creation.

My mother is the new Eve.

Through me, evil will be conquered forever.

_____

c. I was the first son born to Adam and Eve.

I offered to God the best fruit of my land.

I killed my brother out of jealousy.

_____

CAIN

a. We built the tower of Babel.

We were proud and forgot God.

God could not understand us; now we are divided.

_____

b. God called upon me to build an ark.

I took on the ark my family and one pair of every kind of animal.

God and I made a special covenant.

_____

c. I was the first woman.

A serpent convinced me to eat from the tree of knowledge.

I helped to bring sin into the world.

_____

NOAH

Books Puzzle
Complete the crossword puzzle. You can find the correct spelling of the answers in Unit 1 or in the Glossary.

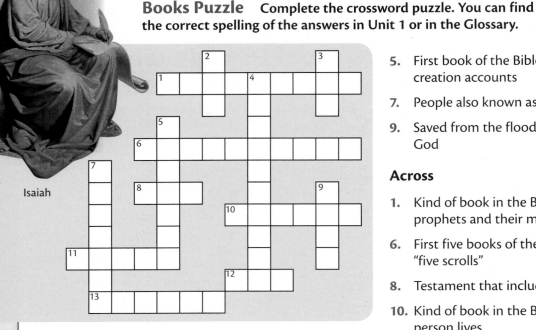

Isaiah

5. First book of the Bible, which contains the creation accounts

7. People also known as Israelites

9. Saved from the flood because he was faithful to God

Across

1. Kind of book in the Bible that tells about the prophets and their messages

6. First five books of the Bible; word means "five scrolls"

8. Testament that includes the four Gospels

10. Kind of book in the Bible that tells how a wise person lives

11. The perfect revelation of God

12. Testament that tells of God's relationship with the Jewish people before Jesus

13. Title given to the one sent to save us

Down

2. Creator of the universe

3. One's free choice to turn away from God

4. Kind of book in the Bible that shows how God cared for the Israelites throughout history

Word Match

Match each Word to Know with its definition.

_____ 1. Torah

_____ 2. stewardship

_____ 3. interpretation

_____ 4. Old Testament

_____ 5. Pentateuch

_____ 6. sin

_____ 7. Law

_____ 8. tradition

A. The history of the Jewish people, which helps us to understand Jesus.

B. The story of creation, the Covenant, and the journey of God's people to the Promised Land. Also known as the Law or the Pentateuch.

C. The beliefs and practices passed down throughout the ages and made a part of the Church's teaching.

D. Disobeying God and his plan.

E. The story of creation, the Covenant, and the journey of God's people to the Promised Land. Also known as the Torah or the Pentateuch.

F. The key to understanding the Bible.

G. Our duty to care for and protect God's creation.

H. The story of creation, the Covenant, and the journey of God's people to the Promised Land. Also known as the Law or the Torah.

Scroll Scramble

Unscramble the letters of these Old Testament books.

1. SMSPLA _____

2. SHAIAI _____

3. ESSNEIG _____

4. DGUJSE _____

5. KEELIZE _____

6. VERPRBOS _____

7. UHTR _____

8. SDOXEU _____

Mosaic of Ruth, Dormition Basilica, Jerusalem.

Which Book Is It?

Use your Bible's table of contents to find which books from Scroll Scramble above match the descriptions below. Write their names.

1. First book in the Bible _____

2. Comes immediately after the book of Psalms _____

3. The second book in the Pentateuch _____

4. The first book of the prophets _____

5. Two of the historical books _____

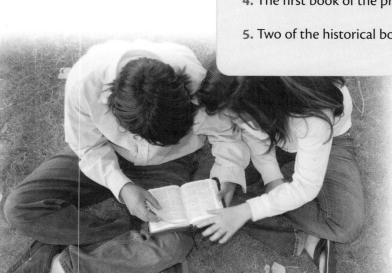

Celebrating

God's Word

Leader 1: We are gathered together in the name of the Father, and of the Son, and of the Holy Spirit.

All: Amen.

Leader 2: We have been created in the image and likeness of God, "who stretched out the heavens and laid the foundations of the earth" (Isaiah 51:13). We have been baptized into God's life. We are his people called to live in his love.

Kim Smith, *The Holy Spirit.*

All: Give thanks to the LORD, invoke his name;
make known among the peoples his deeds!
Sing praise, play music;
proclaim all his wondrous deeds!
Glory in his holy name;
rejoice, O hearts that seek the LORD!
Rely on the mighty LORD;
constantly seek his face.

Psalm 105:1–4

Reader: A reading from the prophet Isaiah.

I, the LORD, your God,
teach you what is for your good,
and lead you on the way you should go.
If you would hearken to my commandments,
your prosperity would be like a river.

Isaiah 48:17–18

The Word of the LORD.

All: Thanks be to God.

(Pause for silent prayer.)

Leader 3: Let us join in a litany of praise for God's wonderful creation. To each of the following, please respond, *We praise you, Lord.*

For the light of the sun . . . ℞

For the moon and stars . . . ℞

For the rain and snow . . . ℞

For the waters of the earth . . . ℞

For the plants and animals . . . ℞

For the creatures of the sea . . . ℞

For the air we breathe . . . ℞

For the food we share . . . ℞

For the gift of life . . . ℞

For the gift of one another . . . ℞

For Christ, our life . . . ℞

(Song: "Your Word, O Lord")

Looking Back at Unit 1

In this unit, you have begun learning about the Old Testament, which is the first part of the Bible. It is through the Bible that God speaks to his people. The Bible is a minilibrary of inspired literature. God inspired the authors of the Bible to share his will for his people and those truths about him that he wanted known.

The biblical authors told stories to explain the mysteries of creation and the beginning of sin in the world. These stories revealed that God created us because of his great love. God wanted to share love and life with the people he created. He asked them to take care of the earth and to use what he gave them to bring joy to others. God wanted his people to be happy, and he knew what would make them happy.

The stories about sin tell us that people wanted to control their lives without God. With the first sin, the mystery of evil came into the world. As sin spread, people separated themselves from God and from one another. But God never abandoned his people. He promised to send a redeemer to conquer sin and death.

Living the Message

Can you give yourself a check (✓) for each statement?

○ I know how to find quotations in the Bible.

○ I understand the religious truths that God teaches in the creation stories.

○ I try to develop the gifts God has given me.

○ I fight the effects of sin by trying to be a peacemaker.

○ When I hear God's Word, I listen carefully and try to live according to it.

Planning Ahead

God made you in his image and likeness, and what God made is very good. However, sin brings separation, conflict, and every type of unhappiness. Read the following verses from the Bible. Write what you will do to preserve the goodness and joy in God's creation.

Psalm 32:5

_____

_____

Psalm 100:1–3

_____

_____

Proverbs 14:21

_____

_____

Sirach 6:5

_____

_____

Family Feature

Our Family of Faith

Before there were churches, Christians would gather in each other's homes to share a meal and celebrate their faith. One's family was not just those people who shared a bloodline; it was also those people who shared traditions, culture, and most important, a belief in God.

This year your child is learning about the Old Testament, which is full of stories about the Chosen People, the Hebrews. As Catholics, we honor the Old Testament because it is also the foundation of our faith. It informed Jesus' own religious upbringing and laid the groundwork for his teachings.

Jesus, Mary, and Joseph were Jewish, the way your ancestors may have been Irish, Chinese, or Mexican. The Holy Family's journey from Nazareth to Bethlehem echoes the journeys of Abraham, Jacob, and Moses. Your ancestors may also have echoed these journeys during the tough trek that immigrants made to the United States. An appreciation of your own family's ancestors will help your children better understand the significance of the Hebrews of the Old Testament, who are their spiritual ancestors.

Think about how the following questions relate to your family.

- Do your children know about their ancestors? Do they get a chance to hear stories firsthand?

- Does your home bear witness to the larger family to which you belong? Are there framed photos of relatives? Do symbols of your Catholic family, adorn your home?
- In the Old Testament and during Jesus' time, names held symbolic significance or honored family forebears. Help your children tap into the power of their names by telling the story of why their names were chosen, what they mean, and how they are significant.

A sense of identity and belonging comes from family rituals and traditions that have been passed down. Think about your own family traditions, formal and informal, and where they came from. Talk with your children about those family rituals that give them a sense of comfort, peacefulness, or security. An understanding of family ritual can help your children better understand and appreciate the rites, rituals, and history of their faith.

Honor Your Family

Ask relatives for copies of family photos, make a poster of your family tree, pull together a collection of old family recipes, or interview your relatives to capture the stories they can remember. Try to include photos and stories of family members' religious experiences, such as stories of what it was like to serve Mass in Latin or photos from your grandmother's First Communion.

Show Your Faith

If you do not display a cross or images of saints in your home, then you might display a family Bible or favorite prayers or sayings printed on a plaque. You might also make it a family project to brainstorm ways to display symbols of your faith in your home. For example, you might make your own religious artwork by finding on the Internet favorite prayers, sayings, and Bible passages and embellishing them with artwork.

The Bible, the Blockbuster

Hoping that its sterling reputation will rub off on other books, writers and publishers have dipped into the Good Book for inspiration, from book titles such as *The Mac Bible* to runaway bestsellers like *The Red Tent* and the *Left Behind* series. And yet when it comes to the pages that fall between its covers, the ordinary Christian sometimes doesn't know where to begin. If you're among the many who can't tell an espistle from an apostle, here are some easy ways to get started.

1. Begin with a book from the Bible that really speaks to your interest or experience. For instance, Psalms is a favorite with people, especially poetry lovers, because it is filled with stirring emotion and color.

2. Work your way through the Bible by following the Lectionary—the readings from the Bible used for daily Mass and weekend worship—and the passages it prescribes for certain days of the year. You can find the order of the Lectionary in leaflets, online, or your parish bulletin.

3. Bible-study groups usually navigate through categories within the Bible—perhaps the historical books first, then the Old Testament prophets—but not necessarily in chronological order. If that sounds like a terrible idea, remember that when relating the story of Luke Skywalker's family in his Star Wars movies, George Lucas jumped all over the chronology through six different films. You can find valuable help from the *Six Weeks with the Bible* series from Loyola Press.

4. The Old Testament offers some of the most exciting and moving tales in literature. David and Goliath, Samson and Delilah, the Book of Ruth, and the story of Queen Esther are all found in the Old Testament. Why not make an Old Testament story the subject of a book-group discussion, or create a Scripture discussion group with your family? Your children will enjoy the exciting stories, you will grow in familiarity and love with the Bible, and your whole family will benefit from reading God's message.

❮ Andrea del Verrocchio, *David with the head of Goliath*, c. 1475.

Growing Together in Faith

The following is a creation story told by the Onondaga, a tribe of the Iroquois Federation. Share the story with your family.

Before the earth was created, there was only water and clouds. Above the clouds was Skyland, which was ruled by an ancient chief. Skyland grew a large, beautiful tree, whose roots faced in the four sacred directions. The tree grew every plant and fruit ever imagined.

One night the chief's wife dreamed that the great tree was uprooted. The chief believed the dream was a sign and uprooted the tree himself. While looking down through the hole left by the tree, the chief's wife lost her balance and fell. As she slipped, she clutched some seeds from the root of the great tree.

Two swans caught the chief's wife as she fell, but the animals knew she could not live in the water as they could. So Muskrat offered to swim down in the water and bring back earth for the chief's wife to stand on. When Muskrat brought back a pawful of earth, a giant turtle offered his shell as a resting place. Muskrat placed the earth on Turtle's back, where it grew until it became the whole world. The chief's wife stepped onto Earth and dropped the seeds she had been holding. Trees, flowers, and grass sprang up. Life began on earth.

The following discussion points may help your children think about the significance of creation stories and how they relate to faith.

- A tree plays an important role in the Onondaga story and in the creation story in Genesis. How are the trees similar in these stories? How are they different?
- What are the differences between how the world is created in this story and how it is created in the Genesis stories?
- Why might have the Onondaga believed that the world was created in this way?
- What are some ways that we, as a family can foster new life? Can we make a commitment to work together on a regular basis to honor God's creation?

A Family Project

A fun family project might be to illustrate this story. Have each member of your family create drawings that illustrates moments from this story. Have the book bound or display it as a collage in your family prayer area.

Caring for God's Creation

There are many ways that your family can work together to care for God's creation. Consider planting and tending to a tree, planting a garden, volunteering together at a homeless or animal shelter, working with a recycling organization, or picking up trash in your neighborhood. Just remember that whatever you choose, everyone in your family should make a commitment to the family project and participate on a regular basis.

Honoring Our Family

Use the outline below to create a family crest. Work with your children to decide what should go on the crest, how your family name should be lettered, and who should be responsible for making each part. When you have finished, frame your family crest and display it in a place of prominence in your home to serve as a reminder of the family from which you come.

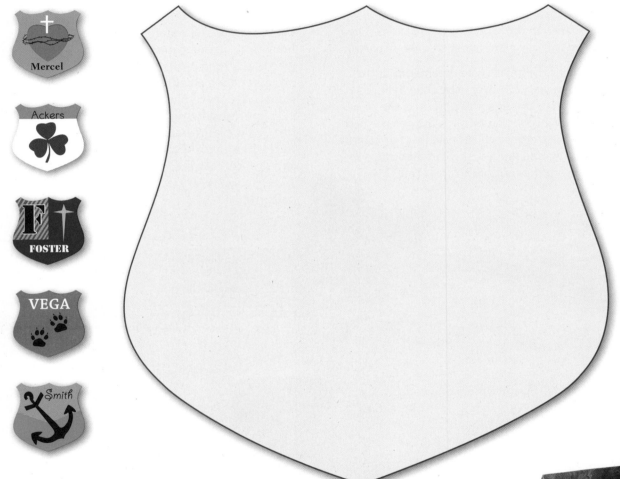

Family Crest Tips

On a traditional family crest, each symbol, line, animal, and color has a meaning. For example, gold represents generosity and an anchor symbolizes religious steadfastness. What is included on a family crest represents strengths, skills, and characteristics particular to that family. If you are creating a traditional family crest, be sure to think about the meaning of each color that you use, and check what different lines and symbols represent. A simple online search will provide you with Web sites detailing the meaning behind different colors and symbols.

Visit **www.christourlife.org/family** for more family resources.

Other Ideas

Instead of drawing elements of your family crest, make color copies of family photos to include.

God Forms a Family of Faith

I will make of you a great nation, and I will bless you.

Genesis 12:2

God Forms a Family of Faith

IN THIS UNIT, you will be learning about how God formed his family of faith, beginning with Abraham.

Abraham Is Our Father in Faith

Abraham was a man of great faith who trusted in God. When God called Abraham to leave his homeland, Abraham responded with a generous and obedient heart. Like Abraham, you are being called by God. You can give witness to your faith by responding as Abraham did. God established a covenant—a sacred agreement—with Abraham. As you learn about God's covenant with Abraham, think about your own baptismal covenant with God. Throughout this unit, you will explore ways of expressing your faith through prayer, sacrifice, and service to others.

The Israelites Journey to Egypt

You will trace the events in the life of Jacob's son Joseph and learn how God brings about good in situations that seem hopeless. We call this God's providence. You will learn how God's providence helps us to be hopeful and encourages us to look beyond the difficulties of the present. You will also learn how Christians have come to see people and events in the Old Testament as hints of the salvation that we find in Jesus Christ.

Jacob Is Chosen by God

Isaac, Abraham's son, had two sons: Jacob and Esau. You will read about the story of Jacob. Just as Jacob received God's blessing, you received God's blessing at Baptism. Like Jacob, you have received a mission: to continue the life and work of Jesus wherever you go.

Jacob

Abraham Is Our Father in Faith

God's Call and Abram's Response

based on Genesis 12

Have you ever been in awe of the power of the sea, the beauty of sunlight, or the strength of the wind? Many centuries before the coming of Christ, people wondered about these things. Nature impressed them greatly. Each element was a mystery to them. Many people worshiped the forces of nature as their gods. They offered prayers and sacrifices to these gods. They did not know the one true God. Faith is a supernatural gift of God that helps people to believe in him.

In those times lived a man named Abram. God chose to reveal himself to the world through Abram. Early in his life, Abram had traveled with his family and relatives from Ur in Chaldea to Haran. There he settled as a shepherd. One day, when Abram was seventy-five years old, God called him to make a journey to the distant, unknown land of Canaan.

God said to Abram:

"Leave your country, your family, and your father's house for the land I will show you.

I will make you a great nation; I will bless you and make your name so famous that it will be used as a blessing."

Abram could not fully understand these words. He only knew in his heart that he must obey them at once.

As Abram set out from Haran on his journey to Canaan, he was also beginning another kind of journey, a spiritual journey. This journey would lead him to a deeper and clearer faith in the one true God.

Abraham ❯

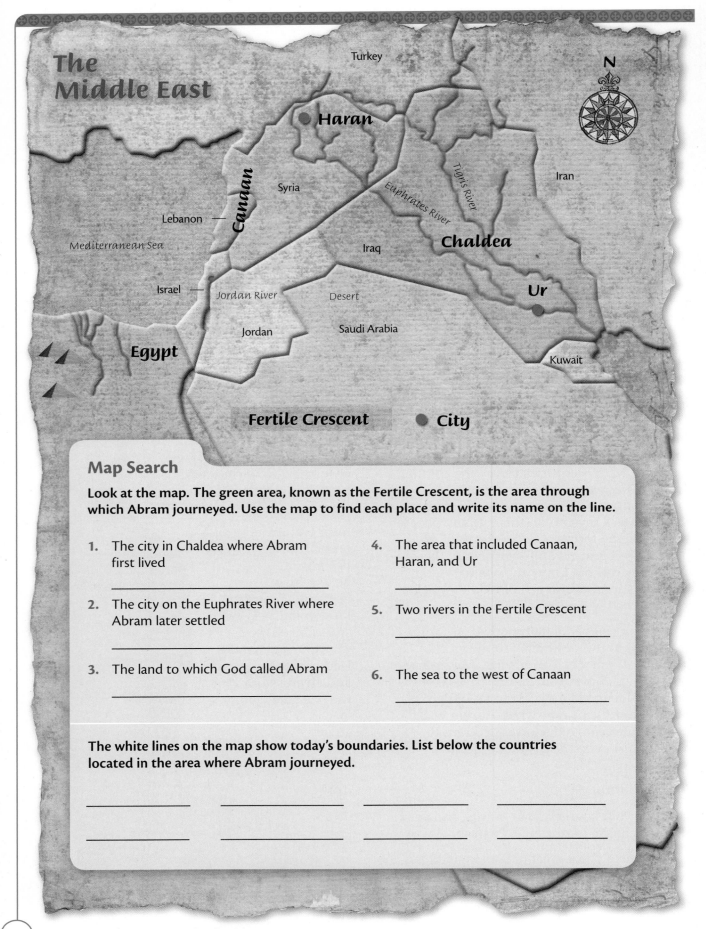

The Middle East

N

Turkey

Haran

Canaan

Syria

Lebanon

Mediterranean Sea

Israel

Jordan River

Jordan

Egypt

Desert

Saudi Arabia

Iraq

Euphrates River

Tigris River

Chaldea

Iran

Ur

Kuwait

Fertile Crescent   ● City

Map Search

Look at the map. The green area, known as the Fertile Crescent, is the area through which Abram journeyed. Use the map to find each place and write its name on the line.

1. The city in Chaldea where Abram first lived

   _____

2. The city on the Euphrates River where Abram later settled

   _____

3. The land to which God called Abram

   _____

4. The area that included Canaan, Haran, and Ur

   _____

5. Two rivers in the Fertile Crescent

   _____

6. The sea to the west of Canaan

   _____

The white lines on the map show today's boundaries. List below the countries located in the area where Abram journeyed.

_____   _____   _____   _____

_____   _____   _____   _____

God's Covenant with Abram

adapted from Genesis 15, 17

After Abram's arrival in Canaan, God continued to strengthen his trust and confidence. God said to him:

"Fear not, Abram! I am your shield; your reward will be very great."

Abram believed God, but he did not understand how all of God's promises could happen. He told God his problem:

"O Lord God, what good will your gifts be? You have given me no offspring, so one of my servants will be my heir."

God took Abram outside and said:

"Look up at the sky and count the stars, if you can. Just so shall your descendants be."

Abram again believed God, and God was pleased with Abram's faith. Then God made a very solemn agreement, called a **covenant,** with Abram. God said:

"No longer shall you be called Abram; your name shall be **Abraham,** for I am making you father of many nations. I will give to you and to your descendants the whole land of Canaan, and I will be their God. As for your wife Sarai, do not call her Sarai; her name shall be Sarah. I will bless her, and I will give you a son by her. You shall call him Isaac."

Within a year Sarah gave birth to a son, even though she and Abraham were very old.

Abraham was the first patriarch, or father and ruler, of the Chosen People. He was the man selected to receive God's promises and pass them on to his descendants. The name *Abraham* means "father of many nations." Abraham's and Sarah's name changes were signs that they were beginning a new way of life. Because of his faith and trust in God, we honor Abraham with the title *Father of Believers.* Like Abraham, who accepted his responsibility to care for and protect his family, we too are called to accept our responsibility to care for and protect others.

In God We Trust

We are believers. Because Abraham is truly our father in faith, we are called to express our faith as he did: with prompt obedience and wholehearted generosity. We are also called to recognize that as a family of faith, we are all brothers and sisters. If we live this way, then we will be open to receiving the blessings that God has promised to those who love him. When we place our trust in God as Abraham did, we are living the First Commandment, which calls us to believe in God, to hope in him, and to love him above all else.

Our Covenant with God

We are free to believe in God. We are also free not to believe in God. Faith is a gift given freely by God, which we can accept or reject. God made a covenant with us when we were baptized. He promises to give us eternal life if we believe in him and live according to those beliefs. In return, we promise to renounce Satan, to believe in God, and to live as Catholic Christians.

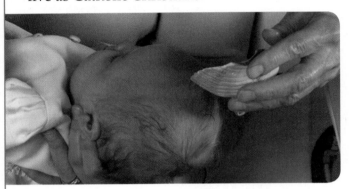

Baptism was the beginning of our journey of faith. We make this journey with God and with the whole Christian community. On the way, we live out our baptismal covenant with God and grow in our relationship with him and with one another. We do this whenever we pray, give witness to our faith in Christlike words and actions, or celebrate the sacraments.

Keeping the Covenant

Write something you will do to live out your baptismal covenant with God. The Holy Spirit, who helps us believe, will assist you.

_____

_____

_____

_____

_____

_____

_____

_____

_____

A Moment with Jesus

In Baptism, you were given the gift of faith and entered into a new life with Christ. Take a moment to thank Jesus for the gift of your Baptism. Ask him to help you to remain faithful to God's law of love. Pray the words of the following psalm:

I will celebrate your love forever, LORD. Age after age my words shall proclaim your faithfulness; for I claim that love is built to last forever and your faithfulness founded firmly in the heavens. Happy the people who learn to acclaim you! LORD, they will live in the light of your favor; they will rejoice in your name all day and exult in your righteousness. Once you said, "I will keep my love for him always. My covenant with him stands firm."

adapted from Psalm 89:1–2,15–16,19,29

A Challenge to Abraham's Faith

based on Genesis 22

When Abraham accepted God's call to leave Haran for Canaan, he did not know what the future would hold. God had chosen him, and that was enough.

Abraham's journey to Canaan meant a new beginning. He had to leave his homeland and his friends. He had to adjust to a new land and a new people. It was a great risk. When he first went to Canaan, his knowledge of God was limited. In the years that followed, Abraham came to know God better. He expressed his faith in God and looked for ways to worship and serve him more generously.

Abraham saw how the Canaanites worshiped. They knew that life was mysterious and they believed that it had to be a gift from a powerful being. To honor this unknown source of life,

the Canaanites followed a practice in which they killed their firstborn children in a religious **sacrifice**. They did this in petition for abundant crops, for strong herds, and for blessings on their families.

When Isaac was born, Abraham might have wondered if God expected him to sacrifice his son the way the Canaanites sacrificed their children. Sacrificing Isaac seemed impossible for Abraham. He loved Isaac, the son of his old age. And if he sacrificed Isaac, how would God keep his promise of making him the father of many descendants? Even so, Abraham was ready to do anything for God.

A Story of Trust

The story of Abraham's trust in and love of God at this time in his life is told in the skit on page 44. The story has been told for many generations since the time of Abraham. It teaches the Chosen People that all human life is sacred and must be treated with dignity. It also teaches that the one true God looks for a sacrifice of our wills rather than for a sacrifice of a human. We sacrifice our wills by saying no to things that would harm us and other people and by saying yes to loving actions.

Abraham's Sacrifice

based on Genesis 22

Characters God Abraham Angel
Isaac Narrator

Narrator: Abraham had lived for many years in friendship with God. One day God called him.

God: Abraham, Abraham, where are you?

Abraham: Here I am, Lord.

God: Abraham, take your son Isaac and go to the land of Moriah. When you arrive, go to the mountain I point out to you and offer Isaac to me as a burnt-offering sacrifice.

Narrator: Although Abraham was saddened by God's command, he rose early the next morning. He saddled his donkey and went out with Isaac and two servants. On the third day of travel, Abraham saw the appointed place in the distance and spoke to his servants.

Abraham: Stay here with the donkey while Isaac and I go to the mountaintop to worship.

Narrator: Isaac carried the wood on his back. Abraham carried the flint and knife as they set off.

Isaac: Father, we have the knife, flint, and wood, but where is the sheep for the sacrifice?

Abraham: God will provide the sheep for the sacrifice, Isaac.

Jacques Tissot, *Isaac Bears the Wood for his Sacrifice.*

Narrator: When they reached the top of the mountain, Abraham built an altar and arranged the wood on it. He then tied up his son and put him on top of the wood. Just as Abraham reached out and took the knife to kill Isaac, an angel of God called out:

Angel: Abraham, stop! Do not harm Isaac, for now I know you fear God. You have not refused him your son.

Narrator: With great relief Abraham looked up and saw a ram caught by its horns in a nearby bush. Abraham knew that God did not want him to sacrifice Isaac. He took the ram and offered it in place of his son. Abraham had responded to God's command with faith. Because of his generous obedience, the Lord made this promise to him.

God: I swear by myself—it is Yahweh who speaks—because you have done this, because you have not refused me your only son, I will shower blessings on you. I will make your descendants as many as the stars in the heavens and the sands of the seashore. In them all nations of the earth shall find blessing—all this because you obeyed my command.

Narrator: By not allowing Abraham to sacrifice Isaac, God taught his Chosen People that he did not want human sacrifice. He also showed that those who believe and trust in him are rewarded with abundant blessings. Abraham's faith in God was shown in his trust. God had led him to a new land, chosen him to be the father of his people, and given him a son. Abraham knew that God loved him, and he trusted in God's goodness. God rewarded Abraham's faith and trust with a renewal of his promises.

Isaac would later marry Rebekah and have two sons. To them he would pass on the promises of God that he had received from Abraham.

Eventually a descendant of Abraham would be the Savior of the world. Through him all nations would be blessed.

Summary

We Remember

What does true faith in God lead to?

True faith in God leads to complete trust in his goodness and prompt obedience to his call.

What did God promise Abraham?

God promised Abraham land and many descendants. He promised that all nations would be blessed through him.

What does it mean to sacrifice our wills?

It means that we say no to things that would harm us or other people and say yes to loving actions.

Words to Know

Abraham   covenant   sacrifice

We Respond

Pray the prayer of faith from Psalm 89 on Page 42. In your journey log, write your thoughts about what it means to celebrate God's love and to live in the light of God's favor.

Things to Do at Home

1. Share with your family the story of Abraham. Stories about him can be found in Genesis 13:1–13 and Genesis 18:20–33. What do you learn about Abraham from these accounts?

2. Work with your family to list qualities that make a good and loyal friend. Talk about which of these qualities Abraham showed in his relationship with God. Discuss which qualities you show toward your friends and family.

3. Abraham was a man of faith who responded to God's call with generosity and prompt obedience. Ask your family members to tell about times when they each were called upon to practice great faith.

4. Make a covenant with a member of your family. Each of you should agree to do a certain favor for the other. After a few days, check to see how well each person has kept his or her part. How is your covenant similar to the covenant between God and Abram? How is it different?

5. Write the story of Abraham and Isaac as seen through Sarah's eyes. Share your story with your family.

Visit **www.christourlife.org/family** for more family resources.

The Man of Faith Use the clues below to write the missing letters in the puzzle.

Across

4. We enter into a covenant with God when we are _____ .

5. Abraham was willing to _____ his son to God.

7. A solemn agreement in which people make a promise is called a _____ .

8. Abraham was the first and greatest _____ of the Chosen People.

Down

1. _____ was the wife of Abraham.

2. _____ was Abraham's son, who carried on the covenant with God.

3. We honor Abraham as the Father of _____ .

6. God called Abraham to _____ and promised this land to his descendents.

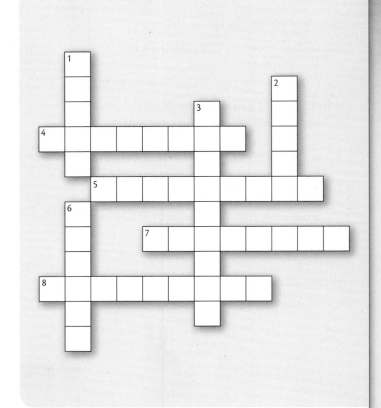

Promises, Promises List four promises that God made to Abraham.

1. _____

   _____

   _____

   _____

2. _____

   _____

   _____

   _____

3. _____

   _____

   _____

   _____

4. _____

   _____

   _____

   _____

Bonus Name two ways in which Isaac was like Jesus.

1. _____

   _____

   _____

   _____

2. _____

   _____

   _____

   _____

David Teniers the Younger, *Abraham giving thanks for having spared his son Isaac*, 1653.

CHAPTER

7

Jacob Is Chosen by God

Sibling Rivalry

We all like to be chosen for things, whether it's for a spot on a sports team, as a member of a club, or for a role in a play. Sometimes we work very hard to be chosen. But not everyone who wants to join is *always* chosen. A play, for example, has only a certain number of roles; not every person who tries out is going to get a part.

Genesis chapter 25 introduces a story that tells us that there was a lot of competition between Isaac's twin sons, Esau and Jacob. Esau was born first but Jacob came out gripping Esau's heel, not wanting to let go. Before their birth, God had told Rebekah, Isaac's wife, that her younger son, Jacob, would play a special role in the life of his people. He was God's chosen one.

Jacques Tissot, *The Mess of Pottage*, c. 1896–1902.

As the firstborn, Esau was to receive his family's birthright. This was the oldest son's right to the greatest part of the inheritance and to a special blessing from the father. The birthright was especially important in Isaac's family. Whoever received the birthright and special blessing would become a patriarch of God's Chosen People. Although all of this was to go to Esau, Jacob wanted it very much.

Jacob did not think he had a chance for this blessing unless he took matters into his own hands. One day Esau found Jacob cooking. Esau was hungry and asked for some of the stew. Jacob knew that this was his chance. He said, "First, give me your birthright." Esau was so hungry that he agreed and even made an oath. Neither son told Isaac of this trade. What does this trade tell you about Esau?

When Isaac was old and nearly blind, he called for Esau to give him his blessing before he died. Rebekah overheard Isaac's words and told Jacob. Jacob was her favorite son. Rebekah wanted him to receive Isaac's special blessing. Instead of trusting that God would make Jacob the leader of his people, she felt that she would have to make it happen.

A Stolen Blessing

Read in your Bible Genesis 27:1–29 to learn how Jacob got Isaac's blessing. Then answer the questions below.

1. Why were Rebekah and Jacob able to fool Isaac? (verse 1)

   _____

2. How was Jacob disguised? (verses 15, 16)

   _____

3. How did Jacob explain how he got the animal so quickly? (verse 20)

   _____

4. Isaac had asked for Esau but was not certain which son had come. What confused Isaac? (verse 22)

   _____

5. What did Isaac ask for Jacob as he blessed him? (verses 28,29)

   _____

Jacob tricked his father into giving him the blessing that should have gone to Esau. God was not pleased with this deceit. Yet, because of his power and love, God would still bring good out of the situation. Jacob was his chosen one, and that choice would not be changed. It would be through Jacob and his family that the promise of a redeemer would be carried out. God continues to care for all of his creation.

Jacob's Dream

based on Genesis 28:10–22

Rebekah found out that Esau planned to kill Jacob because of the stolen blessing. She sent Jacob to Haran, to stay with her brother Laban. Genesis 28 tells us that one night, on the way there, Jacob lay down to sleep at a shrine, using a stone for a pillow. He dreamed about a ramp or stairway leading from the ground to heaven, with angels going up and down. (This stairway is usually referred to as Jacob's ladder.) In the dream, the Lord appeared beside Jacob and renewed the promises he had made to Abraham. The dream symbolized the connection between heaven and earth and reassured Jacob of God's presence. When Jacob woke up he set up the stone as a memorial stone, marking the spot as a sacred place. Later he built an altar there and named the place Bethel, which means "house of God." When we as Catholics gather in the house of God to celebrate the Mass, Christ is truly present in the Eucharist.

Giambattista Tiepolo, *The Dream of Jacob.*

More Tricks

When Jacob went to stay with Laban, he fell in love with Laban's daughter Rachel. He agreed to work for Laban for seven years in exchange for Rachel's hand in marriage. Laban agreed, but later tricked Jacob. On the night of the wedding feast, Laban sent his older daughter, Leah, to Jacob. Because of the veils that Leah wore, Jacob did not realize that he had married Leah instead of Rachel.

It was normal at the time for men to have more than one wife, so Jacob was eventually able to marry Rachel also. However, he had to agree to work for Laban for another seven years! Jacob's trials helped him become a better person. You might enjoy reading about this part of Jacob's life in Genesis 29:15–30.

Jacob Wrestles with God

Eventually Jacob decided to take his family and return home. One night while traveling, when Jacob was alone, a stranger came and wrestled with him until dawn. At one point the man wrenched Jacob's hip socket but did not overcome him. He had to ask Jacob to let him go. Find Jacob's reply in Genesis 32:27–29. Write it here.

_____

Jacob's words showed both great faith and the importance of God's blessing. Jacob was willing to spend all his strength to receive it. He desired to have God act in his own life and through him in the lives of others. When the stranger saw this, he gave Jacob the name Israel, which means "he who wrestled with God." Jacob's new name was a sign of his new mission. He no longer thought only of himself. He was sent forth as the father of God's Chosen People, who would later be known as the **Israelites**.

The visitor did not give his name, but Jacob realized that he had been visited by God himself through a messenger. This divine visit assured Jacob that the blessing he had received from Isaac was truly his. He then returned to his homeland reassured that God was with him. From Jacob's twelve sons came the twelve tribes of Israel.

A Moment with Jesus

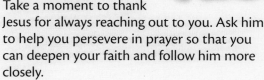

The story of Jacob wrestling with the messenger of God is often used to help us understand our life of prayer. Like Jacob's, our faith requires perseverance. God is always reaching out to us. However, in order to lift our minds and hearts to God, we need to persevere in overcoming distractions. Take a moment to thank Jesus for always reaching out to you. Ask him to help you persevere in prayer so that you can deepen your faith and follow him more closely.

What's Your Name?

Three people you have studied so far have had their names changed by God as a sign of their special calling. Who are they?

_____

_____

_____

At baptism you were given your name. Your parents probably chose it, and it is the name by which God our Father called you to be a member of his family. That name is a sign of your mission. It reminds you to be Christ to everyone you meet.

Some people receive a new name at Confirmation, or when they become a priest, brother, or sister. It reminds them that God calls each of us to become a new person in Jesus Christ. Other people take no new names at these times. They choose to repeat their baptismal names in order to recall their baptismal mission.

Chosen for Mission

We all know how good it feels to be chosen.

What is something you want to be chosen for when you are an adult?

_____

Who would choose you? _____

How could you prepare now? _____

What would you need to be successful? _____

A Chosen Race

Rebekah learned before his birth that her younger son, Jacob, was God's special choice. The blessing that Isaac gave to Jacob was the sign that he was God's chosen one, a patriarch of his people. We do not know why certain people are chosen. God chooses freely, and once he has chosen he does not change his mind. You are also chosen by God.

Which sacrament marked you as one chosen by God to be his child and a member of his Church?

_____

Which sacrament strengthens and confirms your relationship with God as one of his chosen ones?

_____

It is through the Sacrament of Baptism that we enter into the Body of Christ, the Church. The First Letter of Peter (2:9) reminds us that through baptism we become members of "a chosen race, a holy nation, a people of his own, so that you may announce the praises of him who called you out of darkness into his wonderful light." This means that to be chosen is a privilege, and that privilege comes with responsibility. Through baptism, we are chosen to participate in Jesus' mission of bringing

all people together as brothers and sisters. In Confirmation, the Holy Spirit strengthens our relationship with God and with one another so that we can share in Jesus' mission.

Chosen, Not Perfect

Jacob was human, and sometimes he failed to live as God's chosen one. But God did not change his choice. Jacob knew God would always be there to help him. He had received the blessing of the divine visitor. He knew that this blessing would strengthen him to lead his people. You probably find times when you are thinking only of yourself instead of caring for the good of all. But no matter how weak you are, or how many mistakes you make, you will always be one of God's Chosen People. God will always be ready to help you.

What two sacraments can you celebrate often to help you overcome weakness and return to God?

_____

_____

We Remember

Why was the birthright of special importance in Isaac's family?

> The son with the birthright would receive his father's special blessing and become a patriarch of God's people.

What was the meaning of Jacob's dream?

> The dream symbolized the connection between heaven and earth and reassured Jacob of God's presence.

Why was Jacob's name changed and what did his new name mean?

> Jacob's name was changed to Israel, a name that means "he who wrestled with God." His new name was a sign of his new mission.

What mission does every Catholic receive at Baptism?

> A Catholic's mission is to continue Christ's life and work in today's world.

Word to Know

Israelites

We Respond

Ask Jesus to help you understand what it means for someone your age to participate in his mission. Write a prayer asking God to help you always to be faithful to your mission.

⌄ This tree is in Beit El, Israel. It was here that Jacob dreamt of a ladder connecting heaven and earth. He called this place Beit El, or Bethel, which means "House of God."

Things to Do at Home

1. Read Jacob's prayer in Genesis 32:9–13. Imagine how afraid Jacob was as he went to meet Esau. Think about the words he used to pray to God for help. Then write your own prayer asking God to help you with something that you are afraid of.

2. Ask for God's blessing each morning. Each night before you go to bed, think about how you have continued the life and work of Jesus during the day.

3. Jacob's story has many colorful episodes. Choose an episode from Jacob's life. Rewrite it from the point of view of another person in the story.

4. The people God chooses are not perfect. Jacob had his faults and so do we. Choose a famous person, such as a saint or one of your personal heros, who did much good despite a particular weakness. Write a report about him or her.

5. Ask your parents why they chose your name for you. Prepare to share this information with your class.

6. Ask your parents or godparents about your Baptism. Talk about who was present, where it took place, and what it meant to them.

Visit **www.christourlife.org/family** for more family resources.

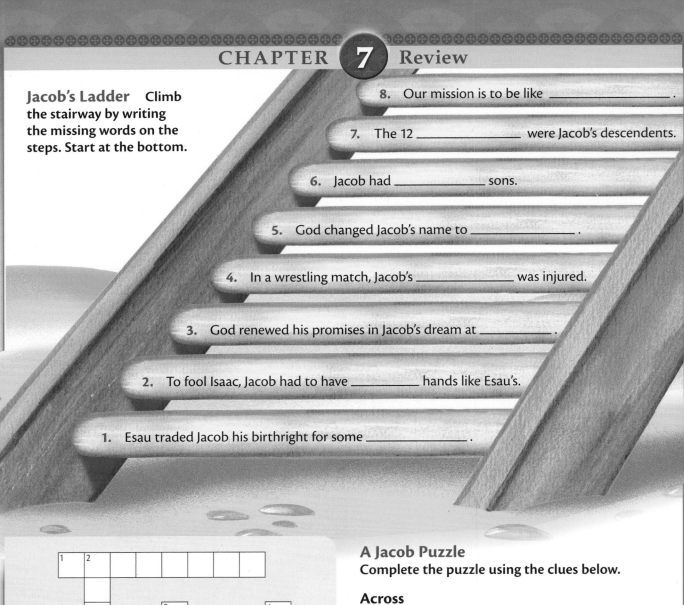

Jacob's Ladder Climb the stairway by writing the missing words on the steps. Start at the bottom.

8. Our mission is to be like _____ .

7. The 12 _____ were Jacob's descendents.

6. Jacob had _____ sons.

5. God changed Jacob's name to _____ .

4. In a wrestling match, Jacob's _____ was injured.

3. God renewed his promises in Jacob's dream at _____ .

2. To fool Isaac, Jacob had to have _____ hands like Esau's.

1. Esau traded Jacob his birthright for some _____ .

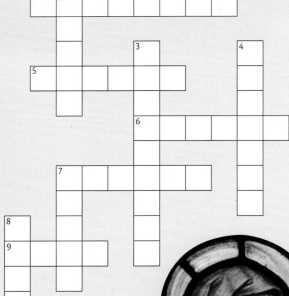

Jacob ❯

A Jacob Puzzle
Complete the puzzle using the clues below.

Across

1. Jacob wanted to receive this from his father
5. After years with his mother's brother, Jacob returned to this land
6. Jacob's favored wife
7. Jacob's name after it was changed by God
9. The brother whose birthright Jacob stole

Down

2. The brother of Jacob's mother
3. The name given to the first leaders of God's Chosen People
4. Jacob's mother
7. Jacob's father
8. Jacob's first wife (the one accidentally married)

The Israelites Journey to Egypt

Joseph, Son of Israel

You may know the story of Moses leading the Israelites out of Egypt and into the Promised Land. But have you ever wondered how the Israelites came to be in Egypt in the first place? The story of Joseph, son of Israel (Jacob), explains how the Israelites came to Egypt.

Israel experienced God's special plan for himself and his twelve sons through some unusual events. These events centered around Joseph, one of Israel's youngest sons. The life of Joseph reminds us that even when we encounter obstacles in life, God provides for our needs and watches over us. We call this **Divine Providence,** which means that God can bring good results from the bad choices that people make. It remains a mystery to us why bad things happen in the world. However, we know that we are not alone when things go wrong—God is always loving and caring for his creation through his Son, Jesus, and through the Holy Spirit.

A Story of Envy

based on Genesis 37

Joseph was Israel's favored son. To show his love, Israel had a fine tunic made for Joseph. When Joseph's brothers saw how much their father loved Joseph, they were envious.

To make matters worse, Joseph told his brothers about a dream he had. "We were binding sheaves when suddenly my sheaf stood up in the center. Your sheaves formed a ring around mine and bowed to it."

"Are you going to make yourself king over us?" his brothers asked. They hated Joseph all the more.

Then Joseph had another dream. He said, "I saw the sun, the moon, and eleven stars bowing to me."

This time even his father scolded him. "Are I, your mother, and your brothers to come and bow to the ground before you?"

One day Joseph's brothers were out tending their father's flocks. Israel told Joseph to check on his brothers and the flocks. His brothers saw him coming and plotted to kill him. "Here comes that master dreamer. Let's kill him. We can say that a wild animal devoured him. Then we shall see what comes of his dreams!"

❮ School of Raphael, *Joseph explaining the dreams to his brothers.*

A Brother Is Sold

Reuben, the eldest, objected to killing Joseph. "We must not take his life. Throw him into that well, but don't kill him." So when Joseph came up to them, his brothers took his splendid tunic and threw him into a dry well.

That night a caravan of traders passed by their camp. Judah asked, "What do we gain by killing our brother? Let us sell him to these Ishmaelites." So Joseph was sold for twenty pieces of silver. He was taken from Canaan to Egypt, where he was sold as a slave to Potiphar, an official of the pharaoh.

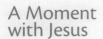

Meanwhile, Joseph's brothers killed a goat and dipped Joseph's tunic in its blood. They sent the tunic to Israel with the message: "We have found this. See whether it is your son's tunic." When Israel identified the tunic, he mourned Joseph deeply and refused to be consoled.

Recall

1. Why did Joseph's brothers hate him?

2. What did Joseph's brothers do to him?

3. How was Israel led to believe that Joseph was dead?

Envy—A Deadly Sin

Joseph's brothers were guilty of envy, one of the seven capital sins. Envy is a feeling of anger, sadness, or resentment because someone has a quality, a talent, or a possession that we want. We call this a capital sin because it can seriously wound the life-giving relationship that we have with God and others. Envy is a sin against the Tenth Commandment. Through our Baptism, God has given us the grace we need to combat envy through good will, humility, and trust in God's providence. When we overcome envy, we are able to live as brothers and sisters, making sure that the material goods of the world are shared by all.

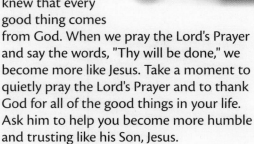

A Moment with Jesus

One of the ways we combat envy is through the practice of humility. To be humble is to be like Jesus, who knew that every good thing comes from God. When we pray the Lord's Prayer and say the words, "Thy will be done," we become more like Jesus. Take a moment to quietly pray the Lord's Prayer and to thank God for all of the good things in your life. Ask him to help you become more humble and trusting like his Son, Jesus.

Dreams and Wonders in Egypt

based on Genesis 39–41

The Lord protected Joseph while he lived in Potiphar's house. Joseph was successful in everything he did. Soon Potiphar put Joseph in charge of all his possessions.

Joseph was a handsome man. After a while Potiphar's wife fell in love with him. She wanted Joseph for herself, but he refused to commit sin with her, for he had great respect for Potiphar and for God's laws.

Angry with Joseph, Potiphar's wife screamed and pretended that Joseph had tried to attack her. Potiphar became furious. He seized Joseph and threw him into jail.

Even in prison the Lord protected Joseph. He won the respect and trust of the chief jailer and was put in charge of all the other prisoners.

Dreams and Wonders in Egypt (continued)

Some time later Pharaoh's cupbearer and the chief baker were imprisoned for offending Pharaoh. Joseph was assigned to guard them.

One night both the cupbearer and the baker had strange dreams. The next morning when Joseph checked on them, he saw that they looked worried. He asked what was bothering them. They answered, "We have had strange dreams, but there is no one to interpret them."

Joseph replied, "Tell me your dreams."

In the cupbearer's dream, he had seen a vine with three branches filled with grapes. "I picked the grapes and squeezed them into Pharaoh's cup. I put the cup into Pharaoh's hand."

Joseph told the cupbearer that in three days he would be released and would again be cupbearer to Pharaoh. He asked the cupbearer to put in a good word for him when he got out. The chief baker, hoping for a similar interpretation, explained his dream. He had seen himself carrying three baskets. In the top one were baked goods for Pharaoh. Birds were pecking at the baked goods.

"In three days," Joseph told him, "Pharaoh will hang you."

Three days later the events happened as Joseph had predicted. But Joseph's attempts to be released were in vain. He remained in prison for two more years. Then Pharaoh had two dreams that no one in his court could explain. The royal cupbearer remembered Joseph and told Pharaoh about him.

Pharaoh summoned Joseph. "I've had dreams that no one can interpret, but I have heard that you can interpret dreams."

Joseph replied, "It is God who will give an answer."

Pharaoh began. "In one dream I was standing on the bank of the Nile. Seven cows, fat and sleek, came up out of the Nile. Behind them came seven other cows, ugly

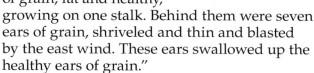

and scrawny. They ate the fat cows. In another dream I saw seven ears of grain, fat and healthy, growing on one stalk. Behind them were seven ears of grain, shriveled and thin and blasted by the east wind. These ears swallowed up the healthy ears of grain."

Joseph said that God had revealed to Pharaoh what he was going to do. In Egypt, there would be seven years of good crops. But those seven years would be followed by seven years of famine. Joseph advised Pharaoh to collect and store food during the good years. That way, during the famine, the people would have food to eat.

Pharaoh was so pleased with Joseph that he made him governor over all of Egypt. For the next seven years, Joseph collected and stored the abundant crops. When famine came in the following seven years, Joseph opened the storehouses to the people. All Egyptians needing food were told to go to Joseph.

Recall

1. What happened while Joseph was in prison?

2. What interpretation did Joseph give to Pharaoh's dreams?

3. What reward was Joseph given?

Solidarity

Joseph set a good example for us by showing how the goods of the earth are meant to be shared by all. God is the creator of all things and he wants his creation to be enjoyed by all. We have the responsibility to care for one another, as Joseph cared for the people during the famine. *Solidarity* is the attitude that leads us to share spiritual and material goods with others.

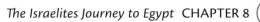

Dreams and Hope

In the Old Testament, the Hebrew people believed that dreams were sent by God as a means of revealing his plan and for inviting a response from his people. When we talk about our own plans in life, we often use the word *dream*. We talk about dreaming of a better life or dreaming about winning the lottery. As Catholics, we believe that God has a plan for us and so instead of simply dreaming, we hope. For Christians, hope is much more than wishing for something. Hope is one of the three Theological Virtues, along with faith and charity. For a Christian, to hope is to have confidence that God will always be with us and will always provide us with what we need. As Catholics, we hope for good things because we trust in God's loving plan for our salvation and well being. It is hope that drives us to struggle for justice and to build a society in which all people's rights are respected.

A Family Reunited

based on Genesis 42–50

The famine Joseph had predicted was experienced everywhere. In Canaan, Israel's family needed food. Israel had heard of the stored grain in Egypt. So he sent all his sons except Benjamin, the youngest, to Egypt to buy food.

Joseph's ten brothers came to him for grain and knelt before him. He recognized them immediately, but they did not know him.

Joseph accused them of being spies. They said they were not spies. They explained that they had left their father and brother at home. Joseph pretended he did not believe them. He kept one brother, Simeon, as a prisoner until they returned with the youngest brother as proof of their story.

When the brothers returned home and told Israel that they would have to take Benjamin to Egypt, he was very upset. Israel cried out, "Must you make me childless? Joseph is gone, Simeon is gone, and now you would take away Benjamin. My son is not going down with you."

But soon they needed food and grain again. So Israel finally agreed to let his sons take Benjamin and return to Egypt.

Joseph received his brothers. When he saw Benjamin, he invited the brothers to dine with him. Although they were worried at first, they accepted. At the meal, Joseph honored Benjamin above everyone else by giving him the largest portion of food.

But Joseph had one more test for his brothers. He had his servant fill their bags with grain and the money the brothers had paid for the grain. Joseph had his own silver cup put into his brother Benjamin's sack.

After the brothers left for home, Joseph sent his guard after them in search of the cup. When it was found with Benjamin, the brothers claimed innocence. But they were ordered to return to Joseph.

A Family Reunited (continued)

As punishment for the theft of the cup, Joseph commanded that Benjamin stay with him as a slave. The brothers begged Joseph not to do this. They told him that their father surely would die if Benjamin did not return.

Moved by their concern for their father, Joseph called them closer. "I am Joseph," he said, "your brother whom you sold into Egypt. But don't feel bad about selling me into slavery. God sent me here first in order to save your lives. Return quickly to my father and tell him to come to Egypt at once. Settle here in the region of Goshen. I will provide for you."

The brothers could hardly believe what they had heard. When they arrived home and told Israel, he was amazed. Immediately Israel, his sons, and their families went to Egypt. There the family rejoiced to be with Joseph.

Years later, when Israel was about to die, he gave each one of his sons a blessing. Judah was promised he would become as powerful as a lion and rule over others. The Messiah, the one promised to deliver all people from sin, would come from Judah's family.

After Israel died, Joseph's brothers were afraid. They thought that Joseph might harm them for what they had done to him. So they went to him to ask forgiveness in their father's name. Moved by their words, Joseph responded, "Do not be afraid. Even though you meant to do evil, God planned that it would bring good. Because of what happened to me, many people have been saved. Do not worry. I will continue to care for you and your families."

The Israelites remained in Egypt for many generations. In time, their families grew large and prospered.

Recall

1. How had Joseph's dreams come true?

2. How did Joseph test his brothers?

3. Which son received Israel's special blessing?

4. What did Joseph answer when his brothers asked forgiveness?

Caring for Our Family

Joseph took care of his family and made sure that they were provided for during their time of need. We, too, are called to do all we can to support not only our own families, but all families. We begin by showing honor and respect for our parents, as the Fourth Commandment calls us to do. The family is the central institution of our society. Our participation in family life and in the life of our community is the key to a healthy society. From the experience of our own families, we come to recognize that we all belong to the family of God and are called to promote the well-being of all people, especially those who are in need.

Providence in Our Lives

Jesus calls us to be forgiving. Joseph took revenge on his brothers and caused his father pain. But in the end Joseph could forgive his brothers because he trusted God. This trust helped him know that God would bring good out of all that happened. Through the events of Joseph's life, God arranged to provide food for the Israelites.

God does the same thing in our lives. He guides our lives so that when evil things happen to us, he makes them work for good if we cooperate with him.

Sometimes it takes a long time for us to see this. Remember, many years passed between Joseph's being sold into slavery and being reunited with his family. One way we can learn to see God acting in our lives is to think about the things that happen to us and others. When we remember that God loves us, we know that no matter what happens he can bring good from it. In prayer we ask God to help us trust and believe in his Divine Providence.

Thy Will Be Done

Jesus taught us to pray the Lord's Prayer. Praying the Lord's Prayer helps us to grow closer to God, to build our trust in him, and to believe in his plan for our lives. Match the following phrases of the Lord's Prayer with the line that describes what we are praying for or about.

___ 1. Our Father

___ 2. Who art in heaven

___ 3. Hallowed be thy name

___ 4. Thy kingdom come

___ 5. Thy will be done on earth as it is in heaven

___ 6. Give us this day our daily bread

___ 7. And forgive us our trespasses, as we forgive those who trespass against us.

___ 8. And Lead us not into temptation, but deliver us from evil.

___ 9. Amen

A. We ask for our needs and for the basic needs of all people.

B. We pray for the growth of God's Kingdom in our lives.

C. We ask that our will and God's will become one.

D. God is truly our Father and that is how we are to address him when we pray.

E. This refers, not to a place, but to God's majesty and his presence in the hearts of holy people.

F. We express our affirmation ("So be it") of all seven petitions of the Lord's Prayer.

G. We ask for God's mercy for our offenses and for the strength to forgive others.

H. God's name is so great that it should be recognized as holy by all people.

I. We ask God to not let us take a path that leads to sin.

Can you recall a time when you felt God taking care of you in a special way? Write about it.

_____

Providence There is a saying, "God writes straight with crooked lines." What does this mean? How is it true in Joseph's story?

_____

_____

We Remember

What is providence?

Providence is God's watching over us and caring for all our needs.

What can we learn from the story of Joseph and his family?

From the life of Joseph we learn that God can bring good out of all things. We also learn how the Israelites came to live in Egypt.

How does praying the Our Father help us to combat envy?

Praying the Our Father helps us to be humble like Jesus. When we pray the Our Father and say the words, "Thy will be done," we become more like Jesus.

Word to Know

Divine Providence

Respond

Lord, help me to love you more and more. Give me light that I may believe in your goodness and trust in your ways.

Peter von Cornelius, *Joseph recognized by his brothers.* ❯

Things to Do at Home

1. Each day, take some time to think about how God has been with you.

2. Find on television, in magazines, or in newspapers stories that show God's providence.

3. Read Luke 12:22–32 to find the words of Jesus about providence.

4. Share the story of Joseph with your family. Talk about what lessons can be learned from Joseph's life. Ask your family about times in which God's providence took care of them.

5. Talk to your parents about how, as a family, you can practice solidarity with people who are in need. Talk about ways that your family can pray for and work to address the needs of people around the world who are suffering.

6. With your parents, design a small prayer card that takes the lines of the Lord's Prayer and includes the descriptions of each line as outlined in the activity Thy Will Be Done on page 58. Decorate the prayer card and make a commitment to pray the Lord's Prayer daily.

Visit **www.christourlife.org/family** for more family resources.

D	E	E	A	C	D	E	Y	A	A
R	R	C	R	A	M	Y	E	E	R
E	E	N	C	R	R	T	P	N	A
A	I	E	F	A	M	I	N	E	A
M	H	D	P	V	J	L	S	L	I
Y	T	I	R	A	D	I	L	O	S
H	M	V	C	N	M	M	Y	E	S
L	L	O	I	O	J	U	D	A	H
O	B	R	R	H	I	H	R	I	E
N	H	P	E	S	O	J	M	A	E

Joseph's Word Maze The following words will help you recall the story of Joseph and his family and what we can learn from this story. Find and circle each word in the word search. Look up and down, side to side, and diagonally. Then identify each word in a short phrase or sentence.

Joseph _____

Jacob _____

Judah _____

humility _____

solidarity _____

caravan _____

famine _____

dream _____

promise _____

providence _____

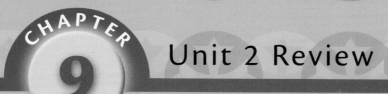

CHAPTER 9

Unit 2 Review

God Forms a Family of Faith

Then and Now

Each of the following incidents is taken from an Old Testament story in this unit. After reading each example, answer the questions that ask about how we can practice the faith today.

1. Abraham responded with faith by doing what God told him to do. What can we do to express our faith today?

   _____

   _____

2. Abraham was willing to sacrifice his son, Isaac, if God wanted him to do this. What might a Catholic sacrifice for his or her faith?

   _____

   _____

3. In the story of Jacob and Esau, Esau chose to trade his birthright for a bowl of stew. For what might a modern-day Catholic be tempted to trade God's grace?

   _____

   _____

4. The brothers of Joseph did not want to leave Benjamin in Egypt. They were concerned about their father and did not want to bring him this sorrow. How can we show concern for our parents?

   _____

   _____

5. Many difficult things happened to Joseph, but he still trusted God. After his brothers had treated him so cruelly, he gave them food and forgave them. How can we show forgiveness to those who hurt us?

   _____

   _____

A Scroll Puzzle Complete the puzzle using the words from the scroll.

Down

2. Any of Israel's descendants is known as an _____ .

3. The father and ruler of God's people was called a _____ .

4. An agreement between God and his people is a _____ .

5. _____ is the land promised to Abraham and his descendants.

7. The one promised by God to deliver all people from sin is called the _____ .

8. _____ is the attitude that leads us to share spiritual and material goods with others.

Across

1. We show _____ when we are like Jesus and know that every good thing comes from God.

6. The first patriarch of God's people was _____ .

9. God's watching over us and caring for our needs is called _____ .

10. God made a covenant with us at our _____ .

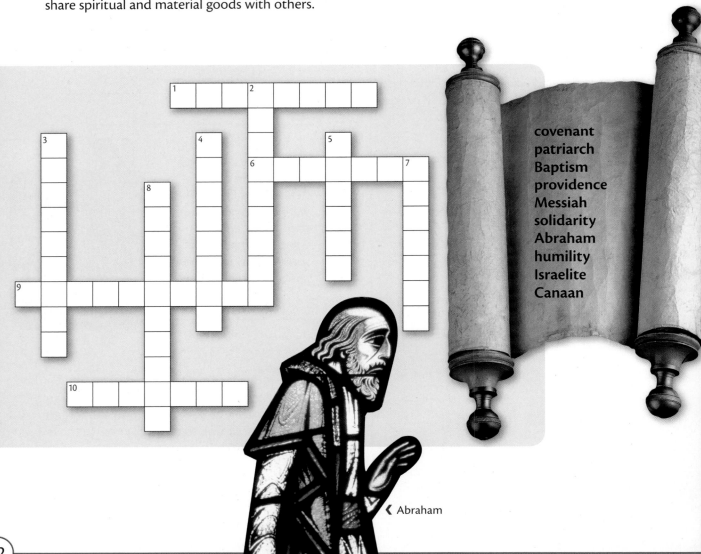

covenant
patriarch
Baptism
providence
Messiah
solidarity
Abraham
humility
Israelite
Canaan

❮ Abraham

Family Tree Fill in the family tree of faith. Read each description and write the name of the person who fits it. For help, look over pages 1–58.

A _____ + S _____

He was the first patriarch of God's people. He is also the Father of Believers.

I _____ + R _____

He was Abraham's son. God promised that through his descendants his promise would be fulfilled.

She received a message from God that her younger son, Jacob, would lead God's people.

E _____

He was Isaac's older son, who sold his birthright for a little bit of food.

J _____ + R _____

He received the birthright from his father, Isaac. Then his name was changed to Israel.

L _____

12 sons, including

J _____

In Israel's blessing, he received the promise that the Messiah would be his descendant.

J _____

He was sold to traders by his brothers. After they came to him in Egypt, he forgave them.

R _____

B _____

P _____

He was the ruler of Egypt who made Joseph the governor.

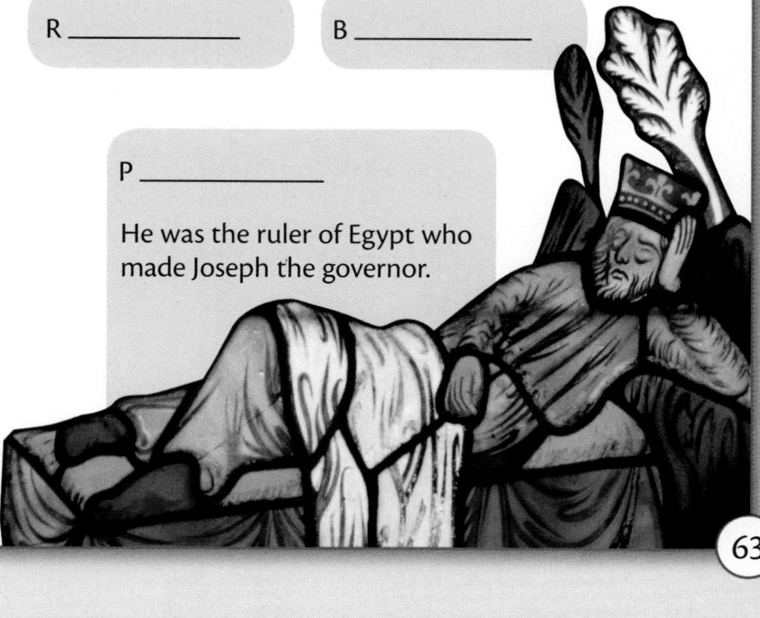

Celebrating

God's Presence

Introduction

Reader 1: Truly God is in this place! This is a dwelling place for the Lord. It is holy and special to us. Let us celebrate!

Leader: God comes to us every day and brings us dawn and life. God greets us in the smiles of our families and friends. God speaks to us deep in our hearts because God loves us so much.

(Song; Procession: Bible, candles)

Leader: Let us begin our prayer together in the name of the Father, and of the Son, and of the Holy Spirit. Amen.

Readings and Responses

Leader: In the Old Testament we read of God speaking to the people he chose. These people would mark in a special way the place where God spoke to them.

Reader 2: A reading from the book of Genesis. *(Read Genesis 12:7)*

Leader: Let us pray.

All: God, come to us today. Speak to us and help us trust in your Word.

(Silent prayer)

Leader: When God appeared to Jacob in a dream, Jacob named the place *Bethel*, which means "house of God."

Reader 1: A reading from Genesis. *(Read Genesis 28:10–22)*

Leader: Let us pray.

All: Father, we meet you in Scripture. We meet you in your Son, Jesus Christ. We meet you in our hearts where you speak to us.

Presentation of Symbols

Leader: We have our own stones to mark God's special message to us. We bring these as reminders that God is truly present in our lives.

(Hold your prayer stone in your hand and extend your arms toward the altar or enthroned Bible as the reader prays.)

Reader 2: This is a special place. This is a special time. Lord, help us remember your loving care for us. Make each of our hearts a "Bethel"—a place where you live. May we pray to you. May we love you. May we share that love with everyone in the world.

(Carry your prayer stone to the altar and place it by the Bible and candles.)

Litany of Love

Leader: We love you, Lord, for you have revealed yourself to us.

All: I will praise the Lord all my life. I will sing praise to my God forever.

Reader 1: You created us, bringing us the joy of life. You are close to us in times of trouble and pain.

All: I will praise the Lord all my life. I will sing praise to my God forever.

Reader 2: You have a plan for our lives. In your providence, you care for us and those we love.

All: I will praise the Lord all my life. I will sing praise to my God forever.

Reader 1: May we be rooted in Christ and built up in him. May we grow strong in faith and be filled with gratitude.

All: I will praise the Lord all my life. I will sing praise to my God forever.

(Song)

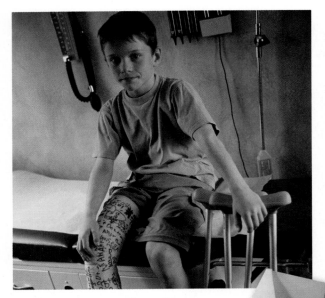

An Encouraging Letter

Jake broke his leg in a bicycle accident. He will be in the hospital for a few weeks. He will miss the soccer games he was scheduled to play.

Imagine you are a friend of Jake's. Write him a letter on a separate sheet of paper. Encourage him by telling him how God's providence could bring good from his accident.

Looking Back at Unit 2

In this unit you have met your fathers in the faith, the patriarchs. These men, Abraham, Isaac, and Jacob, were the ones to whom God chose to reveal himself. From their families God formed his Chosen People. He promised to send his own Son as a member of this people to save all from the power of sin.

When this unknown God began to reveal himself to Abraham, he asked for wholehearted obedience. Abraham obeyed promptly and generously, trusting completely in God's goodness. We hear little of Isaac, but the stories of Jacob and his family are vivid examples of God's providence.

We, too, have been chosen by God, and this choice was marked by our Baptism. Our special mission is to continue the life and work of Jesus wherever we are. We can do this with complete trust in God's providence. We know that in every situation God can draw us closer to him.

Living the Message

Can you give yourself a check (✓) for each statement?

○ 1. I understand the stories of Abraham, Isaac, Jacob, and Joseph.

○ 2. I think about how I am fulfilling the mission given to me at Baptism.

○ 3. I try to show my faith in God by prompt, generous obedience to his calls.

○ 4. I trust God even when things go wrong, because I know God can bring good even from evil.

○ 5. I frequently pray to God and tell him of my faith, my hope, and my love.

Planning Ahead

God chose you to belong to him in a very special way. He chose you to share in Jesus' mission. In Scripture we read, "I have called you by name: you are mine" (Isaiah 43:1). Think how you will respond to God's choice. Write your response below.

_____

_____

_____

_____

_____

_____

Advent:
Past, Present, and Future

In his story *A Christmas Carol*, Charles Dickens invites Ebeneezer Scrooge—and through Scrooge, all of us—to consider Christmas past, present, and future. In the same way, Advent invites us to consider Jesus' coming as man 2,000 years ago (past), his coming to us each day through the Holy Spirit (present), and his Second Coming, which we await for in joyful hope (future). Traditional Advent practices help us prepare to celebrate Jesus' coming in three ways:

1. At the first Christmas

We celebrate the original coming of Jesus by retelling the story of Mary and Joseph and how they found no room at the inn. We recall the angels and shepherds and the visit by the Magi.

2. In our lives right here and now

It is because of our confident hope for the future that we focus our attention joyfully on the present. Jesus promised, "I will be with you all days." That means he has promised to be with us in the midst of our daily lives. During Advent, we take up practices that help us watch and wait for his presence. We pray and we worship. We make time for family closeness, and we give generously to one another.

We acknowledge the yearning in our hearts for the true spirit of Christmas, which is the arrival of Jesus.

3. In the fullness of time

We believe that the Second Coming of Jesus will take place at some future date in history. We anticipate this every time we pray the Eucharistic Prayer, "[May we be] safe from all distress, as we await the blessed hope and the coming of our Savior, Jesus Christ." At Mass, we also pray, "We proclaim your Death, O Lord, and profess your Resurrection until you come again." In this way, we acknowledge our conviction that Jesus will come again to complete his work of salvation.

This Advent season, take time with your family to not only memorialize Christ's birth, but to turn your eyes forward with joyful hope, anticipating the day that God will be fully and completely in our midst. Take time to awaken your consciousness to how Jesus is truly present in your home and family today—even in the midst of all the hustle and bustle of the season.

Family Feature

Christmas Around the World

Christmas is celebrated around the world, but each culture celebrates it a little differently. While you might see a nativity scene in many different cultures, are you familiar with the *Wigilia*, the rooster Mass, or the *posadas*? Share with your family some of these Christmas traditions from around the world.

Wigilia

In Poland, the Christmas Eve celebration gets the greatest emphasis. The *Wigilia* (vee-GEE-lee-ah) is the traditional Christmas Eve vigil supper. It begins when the first star is sighted, usually by the children, at dusk. This first star symbolizes the star of Bethlehem. Traditions of the Wigilia include beginning the celebration with a prayer and the breaking of the Christmas wafer, leaving an extra plate in case a traveler should stop by, eating as many as 12 dishes at supper, and attending the *Pasterka*, or Shepherd's Mass.

Rooster Mass

Christmas in the Philippines begins on December 16, with nine days of Masses called *simbang gabi*. Because these Masses are held at dawn, they are also called "rooster Masses." Often people from the same part of a village will gather in a procession. They sing and carry flowers and banners, gathering followers as they walk to the church. After each Mass, families gather for a special breakfast. Christmas delicacies include *puto bumbong* (a sticky rice with brown sugar and coconut shavings), *bibingka* (rice cake), and *salabat* (ginger tea).

Posadas

The *posadas* is a nine-day celebration in Mexico. It begins on December 16 and ends on *Noche Buena*, or Holy Night (December 24). Each night during the celebration, *Los Peregrinos* (the neighborhood children and adults) reenact the wandering of Joseph and Mary by asking neighbors for lodging. They go to three "inns" (neighborhood houses), finding shelter at the third inn. The Los Peregrinos then kneel around the nativity in that home to pray the Rosary and to sing traditional songs. The posadas ends with the *Misa de Noche Buena*, or midnight Mass.

Caring at Christmas

In many cultures, there is a legend that on Christmas Eve, as a sign of anticipation of the Christ child, animals will be able to speak. In countries such as Germany and Poland, meals eaten on Christmas Eve traditionally do not include meat, out of respect for the animals. As the years passed, this tradition made its way to the New World, where the descendants of German and Polish immigrants honor this custom even today.

This legend can inspire a new Christmas tradition for your family, while showing care and respect for God's creation. Take a cue from Eve Bunting's *The Night Tree*, a story about a family who drives to the woods on Christmas Eve and decorates a tree with edible decorations for the wildlife.

Begin by creating popcorn-and-dried-berry garlands, peanut butter and birdseed pine-cones, and fruit slices attached to hooks or pipe cleaner. Remember to include hot tea or hot chocolate and cookies for your tree-deckers! Once the good-ies are ready, bundle up your family and head out to decorate your tree. Singing carols and drinking hot chocolate while you work keeps the mood festive and fun. Before you head home, offer a prayer of thanks for God's creation, for being able to share what you have with God's creatures, and for the birth of Jesus, who cares for all.

Tips Even if you cannot decorate a tree, you can still care for God's creation. Modify this activity by working with your children to place birdseed or peanut butter-and-birdseed pinecones outside your home. You can also spread bread crumbs or mini-peanut butter sandwiches.

Family Feature

Advent Basket

Work with your family to create an Advent basket, using the materials and directions below. It can be a wonderful way of sharing the spirit of Advent with your friends and loved ones.

Materials:

Medium-sized basket

Copy of Advent Basket Instructions

Candles—3 purple, 1 pink,
        1 larger white

Wreath

Blank prayer cards in an envelope

Small cookie tin

Homemade or store-bought cookies

Christmas story, such as *The Gift of the Magi* by O. Henry or *The Stranger Child: A Legend* by Count Franz Pocci, laminated or bound

After your family has completed the Advent basket, follow the Advent Basket instructions to complete the activities for the first week of Advent. Invite other families to continue passing the basket throughout Advent.

Advent Basket Instructions

This Advent Basket has been created by the _____ family to help those we love celebrate the season of Advent. We invite you to complete the following activities and then pass the Advent basket to the next family.

Activity 1: Work together to write a short prayer on one of the prayer cards. The prayer should be about your family's anticipation of Jesus. Feel free to decorate the card.

Activity 2: Set up the wreath and the candles. The candles should be arranged inside the wreath, with the white candle in the center. Go to www.ChristOurLife.org for information about how to set up the Advent wreath and about which candle to light each week. Then pray together the prayer you wrote.

Activity 3: Share and enjoy the enclosed story and cookies with your family.

Activity 4: Return all items, including the prayer you wrote, to the basket.

Activity 5: Replace the cookies for the next family and pass the basket!

Tip Confirm beforehand which families would like to participate and provide a list of families with the basket so that everyone knows who should receive the basket next.

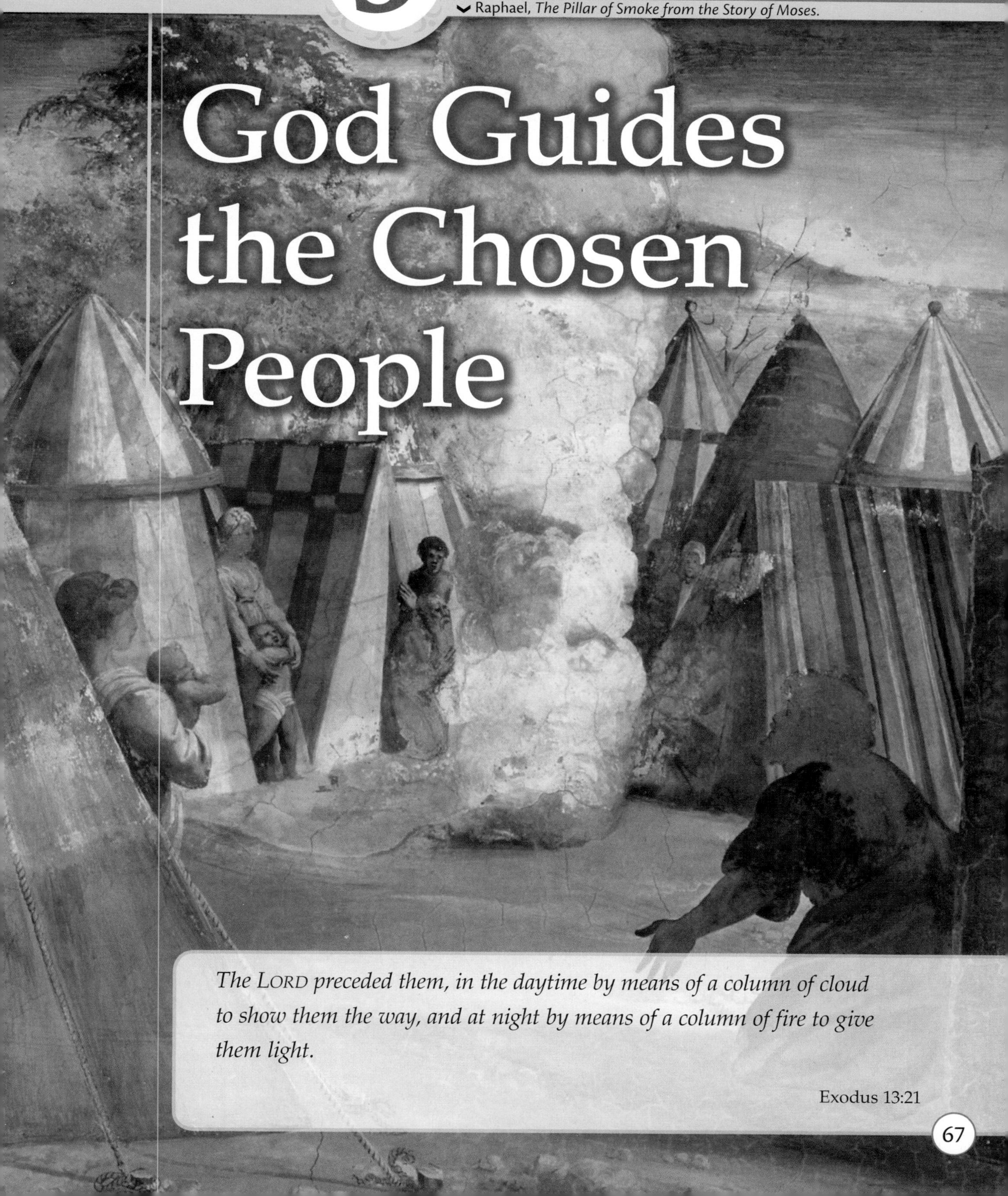

Raphael, *The Pillar of Smoke from the Story of Moses.*

God Guides the Chosen People

The LORD preceded them, in the daytime by means of a column of cloud to show them the way, and at night by means of a column of fire to give them light.

Exodus 13:21

67

God Guides the Chosen People

IN THIS UNIT, you will learn about God's greatest act of saving love in the Old Testament: the Exodus. You will also learn about the Ten Commandments, which are a gift that God has given us so that we might deepen our relationship with him.

God Rescues the Chosen People from Slavery

God's Chosen People became slaves in Egypt, and they cried out for liberation. Through the Exodus event, God delivered his Chosen People from slavery to freedom. Understanding God's saving act in the Exodus story will help you to better understand Jesus' saving actions. You will also learn about the Jewish celebration of Passover.

God Gives Us the Law

God created a loving relationship with his Chosen People at Mount Sinai, where he gave them his commandments. The Ten Commandments teach us how we can live as people of God and attain happiness. The stories of the struggles of the Chosen People in the desert show us that God is with us even during the difficult moments of our lives.

We Live the Commandments Today

The Ten Commandments set the Israelites apart as a chosen people of God. The Israelites were happy to have the Commandments because they saw God's Law as a gift that helped them to become closer to God and to one another. You are invited to respond with grateful love to the gift of God's Law and to learn how to follow the Ten Commandments today.

Learning God's Way

Upon reaching the Promised Land, the Israelites decided that they were not yet ready to march against Canaan. They needed a stronger faith. Because of this, God did not allow them to see the land that had been promised to their fathers. From their example, we learn that we are responsible for our decisions and the consequences of those decisions. You will learn how to make good moral decisions that will identify you as a follower of Jesus.

God Forgives Us

When the Israelites were dying from poisonous snake bites, God saved them through a bronze serpent lifted up on a pole. In the same way, we are saved from the poison of sin by Jesus, who was lifted up on the Cross. Through the Sacrament of Reconciliation, we are healed and are able to grow in virtue.

God's Chosen People Enter the Promised Land

Under the leadership of Moses and then Joshua, the Chosen People finally enter the Promised Land. Their journey to the Promised Land is like our own spiritual journey to heaven. Along the way, we are called to respect just and lawful leaders and to develop our own leadership qualities.

God Rescues the Chosen People from Slavery

Moses, a Man with a Mission

based on Exodus 1–11

Moses is one of the most important people of the Old Testament. God chose him to free his people from slavery in Egypt. The story of Moses' mission is told in Exodus, the second book of the Bible.

For several hundred years, the rulers of Egypt remembered that Joseph had saved them from famine. However, eventually a Pharaoh who did not know about Joseph ruled Egypt. He saw that there were many strong Hebrews, and he feared they might try to take over Egypt. Pharaoh forced the Hebrews into slavery. The Hebrews had to work in the fields, make bricks, and build great cities for the Egyptians.

When the number of Israelites continued to increase, Pharaoh ordered that newborn Hebrew boys be drowned. Hearing this, one Hebrew woman hid her newborn son for three months. When she could no longer safely hide her baby, she placed him in a basket and left him among the reeds along the Nile River. His sister Miriam waited nearby to see what would happen.

Soon Pharaoh's daughter came down to the river with her maids. Noticing the basket among the reeds, she sent one of them to fetch it. When she opened the basket, she saw the baby boy crying. She knew it was a Hebrew child and felt sorry for him. Miriam stepped forth and asked if she could get an Israelite woman to nurse the baby. Pharaoh's daughter agreed, and Miriam went to get her own mother.

When the baby no longer needed to be nursed, his mother took him to Pharaoh's daughter. The Egyptian woman adopted him and named him Moses, which means "drawn from the water."

Moses was brought up as a prince at Pharaoh's court. He grew up to be a strong, well-educated man. But he knew he was a Hebrew, and it bothered him to see his people suffer.

One day Moses saw an Egyptian strike a Hebrew. In anger, Moses killed the Egyptian and quickly buried him in the sand. When Pharaoh found out about it, he sought to put Moses to death. So Moses fled to Midian. There he met the Midianite priest Reuel, also known as Jethro, and went to live with his family. After a time, Moses married one of Reuel's daughters. For many years Moses worked as a shepherd for his father-in-law.

the Old Testament the LORD in small capital letters, it represents the Hebrew name YHWH. In the New Testament, the name Lord is used not only for the Father, but also for the Son, Jesus. This means that we recognize that Jesus is God himself. When we pray the Lord's Prayer, we are asking that the name God revealed to Moses be honored by all people. We bring honor to God's name by recognizing him as our Father and by living as brothers and sisters, helping to create a society that recognizes our need for one another.

God Calls

based on Exodus 2:23–3:15

God heard the cries of his people in Egypt and acted on their behalf. While Moses was tending the sheep grazing on Mt. Sinai, also called Mt. Horeb, God revealed himself to him while still remaining a mystery. Moses saw a bush flaming with fire but not burning up. When he went to investigate, God called his name and told him to remove his sandals for he was on holy ground.

God said, "I have listened to my people, who are suffering greatly in Egypt. I have heard their cries. I will rescue them and lead them into a land flowing with milk and honey. I will send you to Pharaoh to lead my people out of Egypt."

Moses made many excuses. First he asked, "Who am I to go?" God said, "I will be with you." Then Moses asked, "When the Israelites ask me who sent me, what shall I tell them?" God replied, "I am who am. I am the Lord, the God of your fathers Abraham, Isaac, and Jacob."

The Lord

In Hebrew, God's mysterious name, "I am who am" is represented by the letters YHWH. In the Greek Old Testament, God's name is translated as *kyrios* or LORD. When you see in

Moses Responds

based on Exodus 4–5

Moses' next excuse was, "I am a slow speaker and cannot speak well. Isn't there someone else better able to speak for you?" But God answered, "I will assist you, Moses. Your brother Aaron will go with you and speak for you."

Eventually Moses did what God asked and left Midian for Egypt. He met Aaron on the way and explained their mission. Moses and Aaron went before Pharaoh. They delivered God's message: "Thus says the LORD, the God of Israel: Let my people go. They are to celebrate a feast to me in the desert." But Pharaoh refused to let the Israelites leave their work. Instead, Pharaoh ordered the slave drivers to work the Israelites harder. No longer would they be given the straw they needed to make bricks. Now they would have to gather their own straw while still making as many bricks as before.

The Israelites were angry and complained to Moses. He saw their distress and pleaded with the Lord, "Lord, why do you treat this people so badly? My going to Pharaoh has only made matters worse."

The Lord answered, "Now you shall see what I will do to Pharaoh. Forced by my hand, he will send the Hebrews away. I remember my covenant with the Israelites. I will bring you to the land I promised your fathers."

Ten Plagues

based on Exodus 7–11

At God's command, Moses went back to Pharaoh. Aaron threw down his staff, and it became a snake. Pharaoh summoned his magicians, who threw down their staffs, which also became snakes. But Aaron's staff swallowed the magicians' staffs. This showed that God's power would swallow up Pharaoh's power, which he had abused.

Then Moses warned Pharaoh, "The Lord has sent me to tell you to let my people worship him in the desert. If you refuse, I will strike the water of the river and change it to blood. All the fish will die, and the water will be unfit for anyone to drink."

Pharaoh ignored Moses. When Aaron stretched out his staff and struck the river, the Nile turned red. But Pharaoh was not impressed, for the Nile had been polluted before.

Then, at God's command, Moses told Aaron to stretch his arm over the streams and canals. A plague of frogs came upon the land. Frogs swarmed everywhere: in beds, in ovens, in mixing bowls. Pharaoh called for Moses and Aaron. He said, "Pray to your God to get rid of these frogs, and I will let your people go to worship him." So Moses prayed. The frogs died, but Pharaoh did not keep his word.

Moses predicted more plagues, but Pharaoh would not listen. Gnats, and then flies, covered the land. Plagues were sent: disease among the animals, boils on the people and animals, great hailstones, locusts, and days of darkness. Each plague was a sign that God was speaking through Moses, but Pharaoh refused to recognize God.

Finally God told Moses to warn Pharaoh about a final, terrible plague. If Pharaoh refused to let God's people worship him, every firstborn son in the land would die. Pharaoh did not believe this would happen; he still would not let the Israelites leave his land.

Recall

Answer the following questions.

1. What mission did God give to Moses?

2. How did Moses feel about his mission?

3. How did God help Moses when things were difficult?

Your Mission

God is with you as he was with Moses. Write a prayer telling God you believe this.

_____

_____

_____

_____

Moses worked to ensure that God's people were freed from slavery. God is calling you to make sure that all people have a right to life and a right to what they need for personal decency. Write what you think you can do to respond to this call.

_____

_____

_____

God wants you to prepare now for a special mission in life. Write what you could do to prepare for it.

_____

_____

_____

_____

Exodus, a Night to Remember

based on Exodus 12–15

God promised to protect his people from the terrible plague. Moses gathered the Israelites and told them how to get ready for escape. This escape is called the **Exodus.**

One important night, the Israelites gathered as God had told them to. Each family sprinkled the blood of a sacrificial lamb on the doorposts of their house. Then the families prepared and ate roasted lamb with unleavened bread (bread made without yeast), and bitter herbs. They ate with their sandals on their feet and their staffs in their hands, ready for flight. They stayed indoors, as Moses had warned them to.

After midnight, a loud wailing was heard from the houses of the Egyptians. All the firstborn sons had died, even Pharaoh's son. But the houses of the Israelites, which had been marked with the lambs' blood, were passed over and their sons spared.

Pharaoh sent for Moses and Aaron. "Leave at once," he said. "Go and worship the Lord as you have asked. Take your flocks and herds and go." The Egyptians also urged the people to leave. They even gave the Israelites silver, gold, and clothing.

So the Israelites, led by Moses and Aaron, left Egypt. The Lord went before them. By day a column of cloud guided them on their journey, and by night a column of fire. God was truly with his people, leading them to freedom.

A Moment with Jesus

In the Liturgy of the Easter Vigil, when catechumens are baptized, the Church blesses water and recalls God's saving works. In the prayer of blessing of the water, the priest recalls the story of the Crossing of the Red Sea to help us understand how the waters of Baptism liberate us from the slavery of sin. Take a moment to thank Jesus for your Baptism. Pray the following, based on the blessing of water at the Easter Vigil:

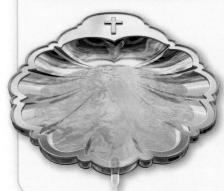

You freed the children of Abraham from slavery in Egypt, bringing them safely through the waters of the Red Sea, to help us see how we are set free through the waters of Baptism.

Through water, you have set me free.

May the waters of Baptism continue to refresh me and cleanse me. Amen.

Crossing the Red Sea

Some days after the Israelites left, Pharaoh changed his mind about letting them go. He ordered his soldiers to capture the fleeing Israelites. By the time the Israelites reached the Red Sea, they could see the Egyptian soldiers coming in their chariots. The Israelites were afraid and cried out to the Lord. Moses said,

> "Fear not! Stand your ground, and you will see the victory the LORD will win for you today. These Egyptians whom you see today you will never see again. The LORD himself will fight for you."
>
> Exodus 14:13–14

Moses raised his staff as Yahweh directed him to do. A column of cloud came between the Egyptians and the camp of Israel. The night passed without the army coming any closer. A strong wind blew all night and made a dry path through the water. The Israelites safely crossed the sea. When the Egyptians tried to follow, the Lord clogged the wheels of their chariots. Yahweh told Moses to stretch out his hand over the sea again. Moses did as God commanded, and the Egyptians in their chariots were drowned.

The Israelites knew that it was God who had saved them, and they sang his praises. Miriam led the women in dancing, singing, and playing tambourines:

> "Sing to the LORD, for he is gloriously triumphant; horse and chariot he has cast into the sea."
>
> Exodus 15:21

God Saves

Through the experience of the Exodus, the Chosen People came to recognize that their God is one who saves. Jesus' name means "God saves." Just as God saved the people of Israel from the bondage of slavery, Jesus saves us from the bondage of sin. We can share in Jesus' saving ministry by paying special attention to the needs of the poor.

The Jewish Passover

Ever since the Exodus, for more than three thousand years, the Jewish people have remembered the night when their houses were "passed over." They celebrate the event each year in the feast of Passover.

There are many preparations for Passover. Houses are cleaned from top to bottom. Tables are set with the best tablecloths, plates, wineglasses, and silver. Candles are placed on the tables, too. There is a special family meal called a seder. *Seder* is the Hebrew word for "order of service." In the seder, families praise God and tell again the story of his saving love. Foods that symbolize the hardships the Israelites endured in Egypt are carefully arranged on the seder plate.

The Christian Passover

Jesus celebrated the Passover each year and recalled with his people how God had freed them from slavery. At the Last Supper, Jesus raised the bread and wine. He prayed a prayer of praise and thanks for all God had done for his people. He said, "Do this in memory of me." But Jesus' meal was more than a memory of freedom; it was a gift of himself.

From that day on Jesus' followers have celebrated the sacred meal in remembrance of him. The Eucharist is the memorial of Christ's Passover from death to new life. His suffering, death, and Resurrection brought about complete freedom for all God's people. Jesus himself was the lamb whose blood saved the world. We celebrate his saving love at every Mass. There we are set free from sin and death.

The Eucharist

For Catholics, the Mass is the heart and summit of our lives. Each Mass is a celebration of the great mystery Jesus gave us as an everlasting covenant. The Mass has two main parts: the Liturgy of the Word and the Liturgy of the Eucharist. Together they form one act of worship.

During the Liturgy of the Word, God speaks to his people. We hear the proclamation of the Word of God: the story of our salvation. We experience God's love for us and for all people as it is recorded in Scripture. The Scripture readings used at Mass are found in a book called the *Lectionary for Mass*. The *Lectionary* has readings for all the days of the year. There are readings for special times, like Easter. There are others for the saints honored throughout the year. There are readings for Masses celebrating the sacraments, special occasions, and votive

Masses. Votive Masses celebrate the mysteries of the Lord or honor Mary and the saints outside of the assigned days.

In the Liturgy of the Eucharist, we give thanks to God our Father for all of our blessings, especially the gift of his Son. Jesus, as the new Moses, makes present his saving acts. He offers himself to the Father for us. We join in his sacrifice. Jesus Christ feeds us with his Body and Blood in Holy Communion. As we join in this liturgical banquet, we are united and strengthened as God's people.

Becoming God's People

It is said that when some sculptors look at a block of stone, they can see the statue inside it. Their hands can create a masterpiece from the stone. We are like that stone. We are masterpieces that want to be freed.

Listening to the Word, celebrating Christ's offering of himself for us, joining him in that offering, and sharing in the holy meal bring us life. Every Eucharist can change us. Usually this doesn't happen suddenly. Like a sculpture, these changes require time and care.

Those who open themselves to God will be filled. There is grace and power in the words of Scripture. There is grace and power in the Eucharistic sacrifice—the banquet of the new covenant.

How will you know if you are becoming the masterpiece you are meant to be? There are many signs. God's Word will come to mind unexpectedly. You will find the strength to think through your actions and responses. You will talk to God more. You will be more concerned about the happiness of others. Slowly your view of life and the world will change—you will mature. You will be a happier person, more at peace.

The eucharistic celebration is not just remembering what God has done in the past. It is also celebrating what God is doing right now, right here, in you.

We Remember

What is the Exodus?

The Exodus is the event in which God led the Israelites out of Egypt to freedom.

What is Passover?

Passover is the Jewish feast that celebrates God's freeing the Israelites from slavery.

What do we celebrate at the Eucharist?

At the Eucharist we celebrate the great mystery of Jesus' sacrifice and the holy meal that unites us, the new people of God, with him and one another.

Word to Know

Exodus

We Respond

Give thanks to the LORD, who is good, whose love endures forever.

Psalm 118:1

Things to Do at Home

1. Read in Exodus 1–15 more about how God called Moses and saved the Israelites. Share with your family what you have read.

2. Research the Jewish celebration of Passover. Write a report about how each of the following are used in the celebration.

   matzoh   bitter herb   haroset
   wine   seder plate   Haggadah

3. With your family, think of ways that you might open yourselves to God. Talk about how opening yourselves to God helps you to become God's people.

4. Prepare in a special way for your celebration of the liturgy this week. Pay close attention to the readings for the Mass. Listen for the message God has for you.

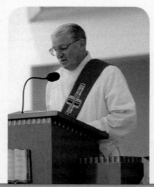

5. Find in your Bible the answers to the following questions.

   Which two cities in Egypt were built by Hebrew slaves? (Exodus 1:11)

   _____

   How many years had the Israelites been in Egypt? (Exodus 12:40)

   _____

   Why did God lead the people by a roundabout way to the Red Sea? (Exodus 13:17–18)

   _____

   _____

   _____

Visit **www.christourlife.org/family** for more family resources.

The Great Escape A Hollywood filmmaker, Cecil B. De Mille, made a famous movie about the Exodus called *The Ten Commandments*. Imagine you are in charge of the props for this movie. Match the props with the scenes that require them.

A. lamb, bread, herbs
B. burning bush
C. frogs
D. chariots
E. basket that floats
F. sheep
G. bricks
H. red water

_____ 1. Early months of Moses' life

_____ 2. Hebrew slaves forced to labor for Egypt

_____ 3. Moses goes to Midian because of his crime

_____ 4. God speaks to Moses

_____ 5. The first plague

_____ 6. Another plague

_____ 7. Passover meal the night the firstborn die

_____ 8. Death of the Egyptians in the Red Sea

Identify the characters in the movie. You will not use all of the characters.

A. Moses
B. Aaron
C. God
D. Miriam
E. Pharaoh's daughter
F. Reuel
G. Pharaoh
H. Hebrews
I. Egyptians

_____ 1. "I am who am."

_____ 2. The Chosen People; descendants of Abraham

_____ 3. Moses' sister

_____ 4. Woman who adopted Moses

_____ 5. Ruler who would not let the slaves in his land go into the desert to worship their God

_____ 6. A poor speaker through whom God sent plagues to Egypt and rescued his people

_____ 7. Moses' brother

Three Sacred Meals
Read each phrase and write the letter of the meal it matches. Phrases may have two answers.

A. Passover

B. Last Supper

C. Eucharist

_____ 1. The celebration of the Jewish Passover by Jesus and his apostles

_____ 2. The Christian commemoration of Jesus' saving acts

_____ 3. The sacrifice of the Lamb of God on the cross

_____ 4. Eaten in memory of God's saving his people from slavery in Egypt

_____ 5. Called "seder meal"

_____ 6. Includes readings from the *Lectionary for Mass*

_____ 7. Roasted lamb is eaten

_____ 8. Brings about God's saving his people from sin and death

↑ School of Raphael Sanzio, *The presentation of the tablets of law to the Hebrews.*

God Gives Us the Law

Beginning a New Way of Life

Moving to a new community or transferring to a new school can be exciting, but also very hard. Think about a time when you were new to something: a new neighborhood, a new school, a new team. What was difficult about that experience?

Struggles in the Wilderness

based on Exodus 15–17

Free from the Egyptians, the Israelites set out for the Promised Land. However, they were about to face many new difficulties. They were used to city life in Egypt and were not prepared for the hardships of the wilderness. The direct route to the Promised Land was very dangerous. To keep the people safe, God had Moses and Aaron lead the people by a longer, more indirect, route.

Water in the Desert

After leaving Egypt, the Israelites traveled three days without water. Finally they reached Marah, an oasis, but the water was so bitter that no one could drink it. When the people grumbled, Moses cried out to the Lord. God pointed out some wood and told Moses to throw it into the water. When Moses obeyed, the water became fresh. Then God laid down a law for the people, saying, "Listen carefully to the Lord your God and do what is right in my eyes. Keep all my commandments, and I will be your healer."

Bread from Heaven

Almost two months after the Israelites had left Egypt, they reached the Desert of Sin. Once more they complained to Moses and Aaron: "Would that we had died at the Lord's hand in Egypt, as we sat by our pots of stew and ate our fill of bread!" Again Moses spoke to the Lord. In the evening, God sent quail. In the morning he sent manna, small white flakes with a sweet taste. The people found manna on the ground every day except the Sabbath. Because manna tasted like wafers, they called it "bread from heaven." In the New Testament, Jesus refers to himself as the "bread that came down from heaven." (John 6:41) As Catholics, we see the story of the manna as a foretelling of the Eucharist.

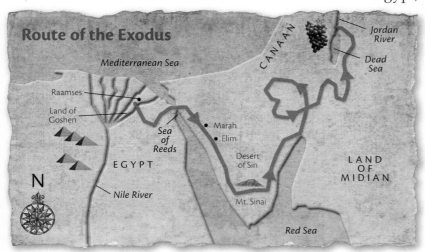

Route of the Exodus

Mediterranean Sea

Jordan River

Dead Sea

CANAAN

Raamses

Land of Goshen

Sea of Reeds

Marah

Elim

Desert of Sin

EGYPT

LAND OF MIDIAN

N

Nile River

Mt. Sinai

Red Sea

The Water from the Rock

One night the Israelites came to a campsite that had no water. Again they complained to Moses. Again Moses told God about the people's complaints. God directed Moses to take his staff and, in front of the people, strike one of the large rocks nearby. When Moses did as God had commanded, water flowed from the rock. Once again God showed love and care for his people.

The Israelites had a lot to learn before they would be ready to enter the Promised Land. God guided them as they wandered in the wilderness for forty years. Forty is a symbolic number that appears often in the Bible. It represents an important period of time during which one's faith is tested. The Israelites were tested and often failed. Jesus would later face temptation in the desert and emerge victorious by remaining faithful to the Father's plan of salvation.

Years later when the Israelites looked back, they remembered God's loving care for them during their desert experience. They had learned that they could trust God's plan for them.

A Moment with Jesus

God provided the Israelites with the basic necessities during their journey: food and water. Jesus taught us that whenever we feed the hungry and give drink to the thirsty, we are serving him. Take a moment to thank Jesus for all of the ways he provides for you. Ask Jesus to help you recognize his presence in others. Ask him to help you be more compassionate about the needs of others and to accept your responsibility to make sure that other people's basic necessities are being met.

Our Journey to Heaven

Like the Israelites, we are on a journey. We are called to trust God and to follow his directions. If we remember that God loves us and is constantly with us, then our journey through life will be a happy one. God is good and wants us to enjoy the blessings he has prepared for us. Match the experiences of the Israelites with ours. Draw lines from the sentences in the first column to those they match in the second column.

The Israelites' Experiences	Our Experiences
1. God saves them by leading them through the waters of the Red Sea.	In this life we must often face hardships.
2. God speaks to them through Moses.	God feeds us with the Eucharist.
3. Life in the wilderness is difficult.	God saves us through the waters of Baptism.
4. God feeds them with manna and quail	God speaks to us through Jesus, through Sacred Scripture, and through his Church.
5. God makes his presence known in different ways.	God is present in his Word, in the sacraments, and in the good examples of those around us.

A Covenant with the LORD

based on Exodus 19–26

Three days after the Israelites reached the desert of Sinai, Moses went up the mountain to God. There, God gave Moses the Ten Commandments. He told Moses that the Israelites would be his people if they followed his law. The people were grateful for these guides. They believed that what God commands, he makes possible by his grace. They responded, "Everything the Lord has said, we will do!" Moses then took the blood, which is a sacred sign of life, of a sacrificed animal and sprinkled it on the altar and on the people. This action was a way of sealing the Covenant.

A Reminder of the Covenant

based on Exodus 27–34

God gave Moses the laws of the Covenant written on tablets of stone. He told Moses to give the people a visible reminder that he was with them. "Build me a sanctuary," God said, "so that I may dwell among them." The Ten Commandments were to be kept in a special chest called the **Ark of the Covenant.** The Ark was to be housed in a Tent of Meeting, a portable sanctuary.

God promised to speak with his people when they came before the Ark of the Covenant. The Ark was a sign of God's presence and a reminder of the Covenant God had made with his people.

Moses stayed on the mountain for forty days. The people thought he was gone. They asked Aaron to make an image of God that they could worship. Aaron collected gold from them, melted it down, and then fashioned a calf, a symbol of strength. The Israelites sacrificed to it and began celebrating, claiming that the image represented God. When Moses came down from the mountain, he saw the calf and the people dancing before it and worshipping it. In his anger, he threw down the tablets and broke them. Then he melted down the calf and ground it into powder.

Moses knew that the people had broken the First Commandment, which calls us to worship God alone. Moses prayed to God for forgiveness on behalf of the people. He spoke to God as a friend. God renewed the Covenant and replaced the broken tablets.

This would not be the last time that the Israelites fell into the sin of **idolatry,** the worship of false gods. Later in their story, surrounded by pagan neighbors, they would often break the Covenant.

The Covenant with God on Sinai was an important event in the Israelites' journey to the Promised Land. By giving them the Law, God showed his people how to live in love. Obeying the commandments would bring them peace and lead them safely to the end of their journey. The Ten Commandments serve as a preparation for the Gospel of Jesus in the New Testament.

God's Covenant with You

God has made a covenant with you. He has chosen you to be his. But God made you in his own image, which means that you have free will. You can decide for yourself what kind of journey you want to make.

Destination: Heaven

Think of life as a hike to God our Father. Fill in this plan for your spiritual hike.

1. Who will be your guide?

   _____

2. What will help you map your way?

   _____

3. Who will be your fellow hikers?

   _____

4. How can they help you follow the trail God has shown you?

   _____

5. What virtues or good habits would help you feel comfortable and cheerful on the hike?

   _____

6. Take plenty of good food. What food could nourish you and give you the spiritual strength you need?

   _____

7. Take equipment you'll need along the way. What will help you get to your heavenly home?

   _____

8. Be alert for dangers along the trail to heaven. What could harm you or cause delays?

   _____

9. Know first-aid skills for spiritual hurts. How can you help yourself or others who are spiritually hurt?

   _____

10. Obey rules for spiritual hikers. How should you show love and respect for people and things on the way?

   _____

We Remember

What promises were made in the Covenant between God and his people?

In the Covenant, God promised the Israelites that they would be his people. The Israelites promised to do everything the Lord had said.

What gift did God give his people to help them live according to the Covenant?

the Ten Commandments

What was the journey to the Promised Land like?

It was a difficult journey that lasted forty years, during which the people often failed to remain faithful to God. God continued to provide for them throughout the journey.

Words to Know

Ark of the Covenant
idolatry

We Respond

Think of a definite time when you can praise and thank God each day. Write your prayer time here.

_____

Things to Do at Home

1. Imagine what it might have been like for the Israelites to travel through the desert without water. Think about all the ways that clean, fresh water is available to you. Now think about the people in the world who do not have access to fresh water on a daily basis. Write a short prayer for those people and pray it with your family.

2. Draw or make a model of the Ark of the Covenant based on the description in Exodus 25:10–40.

3. Have you ever made a time capsule? Imagine that you are one of the Israelites who experienced the Exodus. List what you might include in your time capsule. Then write a message about why the items in your time capsule were important during the Exodus.

4. Discuss with your family times at which they or you have gone camping. Talk about what it is like to live in the wilderness. Then make a list of the supplies that you would need to take with you.

5. Talk with your family about the "Precepts of the Church" on page 216. Discuss how you and your family follow these Church precepts (laws).

6. Make a list of ways that people break the First Commandment. Use the following questions for help: What do people tend to worship in our society? To what or to whom are people devoting themselves? What are some things that people don't need but say that they can't live without?

Visit **www.christourlife.org/family** for more family resources.

Moses' Log Suppose Moses had kept a journal of events during the journey to Canaan. Fill in the blanks.

The direct route to Canaan is very _____, so we are taking a longer route. We had gone three days without water. We finally reached _____, but the water there was bitter. At God's command, I threw _____ on the water, and it became fresh.

It's been two months since we left. The people long to return to Egypt, where they ate well. Last evening God sent _____, and we were able to have fresh meat. This morning God fed us in an amazing way. When we awoke, white flakes were covering the ground. They were like sweet wafers. We called them _____.

Tonight we had to camp at a place without water. Again the people complained. God had me strike a _____ with my staff, and water flowed out.

What a tremendous gift God has given us! On Mt. _____ he gave us his Law. We sealed a covenant with God by offering a sacrifice and sprinkling its blood on the _____ and on the people.

God instructed me to build a visible reminder of his presence with us. We will make a chest called the _____ and keep it in a _____.

After forty days with God on Sinai, I brought down the tablets on which he had written out the Law. To my horror, the Israelites were worshiping a _____.

They had already fallen into the sin of _____.

GOD   ISRAELITES

Covenant Terms A covenant is like the two sides of a coin. Write God's promise on one side of the coin and the Israelites' promise on the other side.

We Live the Commandments Today

A Sign of Love

Everyone wants to be happy, but people have different opinions about what brings true happiness. What about you? Think about three things that make you happy.

The search for happiness was very real for the Israelites. They had escaped from a foreign country where they had been treated cruelly, and they had journeyed through the desert under harsh conditions. Yet the Israelites had their belief in God to support them. They wanted to be his Chosen People. That is why they were filled with joy when God made his Covenant with them at Sinai. For the Israelites, the commandments were a sign of God's love. The commandments were part of their recipe for happiness. People would see the Israelites and know that their God was close to his people.

The Israelites knew many of the laws before God gave them the commandments. God implants in the heart of each human being **natural laws** as a guide. The natural law is made known to us by God and through human reason. So then why did the Israelites love the Law so much? First of all, the commandments showed them how to be free from ignorance and selfishness. God's Law taught them how to assume their responsibility to build a healthy society. With

the giving of the commandments, the Israelites were assured that obedience to these laws would lead to happiness, a desire that God has placed upon the human heart.

The Israelites' obedience to the commandments would also be a way to unite them to the Lord. God created us to live in communion with him. Because God would not force the Israelites to obey, their free response would be a sign of their desire and love for him.

Finally, these commandments would unite the Israelites, setting them apart as God's Chosen People. The law would help them live together in peace. It would help them live according to God's plan for them and prepare them for the fulfillment of that plan in Jesus.

A Moment with Jesus

The Israelites were thankful for the Commandments. They often expressed their gratitude to God in songs and praise. Take a moment to thank Jesus for his law of love. Ask him for the grace you need to follow the Ten Commandments. Pray Psalm 119:47–48, which the Israelites prayed to express their gratitude to God for his Law.

Ten Commandments, Two Groups, and One Law of Love

The Ten Commandments are often divided into two groups. One group focuses on our relationship with God. The other group focuses on our relationship with others. When Jesus spoke of the Law, he used this division. All of the commandments form one single law of love. All of God's laws call us to protect and promote our own lives and the lives and dignity of others. Guided by the Holy Spirit, and with the help of God's grace, the Church tells us how God's laws apply from age to age.

1. I am the LORD your God: you shall not have strange gods before me.

2. You shall not take the name of the LORD your God in vain.

3. Remember to keep holy the LORD's Day.

4. Honor your father and your mother.

5. You shall not kill.

6. You shall not commit adultery.

7. You shall not steal.

8. You shall not bear false witness against your neighbor.

9. You shall not covet your neighbor's wife.

10. You shall not covet your neighbor's goods.

Jesus Summarizes the Commandments

Read Mark 12:30–31. Write the words of Jesus that summarize the first group.

_____

_____

_____

_____

Write the words of Jesus that summarize the second group.

_____

I Say "Yes!"

Whenever we say yes to one thing, we automatically say no to other things. For example, if you say yes to piano lessons on Wednesday evenings, you will have to say no to invitations from your friends to go out on that night of the week. In order to give yourself fully to piano lessons, you have to say no to things that might get in their way.

Sometimes people think that the Ten Commandments are all about saying no. The truth is, the Commandments are all about saying yes. God said yes to us by entering into a covenant with the Israelites. God made it clear that he wants to give of himself in a loving relationship with his people. The people of Israel said yes in response to God's invitation. God gave them the Ten Commandments to safeguard this loving relationship. The Ten Commandments help us to say yes to loving God and our neighbors. In order to do this, we have to say no to those things that get in the way of giving ourselves fully to God and others. Saying yes to God means accepting the responsibility to make sure that all people benefit from this relationship with God.

By dying on the Cross, Jesus showed us that the only way we can fully give ourselves to God is to give of ourselves to others. In other words, to say yes to God is to say yes to our neighbors. The Ten Commandments teach us that love of God and love of neighbor cannot be separated. The Church helps us to love God and one another by organizing our efforts of charity and our work for justice. By working for **social justice**, we challenge society to say no to certain things that get in the way of our ability to live together as brothers and sisters. The Ten Commandments guide our efforts in charity and social justice.

Loving God

The First Commandment reminds us that we are to love God with our whole heart, soul, mind, and strength. Like the Israelites, we can express our love for God by obeying the commandments. Loving God means we respect him, speak to him, listen to him, and speak reverently about him. Loving God means wanting to spend time with him in prayer and worship.

In his goodness God created all things. In Jesus he has revealed his tremendous love for us. To trust in people or in things more than in God shows we do not really know and love him.

Choose one of the following practices. On a separate sheet of paper describe how belief in that practice shows a lack of trust in God.

- superstitions, good luck charms
- astrology
- fortune tellers, palm readers
- chain and prayer letters
- ouija boards
- seances, spiritualism

The Language of Love

God wants us to stay in touch with him. He wants us to keep him in our lives. This staying in touch is called *prayer*. In prayer, we raise our hearts and minds to God. Look at the many ways that prayer can be simple and spontaneous.

Sharing love with family and friends often leads to recognizing our Father's care.

The words of a song may make us think of God.

Talking to God before we go to sleep and when we wake up keeps us in touch with God.

A beautiful, crisp autumn day may help us turn our hearts to God.

Visits to church and celebrating the Eucharist help us remain close to God.

Honoring God's Name

Our names are special. They identify us as unique. God calls us each by name. God's name is special, too. The Second Commandment teaches us to honor God's holy name as a sign of our of love for him.

Read the following words and definitions. If the word describes a respectful use of God's name or a gift of speech, place a (✓) in front of it. If the word describes a disrespectful use, place an (X) in front of it.

———— 1. **blessing**—a prayer asking God to make someone or something holy is a **blessing**

———— 2. **oath**—calling on God to witness to the truth of what someone says

———— 3. **perjury**—lying while under oath or asking God to witness a lie is **perjury**

———— 4. **cursing**—calling down evil on someone or something

———— 5. **blasphemy**—speaking against God in a hateful manner is **blasphemy**

———— 6. **profanity**—speaking of a blessed person, place, or thing with disrespect

———— 7. **prayer**—lifting up the mind and heart to God

———— 8. **Sign of the Cross**—Praying in the name of the Father, and of the Son, and of the Holy Spirit

Keeping Holy the Sabbath Day

Work is an important way in which we participate in God's creation. However, we also need to take a rest from work. God knows his people need time for rest, so he invites us to observe and to keep holy the Sabbath. This day is a time to forget about ordinary matters and everyday problems. It is spent trusting in the Father's love and care.

This day is also a time for the community to come together and renew their relationship with God. We are not alone on this journey to heaven. We can find joy and strength in worshiping God with the Church at Mass. This is our greatest form of communal prayer. As the People of God, we are sent forth from the Mass to participate in society and to promote the well being of all people, especially the poor and vulnerable.

Catholics honor the Third Commandment through our worship in Sunday Mass. Sunday, the Lord's Day, reminds us of the creation of the world by the Father, the Resurrection of Christ, and the coming of the Holy Spirit on Pentecost. Every Sunday we celebrate the Lord's Resurrection. We also have days set aside for special celebration, which are called **Holy Days of Obligation.** They are listed on page 219. On these days Church law obliges us to honor Jesus, Mary, or the saints at the Eucharist. Which holy day of obligation is next on the calendar?

The Life of Christ— The Life of the Church

The life, death, and Resurrection of Jesus are remembered and celebrated in the Church throughout the year. These celebrations make up the liturgical year, or church year. See the diagram of the liturgical year on page 176.

Georges de La Tour, *Nativity.*

The early Christians celebrated only one feast: Easter. Soon they began to include a celebration of Christ's birth. Easter and Christmas were celebrated with special readings from the Scriptures. The weeks before these two great events were spent in preparation. The time before Christmas is called Advent; the time before Easter is called Lent.

Ordinary Time is the time between the seasons of Christmas and Lent, Easter and Advent. During Ordinary Time, the readings center on the teachings of Jesus and his life.

Eventually a whole calendar of feasts and celebrations for the church year was formed. The liturgical year begins with the First Sunday of Advent and ends with the Feast of Christ the King. Over the course of a year, the whole mystery of Jesus unfolds—from the anticipation and celebration of his birth to his death, Resurrection, Ascension, and the arrival of the Holy Spirit at Pentecost.

The Sunday Scripture readings are divided into three cycles: A, B, and C. It takes one year to complete each cycle. After three years, the community has heard many of the most important readings from Scripture. Again and again, we recall God's plan of salvation and his overwhelming love for us.

We practice love of others in our friendships. We all want and need friends. We like to share our thoughts and feelings with them. We need to know that we are loved. We need to know that others accept us. But we must always remember that love is a two-way street. We must learn to accept responsibility. We must give love and acceptance if we wish to receive them.

Jesus understood our need to be with people and to share our lives with them. He was aware of the difficulties that come with living with others. So he gave us the example of his own life to show us how to love. He also gave us other guidelines.

Read Matthew 7:12. What do we call this teaching?

_____

Write Jesus' advice here.

_____

_____

A Heart for Others

The Fourth through the Tenth commandments call us to love our neighbor. By following these commandments, we show honor for the following:

- our parents
- all human life
- sexuality
- the goods of the earth
- the truth
- relationships
- possessions

A New Commandment

On the night before he died, Jesus gave his followers a new commandment. It was a command of love. This love was to be the sign of the Christian. Although the Ten Commandments demanded love, Jesus now demanded more.

Write the New Commandment found in John 13:34–35.

_____

_____

Some people follow the rules and keep the commandments, but do not really love. Jesus spoke out against this empty kind of loving. God wants our hearts.

▲ Peter Paul Rubens, *The Last Supper*, 1630.

We Remember

Why were the Israelites so thankful to receive the commandments?

The commandments helped the Israelites to be free from selfishness and ignorance, to be united with God, and to be united with one another as the Chosen People of God.

What are the two great commandments?

The first great commandment is that you shall love the Lord your God with all your heart, with all your soul, with all your mind, and with all your strength. The second is that you shall love your neighbor as yourself.

What new commandment did Jesus give at the Last Supper?

At the Last Supper Jesus said, "I give you a new commandment: love one another. As I have loved you, so you also should love one another." (John 13:34)

Words to Know

blasphemy
blessing
Holy Days of Obligation
natural law

Ordinary Time
perjury
social justice

We Respond

"No one has greater love than this, to lay down one's life for one's friends."

John 15:13

Lord, I will try to remember your special love for me today. I will try to show my gratitude for this love by _____

_____.

Things to Do at Home

1. Write on separate note cards each of the Ten Commandments. Write each commandment's number on the back of its card. Use the cards as flashcards to help you memorize the commandments. When you know them by heart, ask each of the following people to listen to you recite the commandments without help. Have each person place a check (✔) in the appropriate circle below.

   ○ Adult Family Member

   ○ Teacher

   ○ Classmate

2. Interview adult family members about how they spent Sundays when they were children. Compare Sunday customs of today with those of the past. Present to your class the information you find.

3. For one day, list all the acts of love that you observe from the time you wake up until the time you go to bed. Share with your family what you observed. Together, say a prayer of thanks for all the goodness in your life.

4. Talk with your family about the importance of words and the effect they have on people. Discuss ways that words can bring happiness and ways that words can hurt others. Then work together to list ways that your family can use words to bring happiness to others.

5. Memorize one of the following Scripture passages: Mark 12:29–31; John 13:34–35; Matthew 5:1–10. Recite the passage to your family, and discuss what can be learned from it.

6. Listen carefully to the lyrics of several popular songs. Make a list of those that show a true understanding of love and friendship and those that do not. Then write your own song or poem on the same theme.

Visit **www.christourlife.org/family** for more family resources.

A Test of Love Draw a heart on the line before each true sentence.

_____ **1.** The Ten Commandments were a sign of God's love.

_____ **2.** The Israelites resented having to keep the Ten Commandments.

_____ **3.** The commandments led to true happiness.

_____ **4.** The commandments united the Israelites.

_____ **5.** God's law made the Israelites like all other peoples.

_____ **6.** It is not enough to follow the commandments; we must do so out of love.

Moses ❯

What's the Law?   Match the laws with their identification.

A. The Ten Commandments

B. The two great commandments

C. The Golden Rule

D. Jesus' new commandment

E. Love

_____ **1.** Love God and love your neighbor as yourself.

_____ **2.** This law was given on Mt. Sinai.

_____ **3.** It summarized all the commandments.

_____ **4.** Treat other people as you would like to be treated.

_____ **5.** Love one another as Jesus loves us.

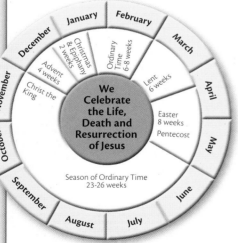

The Liturgical Year Here is a diagram of the liturgical year. Refer to it as you do the following activities.

1. Color Advent and Lent violet.

2. Color the seasons of Ordinary Time green.

3. Leave Christmas and Easter white.

4. The longest season of the liturgical year is

_____.

5. The new Church year begins on

_____.

6. The year ends on the feast of

_____.

7. What does the Church recall and celebrate during the year?

_____

_____

8. Name two Holy Days of Obligation.

_____

_____

9. What must we do to celebrate a Holy Day of Obligation?

_____

Learning God's Way

Learning to Live as God's People

Most of us do not like to wait. When we want something, we want it right away. If we have to wait a long time, we often become impatient. We are not different from the Israelites. They wanted the Promised Land immediately. But they were not yet ready. The fulfillment of God's plan for them took many years in the desert. After more than a year at Sinai, they were on their way again, following the cloud, the sign of God's presence, to Canaan.

A Fearful People

based on Numbers 13, 14:1–38

When the Israelites reached Canaan, Moses sent a leader from each of the twelve tribes to survey the land. Forty days later they returned, two of them carrying a branch with a cluster of grapes. The scouts reported, "We went into the land to which you sent us. It does indeed flow with milk and honey, but its people are fierce. The towns are fortified and strong." Caleb of the tribe of Judah proclaimed, "We ought to seize this land. We can do it." Moses and Aaron agreed. Read Numbers 13:31–33 to learn how the other men described the land and people of Canaan. How would you have felt after hearing about Canaan?

The people were afraid to engage the Canaanites in battle. They wanted to choose a new leader and return to Egypt. Joshua, another tribal leader who had surveyed Canaan, joined Caleb to defend Moses and Aaron. Joshua and Caleb said to the people, "If the Lord is pleased with us, he will lead us into this land and give it to us. Do not rebel against the Lord. Do not be afraid of the people of this land, for the Lord is with us." The people did not listen and threatened to stone Joshua and Caleb. The Israelites had made their decision: they would not march against Canaan.

Suddenly the glory of the Lord appeared at the Tent of Meeting. God asked Moses, "How long will this people insult me? How long will they refuse to believe in me despite the signs I have performed among them?" God said he would strike them with sickness and disown them.

Knowing that it was God's desire to save all people, Moses offered a prayer of **intercession,** meaning that he prayed on behalf of the people. God agreed not to destroy them. In his mercy, he forgave them, but he let them suffer the results of their sins. The people that had complained would not see the land that God had promised their ancestors. Instead, they would spend forty years in the wilderness, moving slowly to the east side of Canaan. Only Caleb and Joshua, who had followed God faithfully, along with some of the young children, would live to enter Canaan.

A Complaining People

based on Numbers 20:1–13

During these years of wandering, the people could not quite put their faith totally in the Lord. Each time they met a problem, they grumbled and complained. They blamed Moses and Aaron. They wished they were back in Egypt—or even dead. But God understood his people. Whenever Moses prayed for them, the Lord provided for them in some new way.

Can you recall two ways in which God provided for his complaining people?

Sadao Watanabe; *Moses smiting the Rock at Meribah,* 1972. ❯

_____

_____

_____

When the Israelites arrived at Meribah, they complained because again there was no water to drink. The livestock was dying, and the land did not have figs, vines, or pomegranates. Moses and Aaron again pleaded with the Lord. God told Moses to call the people together and to cause water to flow from a rock by striking it with his staff. Moses questioned whether

God would have mercy on the rebels. Moses allowed his prayer to be tempted by a lack of faith.

Then Moses struck the rock, not once, but twice, perhaps because his faith was weak. God answered Moses' prayer, but he was not pleased that Moses had felt the need to strike the rock twice. The Lord spoke to Moses and Aaron, "Because you were not faithful to me in showing my sanctity to the Israelites, you shall not lead this assembly into the land I will give them."

God was unhappy because of Moses' lack of faith in God's unfailing love for the people. This story shows that we must accept the results of our actions and decisions.

A Moment with Jesus

Sometimes in your prayer, you may be tempted by a lack of faith. Other times, you may simply get distracted or feel empty. If you feel that your prayer has not been heard, you may experience a lack of trust. Take a moment to ask Jesus for the grace you need to pray with faith, enthusiasm, and trust. Ask the Holy Spirit to teach you to pray and to help you to pray without ceasing.

The Desire for Happiness

Like all people, the Israelites wanted to be happy. As they struggled through their desert experience, however, they often complained. We also seek happiness and, like the Israelites, we often complain along the way. Many times we seek happiness where it cannot be found. Jesus taught us that true happiness is found only in God. In his Sermon on the Mount, Jesus gave us the Beatitudes—a recipe for finding happiness in the Kingdom of God. Read them in Matthew 5:3–12

A Power to Judge

The Beatitudes give us choices that help us learn to love God above all else. We are free to make choices that lead us either to God or away from him. How do you know what is a good choice and what is not? Some things, such as murder and theft, are wrong by nature. All people have the ability to judge how good or bad an act is. This ability is conscience.

Our conscience is a wonderful gift. We should educate it according to the teachings of Christ and act according to our conscience's advice.

In some ways, conscience can be compared to an Internet search engine. If a search engine is given accurate data, it will take you to Web sites that have the information you are looking for. If it is given the wrong data, it will take you in the wrong direction. The more information you put into your search, the better the chances that you will find what you are looking for. In a similar way, your conscience needs to be fed as much accurate information as possible so that it can lead you to the truth: happiness in God. There is, however, a big difference between conscience and a search engine on a computer. A computer is a machine. Conscience is an ability of a human being and can be guided by the Holy Spirit.

Decision-Making Vocabulary

To learn how a computer works, we must study some computer terms. To learn how conscience works, we must also know the meanings of some important words.

Obligations are duties that we have because we have agreed to them. Because we are God's people and have agreed to do what he wants, the Ten Commandments are obligations for us.

Principles are truths we believe in strongly enough to act on them. They help us decide how to act in different situations. For example, Catholics believe in the principle that all human life is sacred and that all people must be treated with dignity. Jesus gave us many principles in his Sermon on the Mount and at the Last Supper.

Consequences are the results of choices. Sometimes we can be sure of consequences; at other times we cannot. Sometimes we can be sure of only some of the consequences.

Making a Decision

All people have decisions to make. People who want to follow Jesus will ask the Holy Spirit to guide them in making their decisions. Through faith and prayer, the Word of God informs our consciences.

Conscience helps us make decisions in particular situations. A well-formed conscience helps us to make decisions according to God's law of love. We decide if we have any *obligation* to make one special choice. We then ask ourselves if our *principles* demand a certain choice. Finally, we look at the possible *consequences*. We ask if a choice would weaken our friendship with God or be harmful to others or to ourselves. After we do this, conscience makes its judgment. Conscience always judges in favor of what it sees as good.

After conscience has made its judgment, we are obliged to follow it. Feelings or desires can oppose our choice if we let them.

Once we have made a decision and acted on it, conscience goes back to work. It informs us whether our choice was good or bad. If we have made a good choice, we will be at peace. If conscience tells us the choice was not good, we will be uneasy and unhappy. This uneasy feeling is a warning signal that we are going away from God. It helps us realize that we must follow our conscience to find real happiness. A guilty conscience is a sign of hope that can lead us to conversion. Likewise, conscience can lead us to recognize the needs of others, especially those who are poor and vulnerable, and to increase our efforts to address their needs.

As you can see, conscience is a big help in daily decision making. We must remember to listen to and follow its judgment. When we follow the judgment of a good conscience, we become more like Jesus. We are then on our way to discovering true happiness in God's Kingdom.

Joose de Momper the Younger, *The Sermon on the Mount*, 1479.

We Remember

What is Jesus' recipe for happiness?

Jesus gave us the Beatitudes to help us recognize that true happiness in found only in God.

How does our conscience help us with our decisions?

Conscience helps us to make decisions based on our obligations, on our principles, and on the consequences.

Word to Know

intercession

We Respond

Write a prayer asking the Holy Spirit to teach you to make Christlike decisions.

Things to Do at Home

1. Show your parents the Decision-Making Vocabulary on page 93. After watching a TV program together, discuss the decisions that were made. Were the people aware of their obligations? Do you know any of the principles on which they based their decisions?

2. Read the Sermon on the Mount (Matthew 5–7). Pick three principles that are very important in the life of a Catholic.

3. After looking at the newspaper or watching the news on TV, spend at least five minutes praying for those who are in need of God's forgiveness. Ask God to forgive them and to help them make up for their sins. Pray Moses' prayer (Numbers 14:13–19) if you wish. Pray a Hail Mary as a reminder that we are all sinners in need of forgiveness.

4. The law required the Israelites to tithe, or give 10 percent of all they owned as a religious tax. Some of the tax was used to provide for the needs of the poor. Think about giving a certain percentage of any money you receive to the Church or to the poor.

5. Ask your parents to talk about the consequences they have faced because of a decision they made. Discuss which principles they followed or ignored when making their decision.

6. List things that truly make you happy. Ask yourself which things on this list draw you closer to God and which get in the way of long-lasting happiness.

Visit **www.christourlife.org/family** for more family resources.

Know Your Numbers Find in the puzzle the eleven hidden words. Look up and down, across, and diagonally. Use the clues below to help you.

1. God led the Israelites through the desert to _____.

2. Canaan was also called the _____.

3. _____ sent one leader from each of the twelve tribes to survey the land.

4. The scouts reported that the land flowed with _____.

5. _____, of the tribe of Judah, told the people that they should seize the land.

6. The Israelites wandered the desert for _____ before reaching the Promised Land.

7. When God threatened to disown the complaining Israelites, Moses offered a prayer of _____.

8. The ability to judge whether an act is good or bad is our _____.

9. Duties that we have because we agreed to them are our _____.

```
Y O B L I G A T I O N S
E E K C C S E Y O U N Y
N O I S S E C R E T N I
O E Y I O C O O E F F I
H R N A A N N S D C O C
D N A L D E S I M O R P
N C E N S U C M N C T B
A B S I U Q I A O P Y O
K O E N A E E D N S Y O
L A N D R S N N E A E C
I I T Y B N C S S E A S
M S L S L O E I Q C R N
R P R I N C I P L E S M
```

10. Truths that we believe in strongly enough to act on them are our _____.

11. The results of our choices are called _____.

Decisions, Decisions! Answer the following using the decision-making vocabulary you have learned.

1. The Israelites had promised to do whatever God asked. When God asked them through their leaders to go into Canaan, they had an _____ to do so.

2. The Israelites knew that God was with them and would help them and that therefore they could trust God. They should have acted on this _____.

3. Whenever the Israelites did not follow God's Law, they suffered. They should have considered this _____ when they decided not to go into Canaan.

4. As they wandered in the desert and realized they had made the wrong decision, the Israelites' _____ probably bothered them.

CHAPTER 14

God Forgives Us

A Bronze Serpent

based on Numbers 21:4–9

Have you ever seen a snake in a field or yard? How did you feel? What did you do? Many people are afraid of snakes, even the ones that are harmless. They do not trust any snake. As the following story shows, the Israelites had good reason to dislike snakes.

Throughout the Israelites' years in the wilderness, God had provided for their needs. But eventually they grew tired of the manna God had given them. They said, "We are sick of this tasteless food." They complained about Moses and even about God.

The Bible tells us that as punishment for their complaining, God sent serpents among them. The bites of these snakes caused death. Only after many people had died from poisonous bites did the Israelites realize their sinfulness.

The people went to Moses and admitted that they had sinned by speaking against him and against God.

They asked Moses to intercede for them so that God would save them from the snakes. Moses prayed, and God answered his prayer. He told Moses to make a bronze snake and to put it on a pole where the people could see it. People who had been bitten by a snake came to see the bronze serpent. They had faith in God's power to heal them. These people lived. They were healed of the terrible snakebites.

Jesus Is Lifted Up

Over one thousand years later, when the Gospel of John was written, the story of the bronze serpent was remembered. John tells us about a conversation between Jesus and Nicodemus, a Pharisee. In this conversation, Jesus refers to Moses and the bronze serpent.

❮ Peter Paul Rubens, *Christ on the Cross.*

> "And just as Moses lifted up the serpent in the desert, so must the Son of Man be lifted up, so that everyone who believes in him may have eternal life."
>
> John 3:14–15

Who is the Son of Man? ———————————

How was the Son of Man lifted up?

————————————————————

What happened when people looked at the serpent Moses lifted up?

————————————————————

————————————————————

What will the Son of Man do for us now that he has been lifted up?

————————————————————

The lifting up of the snake hinted at what would later happen to Jesus. We say it *prefigured* Jesus. The healing of the people who looked at the bronze serpent prefigured the healing of those who would believe in Jesus.

When Jesus was lifted up on the cross, he offered a perfect sacrifice of obedience to the Father. He died for our sins so that we might have salvation. He offered his sacrifice in the name of all sinners, totally making up for sin. We are called to have faith in his sacrifice. One of the ways we show our faith in his sacrifice is to display a cross or a crucifix in our homes.

Other ways that we can show our faith in the sacrifice of Jesus are

- being sorry for sin.
- being willing to make up for sin.
- trying to live according to the law of love.
- trying to become more and more like Jesus.

With faith like this we will become reconciled to God. Our relationship with him will grow.

A Moment with Jesus

We can be healed and reconciled with the Father because Jesus, the Son of God, was lifted up on the cross and experienced death. We can also share in his Resurrection and ascension into glory. Take a moment to rejoice with Jesus and to praise him. Thank him for his death, which is the promise of our life. Thank him for his Resurrection. Ask him to help you to serve him by serving others.

Reconciliation in Our Lives

Sin is the worst evil in the world. It is the cause of many other evils. It caused the death of Jesus, but by his death Jesus broke the power of sin. His sacrifice has the power to help us overcome sin in our lives and in the world. Through Jesus our relationship with God and with others can be restored and strengthened.

We know that people are weak. Even though we love God and try to serve him, we sin. Our sins do not bring happiness. They damage our relationship with God, with other people, and even with ourselves.

God recognizes our weakness and is not surprised by our sins. He always loves us and wants to give us his forgiveness. All we need to do is turn to God, express our sorrow, and promise to do better. Then we will be reconciled. Our relationship with God and with others will grow stronger and we will experience new life in the Holy Spirit.

Receiving Forgiveness

God in his goodness has given us several ways to be reconciled with him when we have sinned. They are

- the Sacrament of Penance and Reconciliation (also called Reconciliation or confession).
- an act of love.
- an act of contrition.
- the Eucharist.

The following paragraphs explain each of the ways of receiving forgiveness. After each section, identify the type of reconciliation being described.

When we have said or done something that hurts a friend, we feel unhappy until we apologize. If this is true with our friends, it should be even truer with God. As soon as we recognize that we have sinned, we should ask God's forgiveness, for no other reason than our love for him. God's answer will not be heard with our ears, but we will know it in our hearts: "Your sins are forgiven" (Luke 5:20).

_____

Sometimes we want to do more than apologize when we hurt others. We want to do things that show that we are sorry. We want to love them and help them. We can also be reconciled with God by doing things for others that show how much we love him.

_____

In the Eucharist we remember that Jesus loved us enough to suffer and die for us. He offered this sacrifice to restore us to perfect relationship with his Father. In every Mass Jesus offers this same sacrifice for us. As we participate, we express our sorrow for anything we have done to separate ourselves from the Father and from one another. We ask Jesus to help us to make up for our sins, to become more like him, and to recognize that we are all brothers and sisters.

The fullest sign of God's forgiveness comes when Jesus gives himself to us in Holy Communion. He who is all holy takes away anything that separates us from himself.

_____

When we confess our sins with sorrow to a priest, we make a commitment to avoid this sin in the future. We can be sure that Christ will heal us. He will restore our relationship with God no matter how serious our sins are.

_____

Mortal Sin and Venial Sin

We have committed a **mortal sin** if

- we have done something that is *seriously* wrong,
- we *knew* it was seriously wrong, and
- we *freely* and *willingly* chose to do it.

A serious sin is not always a mortal sin. If one of these conditions is missing, the sin is not mortal. If the person did not know that something was seriously wrong, it was not a mortal sin. If something happened so quickly that a person did not really have time to choose freely, it was not a mortal sin.

A **venial sin** is a lesser sin. Such sins can be forgiven in other ways, but it is good to confess them in the Sacrament of Reconciliation. We receive special help to overcome them in this sacrament. The priest can help us to get at the roots of our sins and bad habits.

the number of times we have committed each mortal sin. The priest tells the person to perform certain acts of penance, or satisfaction, to repair the harm caused by sin. The acts of penance also help the person to replace bad habits with virtues.

Healing and Growth

Through the Sacrament of Reconciliation our mortal and venial sins are forgiven. The wounds in our minds and wills that have been caused by sin are healed. We are reconciled with God and with the Church. Grace, the life-giving power of this sacrament, remains with us in our daily life. The sacrament fills us with peace and allows our conscience to rest. It strengthens us so that when we are tempted again, we will be more likely to say no to temptation and say yes to God. It also helps us to participate fully in our community, working for the well-being of all, especially those who are poor and vulnerable.

The Sacrament of Reconciliation helps us know ourselves better. Examining our conscience is like looking in the mirror. We see the times we have accepted God's **grace,** which is the life-giving power that this sacrament gives us. We see our good habits and our bad habits. We see where we are weak and where we are strong.

Each time we receive forgiveness in the Sacrament of Reconciliation, we grow stronger in God's life and love. This sacrament helps us correct our bad habits and form good ones. It helps our conscience recognize the good and strengthens our will to choose it.

As the good becomes a habit, we grow in **virtue.** A virtue is a habit of doing something good. We do it because it is what God wants for our own happiness and the happiness of others.

Reconciliation

In the Sacrament of Reconciliation, a person performs three actions: repentance, which is a desire to change; confession of sins to the priest; and a commitment to repair the harm caused by the sin. A person who commits a mortal sin should immediately ask God's forgiveness in his or her heart. Then, after doing an examination of conscience, the person must confess the sin to a priest in the Sacrament of Reconciliation. Until this is done he or she should not receive Communion.

A mortal sin should be confessed with enough information to let the priest know how serious the sin is. We must also confess

We Remember

How were the Israelites healed of their snake bites?

God told Moses to make a bronze snake and to put it on a pole where the people could see it. People who had been bitten by a snake came to see the bronze serpent. Because of their faith, they were healed of the terrible snakebites.

What are four ways of being reconciled with God?

Four ways of being reconciled with God are the Sacrament of Reconciliation, an act of contrition, an act of love, and the Eucharist.

What conditions must be present for a sin to be considered mortal?

The action must be a serious wrong, we must know that it is seriously wrong, and we must have committed it freely and willingly.

Words to Know

grace   venial sin
mortal sin   virtue

We Respond

Use the Examination of Conscience on page 222 as a guide for writing in your reflection notebook over the next several days.

Things to Do at Home

1. Find out when your parish celebrates the Sacrament of Reconciliation. Do an examination of conscience (see page 222) in preparation for celebrating the sacrament. Make a commitment to practice the penance your priest suggests as a way of repairing the harm caused by sin.

2. Ask someone who knows you well to tell you what he or she thinks is your most outstanding virtue. Thank God for this gift and try to make it grow even stronger. Ask God to help you with his grace.

3. Ask for an old missalette from your church. Cut out the prayers of the Mass that call us to reconciliation. Put each one on a card and label it. Talk with your family abut what each prayer means and why it is important.

4. Memorize Psalm 65 and pray it whenever you think of God's loving forgiveness.

5. Pray the Stations of the Cross (see page 213) with your family. Take turns having family members pray each of the fourteen stations along the Stations of the Cross.

6. If your family does not have a cross or crucifix (a crucifix is a cross with the body of Jesus on it), make arrangements to acquire one. Display it in your home as a reminder of how we are healed through Jesus' death on the cross.

Visit **www.christourlife.org/family** for more family resources.

From Death to Life Use the clues to fill in the acrostic.

1. Jesus Christ gives himself to us—his Body and his Blood—in this sacrament.

2. The serpent that Moses made hinted at, or _____, what Jesus would do.

3. The serpents appeared and bit the Israelites after they _____.

4. Jesus' death on the cross _____ us with the Father.

5. Both the serpent in the desert and Jesus brought _____ to wounded people.

```
_ _ _ H _ _ _ _ _
  _ E _ _ _ _ _ _ _
_ _ _ _ A _ _ _
_ _ _ _ _ _ L _ _
      _ I _ _
  _ _ _ N _ _
    _ _ G _ _
```

6. The Israelites were healed of their snakebites when they looked at the _____ serpent on the pole.

7. When we sin, God is always ready to _____ us if we are sorry.

Forgiveness Facts Imagine that you are writing this E-mail to a friend. Fill in the missing information to complete the E-mail.

To: _____ From: _____

Hi _____,

Today I learned about reconciliation and forgiveness. Did you know that there are four ways to be reconciled with God? They are the Sacrament of _____ , an act of _____ , an act of _____ , and the _____.

The Sacrament of Reconciliation is pretty interesting. Through it, _____ sins and _____ sins are forgiven. The wounds in our minds and wills that are caused by sin are _____. This sacrament gives us _____, which is a power that strengthens us against temptation. It also helps us replace our bad habits with _____.

You might be wondering what the differences are between mortal sins and venial sins. Well, we have committed a mortal sin if these three conditions are met: We have done something seriously _____. We _____ that what we did was seriously wrong. We freely and willingly _____ to commit the sin.

I'll be learning about Moses and Joshua next. I'll keep you posted!

Your Friend,

_____

⌃ School of Raphael Sanzio, *Crossing of the Jordan.*

God's Chosen People Enter the Promised Land

A Team Leader

Suppose you and your friends want to form a basketball team. One of the first things you will probably do is choose a captain. The captain will be the leader, the person who will make decisions and get the team organized.

Moses—A Great and Wise Leader

based on Deuteronomy 31–34

Moses was the leader of the Israelites for many years. He received from God the authority to lead the people. He helped organize the tribes into a nation. He spoke to God for the people and made decisions based on God's Law. Moses served the people by caring for their needs. He led them through the desert until they came to the plains of Moab, not far from Canaan, the Promised Land.

When Moses was one hundred and twelve years old, he told the Israelites that he was about to die. He reminded them of all the Lord had done for them. God had delivered them from the Egyptians. He had given them food and drink in the desert and had watched over them with loving care.

God had formed them into a people by giving them his law through Moses, thus renewing the covenant he had made with Abraham.

Then Moses called Joshua, a military leader, and said to him, "Be brave and faithful, because you must bring these people into the land which the Lord swore to their fathers he would give them."

Encouraging the people to love God and listen to his word, Moses spoke a blessing to each of the twelve tribes. Then he went alone up Mount Nebo. There God showed him the Promised Land, saying, "This is the land that I swore to Abraham, Isaac, and Jacob that I would give to their descendants. I have let you see it, but you shall not cross over."

Moses died on Mount Nebo at an old age and was buried in the valley of Moab. For thirty days the Israelites mourned his passing. As a true leader, Moses had obeyed God as he served the people. He had taught them how to walk in the way of the Lord. Scripture tells us that there has never been such a prophet in all of Israel as Moses, the man whom the Lord knew face-to-face.

❮ Mount Nebo

Joshua—A Strong and Fearless Leader

based on Joshua 1

After the death of Moses, Joshua became the leader of the Israelites. He was filled with the spirit of wisdom, for Moses had laid his hands upon him. The name *Joshua* is the same as the name *Jesus*. It means "God saves." The Lord spoke to Joshua, saying:

> "Prepare to cross the Jordan here, with all the people, into the land I will give the Israelites. . . . Be firm and steadfast, taking care to observe the entire law which my servant Moses enjoined on you. Then you will have success. Do not fear, for the LORD, your God, is with you."
>
> adaptation of Joshua 1:2,7–9

Joshua called together the officers of the people. He ordered them to go through the camp and tell the people to get ready to cross the Jordan in three days. Now, Moses had already given land on the east bank of the Jordan to three tribes. Joshua called for the men of those tribes. He told them that even though they already had their land, they were to cross the Jordan and help win the rest of the land.

The Israelites believed that God was with Joshua, and they followed his directions. All prepared to cross the Jordan and enter the Promised Land.

The Laying on of Hands

What happened to Joshua when Moses laid hands on him?

_____

The act of laying on of hands is an ancient way of giving a blessing. To the Israelites, a blessing was a reality that could be passed from one person to another. In order for Joshua to assume a position of leadership, and to receive the power and authority that go with that position, he needed to be filled with the Spirit. In the Acts of the Apostles 8:14–17, the apostles laid their hands on the baptized so that they could receive the Holy Spirit. In the Sacrament of **Confirmation,** the baptized are anointed on the forehead with chrism, a holy oil, as the bishop says "Be sealed with the gift of the Holy Spirit." He then lays hands upon the baptized as a sign of conferring the gift of the Holy Spirit.

Through the Sacrament of Confirmation, you receive the grace you need to assume responsibility in the Church and to participate in fostering a community spirit and promoting the well-being of all people.

The Promised Land at Last!

based on Joshua 3–6 and 24

Joshua led the people to the banks of the Jordan as God directed. There they camped to make the final preparations for crossing the river and entering the Promised Land. On the third day, the people were told to follow the priests carrying the Ark of the Covenant. Joshua said to them, "Sanctify yourselves, for tomorrow the Lord will perform wonders among you."

The next day Joshua directed the priests to take up the Ark of the Covenant and lead the Israelites through the river. As soon as the priests set foot in the Jordan, its waters stopped flowing! As during the Exodus at the Red Sea, God kept his promise that the people would be able to cross the river on dry ground. The priests stood with the Ark of the Covenant to one side of the pathway across the Jordan. After all the people had crossed the river, the waters of the Jordan again flowed freely. This reminded the Israelites of how their fathers had walked on dry ground through the Red Sea. It was a sign to them and to all who would come after them that God is powerful. He is always with his people.

The Battle of Jericho

When the tribes in Canaan heard of God's care for his people, they were afraid. The first city to be attacked by the Israelites was Jericho.

Each morning for six days the priests took up the Ark of the Covenant. Seven priests carrying ram's horns marched in front of the Ark. In front of the priests marched specially selected troops. Once each day they circled the walled city of Jericho in this manner, with the priests blowing the ram's horns. On the seventh day they marched around the city seven times. On the seventh time around the city, Joshua

commanded the people to shout, for the Lord had given them the city and everything in it.

As the horns blew and the people shouted, the wall collapsed and Israelites stormed the city. Word of Joshua's success spread throughout the land.

Victory

It was no easy job to conquer Canaan. The people living there were strong and experienced in war. The Israelites had poor weapons and no regular army. Yet one city after another fell to the Israelites under Joshua's command.

After they had conquered the land, the Israelites assembled in Shiloh, where they set up a tent to house the Ark of the Covenant. This was a place of worship for them and a reminder of God's continued presence among them. Before the tent, Joshua divided the land among the tribes that had not yet received a part, except for the tribe of Levi. The Levites were the priests, and the Lord was to be their inheritance. They were given cities in the lands of the other tribes, which they would serve.

Before he died, Joshua called all the tribes together in Shechem. By this time other people had joined them. He reminded the Israelites of the goodness that God had shown to them. He pointed out that the Lord had kept his promise. He had given them the land of Canaan. Joshua then asked the people to decide which gods they would serve. They said, "We will serve the Lord, our God, and obey his voice." Joshua renewed the covenant. Then he sent the people to their own lands, the lands promised to them as the descendants of Abraham.

The Promised Land

Reaching Heaven

Like the Israelites, we too have a promised land. It is **heaven.** We journey every day in hope of one day reaching our goal. During our human life we can either accept or reject God's grace. When we die, we will be judged according to our works and faith. As a result of this particular judgment, a person may be united with God in heaven; may undergo a purification in **purgatory** before being united with God; or, because of his or her choices, may enter **hell,** which is total separation from God.

God sent the Israelites a leader, Joshua, to bring them to their homeland. To us he sent his very own Son, Jesus Christ, who suffered, died, and rose from the dead in order to open the gates of heaven.

The Israelites wandered many years in the desert before they were ready to enter the Promised Land. If we die without having made up for our sins, we cannot go directly to heaven. Instead we must first be purified in purgatory, an experience that readies us to live with God forever.

Those Israelites who were not faithful to the true God never reached the Promised Land. The same is true for those of us who destroy our relationship with God through serious sin and who do not repent before death. Such sin prevents a person from knowing the joys of heaven.

Before the Israelites could possess Canaan, they had to fight many enemy tribes. We also have enemies to fight. We have to fight our own selfishness and pride. We also have to fight hate, distrust, impurity, dishonesty, and other forms of evil in the world. God can give us the strength to conquer these enemies and enter into the Promised Land.

The Israelites had the Ark of the Covenant as a sign of God's constant presence. We have something much greater. We have God's own divine Son in the Eucharist. We have his words

and teachings in the Gospels. We have his presence in the Church and in the sacraments.

We receive the guidance and grace of Christ through his representatives on earth:

- The Holy Father: the Vicar of Christ, or Christ's representative, who is the visible leader of the Church.
- The bishops: the successors of the apostles, who are the Church leaders in the different dioceses.
- The priests and deacons: the Church leaders in the parishes of each diocese.

These leaders receive their authority from the Church through the Sacrament of Holy Orders. In this sacrament, the bishop lays hands upon those being ordained, just as Moses laid his hands upon Joshua. The bishop also prays a prayer of consecration, asking God to grant those being ordained with the graces of the Holy Spirit, which they will need for their ministry.

God shows us the way to heaven and gives us the means to get there. As members of God's Church we are called to live in obedience, so that one day we will enjoy life with God forever.

A Moment with Jesus

In Matthew 25:32–46, Jesus speaks of the final judgment that we will all face before God. Jesus tells us how all people will need to answer to God for the decisions they have made in life. Take a moment to read this Scripture passage. Think about Jesus' description of the ways people should be treated. Talk to Jesus about some ways that you can do these types of things. Ask Jesus to help you recognize him in all people, especially in those who are poor and vulnerable.

We Remember

How did the Israelites finally enter the Promised Land?

Moses appointed Joshua as the new leader. Joshua directed the priests to carry the Ark of the Covenant and to lead the people into the Jordan River. The waters stopped flowing, allowing the people to cross safely. Joshua led the people to surround Jericho and, after circling the city seven times, he directed the priests to blow the horns and the people to shout. The walls of Jericho fell, allowing the Israelites to enter.

❮ Tamas Galambos,
The Fall of Jericho, 1996.

Who leads us to our promised land the way Joshua led the Israelites to Canaan?

Jesus and his representatives in the Church lead us to heaven.

Words to Know

Confirmation	hell
heaven	purgatory

We Respond

Thank you, Lord, for showing us the way to heaven. Thank you for giving us leaders to guide us there. Bless especially our Church leaders. May they lead us in your way. Amen.

Things to Do at Home

1. Every person is meant to be a leader in some way. One way is leading by example. Brainstorm with your family ways in which ordinary people can become leaders. Share your list with your classmates.

2. Moses and Joshua were good leaders because they prayed. Discuss with your family praying together, if you do not already do so. Some questions you might ask are: Is it possible to set aside a time once a week to pray together? What suggestions do you have for this time of prayer?

3. During family prayer time, remember to pray for the leaders of the Church. Consider asking an adult in your family to invite your parish priest or deacon to visit your home for dinner and to participate in your prayer time.

4. Learn the traditional song "Joshua Fought the Battle of Jericho."

5. Both Moses and Joshua were good leaders. Go through the story on page 103 and list leadership qualities that Moses had. Then talk with someone in your family about which leadership qualities you share with Moses.

6. Identify people you consider to be leaders: at home, at school, in your extracurricular activities, in your community. Think about leadership qualities that they have that you would like to strengthen in yourself.

Visit **www.christourlife.org/family** for more family resources.

Two Homelands Fill in this chart comparing the Promised Land of Canaan to our promised land.

	Canaan	Heaven
People promised the homeland		
Leader		
How God is present with his people		
Time of formation, testing, and preparation		
Enemies to be overcome		
Help from God		

People and Places Complete the following sentences. Use the words in the word bank. Some words may be used more than once.

Shiloh	Pope	Jericho
Joshua	Moses	Jordan
Shechem	Levites	Jesus

1. The greatest prophet of Israel was _____.

2. The _____ were the tribe of priests who did not receive land in Canaan.

3. _____ was the city in Canaan where the Israelites renewed their covenant with God.

4. _____ led the Israelites into Canaan.

5. The city whose walls fell when the Israelites blew horns and shouted was _____.

6. _____ died on Mount Nebo.

7. The visible head of the Church, the _____, represents Christ.

8. After settling in Canaan, the Israelites kept the Ark of the Covenant in _____.

9. The Israelites had to cross the river _____ to enter Canaan.

10. The names _____ and _____ mean "God saves."

Shechem ❯

Unit 3 Review

❮ Moses with commandments.

Living the Commandments

The Ten Commandments are often identified by two categories: love of God (the first three commandments) and love of neighbor (the fourth through tenth commandments). For each example below, decide which category the person or people belong to. Write *A* for love of God and *B* for love of neighbor.

_____ 1. Students in the sixth grade class at St. Jerome school are writing letters to their elected officials, asking them to support legislation that respects the dignity of human life.

_____ 2. Andy strives to bring honor to the name of Jesus through his words and deeds.

_____ 3. Maria avoids the gossip that many of her friends seem to enjoy so much.

_____ 4. Kenna always makes sure to fast for an hour before receiving Jesus in the Eucharist.

_____ 5. Olivia is making a special effort to help her mother around the house while she recuperates from surgery.

Help these students decide what to do. Write the commandment and its number that would best help each person.

1. Chelsea: It is Sunday morning. I am very tired. I don't feel like going to church.

_____ : _____

2. I am walking through the store after school and I am hungry. It would be easy to pick up a candy bar and put it in my pocket.

_____ : _____

3. Eddie: Mom told me to take out the garbage. I don't feel like doing it.

_____ : _____

4. Victor: I am not supposed to play my brother's stereo without asking him. But I have a new CD I want to listen to, and my brother isn't home.

_____ : _____

5. My friends are planning on making up a story to get an unpopular classmate in trouble. I don't want them to think I'm a baby, so I might go along with them.

_____ : _____

_____

Celebrating

God's Guidance

Introduction

Leader: We begin our prayer as we begin all things, in the name of the Father, and of the Son, and of the Holy Spirit.

All: Amen.

Leader: Let us praise the God of wisdom, knowledge, and grace. Blessed be God forever.

All: Blessed be God forever.

Leader: Lord God, you have guided your people in many wonderful ways. You led them through the wilderness. You made them a holy nation when you gave the Ten Commandments. You gave them good, strong leaders. You continue the loving care of your people today, Lord. You are leading us through the wilderness of this earth to the glory of your eternal kingdom. You are always with us. We have come together to praise and thank you for your goodness.

(Song: One that thanks or praises God for his loving care)

Procession

Leader: Lord, you have spoken to us in your holy Word. We rejoice in that Word and proclaim that you alone are our God.

(Everyone joins the procession led by students carrying the Bible and candles.)

Readings and Responses

Leader: The Bible tells of God's loving care for his people. Let us listen now to God's command to Moses in a reading from the Book of Deuteronomy.

Reader 1: A reading from Deuteronomy 31:19–22. *(Read from the Bible.)*

The Word of the Lord.

All: Thanks be to God.

Leader: Psalm 119 praises God for guiding us on our way to eternal life with him. Let us listen to some of the verses of this psalm. After each verse, please respond by saying "Proclaim the name of the Lord. O tell the greatness of our God."

(Students read verses selected from Psalm 119. All repeat the response.)

Prayers of Thanks and Petition

Leader: Eternal Father, you are the Lord our God. You have taught us how to live as your people. Listen now to our prayers of praise and thanksgiving.

Reader 2: For the leaders of the Church—the pope, bishops, priests, and deacons who lead us to you,

All: We praise you and give you thanks.

Reader 3: For the Sacrament of Reconciliation, in which you forgive our sins and give us your grace,

All: We praise you and give you thanks.

Reader 4: For your commandments, which you gave us out of love so that we could love you more,

All: We praise you and give you thanks.

Reader 5: For your Holy Word, which reveals your goodness and love,

All: We praise you and give you thanks.

Conclusion

Leader: Let us now stand and pray the Lord's Prayer, which Jesus himself taught us to pray.

All: Our Father . . .

(Song: A joyous hymn of praise)

James Jacques Joseph Tissot,
The Sermon on the Mount, c. 1886-96.

James Jacques Joseph Tissot, *Moses Sees the Promised Land From Afar.*

Looking Back at Unit 3

In this unit, we have accompanied the Israelites as they left their lives of slavery in Egypt and journeyed through the desert to the Promised Land. Desert living was a new way of life for the Israelites. Because of their hardships, they often failed to respond to God's love. However, God was faithful to his word. He had chosen this people to belong to him in a special way. He had made a covenant with them. He asked them to live according to his law of love. God promised that he would be with them, to care for them no matter how hard things got.

When the Israelites failed to keep their part of the Covenant, God always forgave them. He loved them and cared for them constantly. Their task was to repent and turn toward God's mercy. Through the leadership of Moses and Joshua, God finally led his people to the Promised Land.

We are also God's people. He asks that we live by his law. God asks us to base our decisions on the principles we learn from his Son, Jesus. Jesus gave us a new commandment, "As I have loved you, so you also should love one another." (John 13:34) When we commit sin, Jesus will always reconcile us with his Father if we are truly sorry.

Planning Ahead

Look up the following Scripture passages. Choose three that you will try especially hard to follow. On the corresponding lines below, write each passage in your own words.

___ Matthew 6:1	___ Matthew 6:19
___ Luke 11:9	___ John 8:47
___ Matthew 6:14	___ Luke 6:27–28
___ Luke 14:10–11	___ John 15:17

1. _____

_____

_____

2. _____

_____

_____

3. _____

_____

_____

Living the Message

Can you give yourself a check (✓) for each statement?

○ 1. I know several of the stories about what happened while the Israelites wandered in the wilderness for 40 years.

○ 2. I can explain how the commandments are a sign of God's love.

○ 3. I understand how my conscience helps me to make decisions.

○ 4. Before making a decision, I stop and think about my obligations, my principles, and the possible consequences.

○ 5. I have decided to celebrate the Sacrament of Reconciliation regularly in order to be reconciled with God and grow in virtue.

Rituals and Identity

The Catholic experience is one steeped in ritual, and those rituals are often ingrained into the very identity of those raised in the Catholic faith. The scent of incense, the play of candlelight on stained-glass, or the cadence of a prayer or hymn can bring back not only memories and ideas of our faith, but for many of us, memories of our earliest childhood. There is often a soothing comfort associated with the rites and rituals of our faith, because they represent both a continuity in our own lives and a continuous connection with our Catholic brothers and sisters.

Families have their own rituals, which can offer many of the same feelings of comfort and connectedness. One family might have a large Sunday dinner, in which they indulge in family recipes and catch up on the week's events. Another family might have a special way of saying good night before bedtime. Your own family probably has rituals unique to itself, rituals that you and your children rely on as touchstones in a hectic world.

Rituals don't have to be fancy to have an effect on us. Their power lies in being a reminder of what is important to us on a daily, weekly, or even yearly basis. When you carve out time for what's important—whether it's eating together, biking together, or going to Mass and praying together—you not only improve upon what your family decides to do together, you also strengthen your relationship to one another. Your children may remark that weekly Mass is "always the same thing." These complaints are an excellent opportunity to open up a discussion about ritual. Point out that a birthday party is a ritual: there is a decorated cake, candles, presents, and the singing of "Happy Birthday." Challenge them to imagine a birthday celebration without presents or a cake. Explain that for a ritual to have its desired effect, it must have a "sameness" that we can count on week after week, year after year. In a similar way, the ritual of the Mass, as well as the rituals of all the sacraments, provides us with a sameness that allows us to easily gather as a community and worship God. That sameness allows us to celebrate the ritual of the Mass anywhere in the world—even in a different language—and still participate fully.

Family life is fast-paced and ever-changing. This makes rituals all the more important. Pay attention to the rituals that punctuate your life daily, weekly, seasonally, and yearly. They can help strengthen your family's faith.

Habits That Help Us

Rituals remind us we have a safe and dependable place in the world, as well as the love, support, and acceptance we need to navigate life. As a parent, you try to create for your child an environment of safety and love. As Catholics, we experience an elevated sense of love and belonging by making a habit of going weekly to Mass, and as extensions of us our children, we share that experience. But the power we tap into at Mass will have a much richer meaning—for ourselves and our kids—if we are already practicing certain habits at home:

1. **Pray together.** Whether it's a quick thank-you for the food on the table, or asking for God's protection when children are prone to nightmares, we all feel better when we remind ourselves that God is listening lovingly to our needs. We can rely on traditional prayers of the Church, such as the Our Father, or we can simply speak to God in our own words. Whatever the form of prayer, when your family prays together, your child learns that with God, all things are possible. When we pray together at home, kids learn why it's important to pray together as a parish family.

2. **Eat together.** Meals are powerful proof that we feed more than our bodies when we sit down around a table and pass platters of food. Meals help feed our sense of belonging and our shared beliefs. Over bread and butter, we share laughter over old jokes or swap stories about family members whom we admire or

miss. Family meals remind us of the importance of celebrating and thanking our loved ones—and of celebrating and thanking God for placing those we love in our midst. The more meals that your family shares at home—meals of food and conversation rather than of TV—the more your children will instinctively learn the importance of coming together at Mass to celebrate the lifesaving meal of the Eucharist.

3. **Forgive, forgive, forgive.** Forgiveness might be described as "the oil" that makes a family run. A family's ability to working smoothly together gets bogged down when we hold on to grudges or nurse resentments. By practicing forgiveness on a daily basis—knowing that most of the hurts hurled aren't intentional, knowing that people mess up because of low patience, little time, or lack of knowledge—mercy and forgiveness will spill into your family's workplaces, schools, parish, and community. The Church also offers the Sacrament of Reconciliation, an opportunity for forgiveness that is as necessary to the well-being of a family as a tune-up is for a car.

4. **Read and sing together.** Education experts tell us that kids pick up a tremendous amount whenever their parents read and sing to them. Not only are they learning language by hearing repeated words and phrases, but they are soaking up values and attitudes. Reading with your children often also gives the same two-for-the-price-of-one investment that rituals give: strengthening family togetherness even as you underscore the values you wish to impart. Reading and singing can, in fact, become family rituals in their own right. Families who read and sing together at home develop a love of stories and song that often helps them, and especially the children, gain deeper insight from the readings they hear at Mass and greater joy from the songs that fill our worship.

Building Family Identity

Work with your family to help your child recognize the family rituals that make the touchstone of his or her life. Use the scroll below to write family rituals that you practice on a daily, weekly, monthly, and yearly basis. Talk about which rituals each member of your family finds especially comforting and why. If you practice rituals that are family tradition, such as using your great-grandmother's cookie recipe at Christmas or reading your great-uncle's favorite story with your child, talk about the history of the ritual and why it is significant in your family.

Daily Rituals	Weekly Rituals	Monthly Rituals	Yearly Rituals

Learn New Tricks Remember that it is never too late to develop new family rituals. If you don't already, consider setting aside time each week for family prayer. Or your family might turn off the TV one night a week and take turns reading aloud from a book or from the Bible. Rituals can even be as simple as working together to create a themed dinner on Saturday night or planning one specific outdoor activity each week. What other ideas can you and your family think of? Whatever you choose, remember that for it to be a ritual, it must be performed consistently and become part of your family identity.

Building Catholic Identity

How well does your child understand the rites and rituals of the Catholic faith? How well do you? If knowledge is power, then knowledge of the rituals of Catholicism is a powerful tool in helping you and your child develop strong Catholic identities.

As a long-term family activity, challenge each member of your family to identify each week one thing that they are curious about Catholicism. Examples might include why incense is used in certain rites, where a certain prayer or song came from, or the meaning of the priest's vestment colors. Even questions such as *Who built the church? What is the history behind the artwork in the church?* and *Who have been active members of our parish?* can help strengthen your family's community and Catholic identity. After Mass each week, work together as a family to find the answers to each family member's question.

Visit **www.christourlife.org/family** for more family resources.

History Lessons
Your child may shy away from the idea of "schoolwork" during his or her off-hours. But there are ways that you can make this research activity more fun or worthwhile. You might propose the research as a basis for a trivia game that you can integrate into your family prayer sessions. Or you might award your child or children points for their answers, which they can accumulate to be excused from household chores or to earn a special treat.

Building Family and Community
Participating in community service activities as a family is a great way to develop a new family ritual and practice the virtues of the faith. Work with your family to choose one new community service project each month or every few months and commit to that project as a family. As your family bonds develop by participating in consistent family activities, your child will learn the importance of active participation in the community and develop the habit of applying Catholic virtues to his or her life.

God Leads the Chosen People

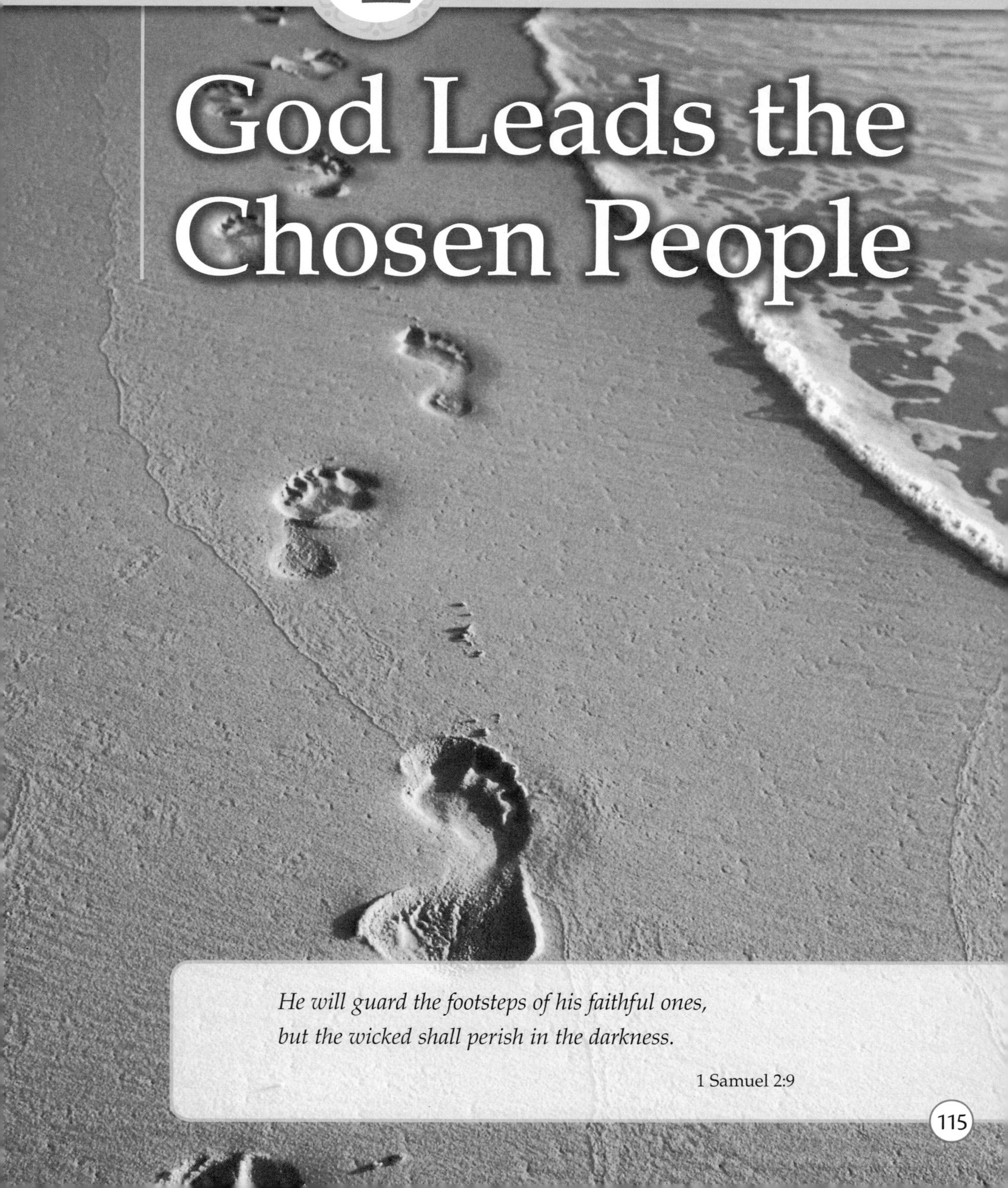

He will guard the footsteps of his faithful ones,
but the wicked shall perish in the darkness.

1 Samuel 2:9

God Leads the Chosen People

IN THIS UNIT, you will learn about how God accomplishes the divine plan of salvation, using human strengths and weaknesses. In particular, you will learn about the roles and contributions of the judges and the first three Israelite kings.

The Period of Judges

In Israel's history, the period of judges was a time of adjustment for the Chosen People. The judges were military leaders who ruled the Israelites before the monarchy was established. As you learn about them, reflect on your own choices of role models, and consider the heroes and heroines portrayed in modern media.

The Kings of Israel

Following the period of the judges, Israel entered into a period of monarchy. You will learn about Samuel, Israel's last and greatest judge, and the first two kings of Israel, Saul and David. The history of the Israelite kings will help you better understand the mission that God entrusts to those in authority.

David and Solomon

King David united the tribes of Israel into one great nation. One important way of uniting the tribes was by making Jerusalem the political and religious capital of the kingdom. David's greatness was reflected in his humble repentance for his sins, his deep love of God, and the love he showed in the psalms he wrote. David's son Solomon was blessed with great wisdom in dealing with his people. This wisdom is expressed in his proverbs. David and Solomon teach us that all human leaders, though they may not be perfect, deserve our respect, support, and obedience.

King David and King Solomon,
Byzantine mosaic, 11th c.

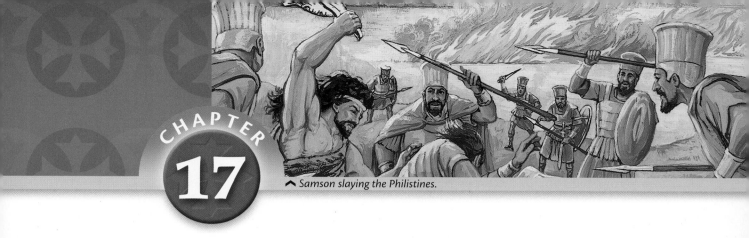

↑ *Samson slaying the Philistines.*

The Period of Judges

Growing Pains

Growing up can be exciting. There is so much to learn and to discover. We look forward to new experiences and more privileges. But along the way there are also rough spots. We make many mistakes. Sometimes we fail. This can be frustrating and painful.

Problems in the Promised Land

Many of our experiences are like those of the Israelites. They, too, had growing pains. They knew what it was like to fail and to have to start over again. The pattern of failing and beginning again is seen throughout the Book of Judges.

There was much to learn about living in the Promised Land. Once the Israelites had been desert travelers. Now they had to plow the soil and plant crops. Once the Ark of the Covenant had been in their midst. Now the tribes were scattered throughout the land.

How did the Israelites deal with these changes? For one thing, they made many mistakes. They often forgot the Lord and all he had done for them. They violated the first commandment, which calls people to believe in God and to love him above all else. Instead, they placed their hope in the god Baal, just as their Canaanite neighbors did.

Then the Israelites found their lives in danger. Invading tribes threatened to take their land.

The Israelites realized that they had forgotten their covenant with the Lord. They hadn't been faithful. They called out to God. They wanted to be forgiven and protected once again.

An Answer to Prayer

God answered the prayers of the Israelites by sending leaders to save them from their enemies. These leaders were called *judges.* These judges did not sit in courtrooms. They were usually military leaders. They were leaders of their tribes who were respected for their victories.

The judges were gifted by God with a power called a *charism.* A charism is a special gift of God given to a person for the good of others. The judges had charisms that helped them defeat Israel's enemies.

The time from the death of Joshua to the beginning of the rule by kings is called the period of judges. There are twelve judges recorded in the Book of Judges.

During the period of judges, there was a lot of failure and lawlessness in Israel. It was a time during which God's people did not live like brothers and sisters who were responsible for caring for one another. However, people can learn and grow after making mistakes. The period of judges was a time of growth for God's people.

Heroes of Israel

Some of the judges are very famous. Their stories tell of fantastic battles and acts of courage. The Israelites were proud of their heroes. When the people retold stories about their heroes, they would sometimes exaggerate some of the facts. But those who heard the stories understood their message and found strength and hope in hearing them. Whenever the Israelites found themselves in trouble, they looked back at their history. They recalled how they had turned from the Lord. They also remembered that believing in God and placing their trust in him resulted in amazing consequences for them. They recalled those leaders who helped them to place their trust in God. With all of this in mind, they could deal with new problems.

Deborah: A Faith-Filled Woman

based on Judges 4; 5

Deborah was a judge and prophet of Israel. Seated under her palm tree, Deborah advised people who came to her for judgment. One day Deborah told Barak, a military leader, "God commands you to march on Mount Tabor. He will deliver Sisera into your hands." Sisera, the general of a Canaanite king, had led the Canaanite army against the Israelites for 20 years. Barak would not go to battle without Deborah, so she accompanied the troops into battle. They put every Canaanite soldier to death. The only survivor was Sisera, who fled on foot and found safety at the house of his friend Heber. Sisera, however, was tricked by Heber's wife, Jael, who was loyal to Israel. Jael invited Sisera into her tent, fed him, and then killed him while he slept.

Deborah is a good example of someone who accepted her responsibility to build a healthy society. She took great risks and trusted in the Lord. After the battle, she praised God for all he had done for his people. Deborah's song of praise, found in the Book of Judges, chapter 5, is considered one of the oldest texts in the Bible, originating over 3,000 years ago.

Gideon: An Obedient Judge

based on Judges 6–8

After Deborah's victory, there was peace for about 40 years. However, the Israelites eventually turned away from God again, so God allowed the Midianites to rule over the Israelites. After seven years, the Israelites cried out to God for help.

Gideon's family was the poorest in the tribe. Despite this, he was called by God to save the Israelites from the Midianites. Gideon asked God to perform a miracle to prove that God could give him the power to defeat the Midianites. Gideon laid a piece of fleece on the floor and asked to have dew appear on the fleece while the ground stayed dry. Then he asked that the fleece remain dry while dew fell to the ground around it. God humored Gideon and performed the tasks. Then, to show that trust in God is rewarded, God gave Gideon special directions for his army. Read Judges 7:2–8 and complete this summary of what Gideon was told to do:

_____ his army from 32,000 to _____ soldiers.

You can read about the battle in Judges 7:16–22.

Samson, the Strongman

based on
Judges 13–16

Samson is a colorful and larger-than-life character. To thank God for giving them a son, Samson's parents promised that he would **abstain** from wine, unclean meat, and cutting or shaving his hair. As long as this vow was kept, the Spirit of God would give him great strength. Samson would grow up to take on the Philistines, who were longtime enemies of the Israelites. But he also made many mistakes and often broke God's rules.

As a young man, Samson married a Philistine girl, against the advice of his parents. At his wedding, Samson bet his groomsmen that they could not answer a riddle. If they won, Samson would give each man a set of clothes. When the men could not answer the riddle, they convinced Samson's wife to tell them the answer. Samson was so angry that he flew into a rage and killed 30 men in Ashkelon, taking their clothes to pay off the bet.

While he was in Ashkelon, Samson's bride was given to another man. In anger, Samson tied torches to the tails of 300 foxes and set them loose in the Philistines' crops. When a thousand men came to capture Samson, he slew them with the jawbone of a donkey.

A while later, Samson fell in love with a woman named Delilah. The Philistines paid her to find out the secret of Samson's strength. After asking three times, Delilah wore Samson down. He told her that he would lose his strength if his hair was cut. One night while Samson slept, Delilah cut his hair, leaving him powerless. The Philistines seized him, blinded him, and put him in prison.

Samson did not lose his strength just because his hair was cut, but rather because he had broken the vow that his parents had made at his birth. Having his hair cut was the last straw, so God took his strength away.

At a Philistine festival, Samson was brought out to amuse the people. He asked God for the strength to destroy the Philistines. God granted Samson's last request. Samson pushed against the pillars of the building where the Philistines were gathered. The building collapsed and killed them all, including Samson.

Despite Samson's failures, he is considered a great judge because he realized that his strength came from God. As people of hope, we too are called to patiently place our trust in God.

Ruth, the Foreigner

based on the Book of Ruth

Ruth's story is one of loyalty and commitment. Although she was not a judge herself, her story took place during the period of judges.

Naomi, a Hebrew woman, was married to a Hebrew man whose family had come to Moab during a famine. Naomi's two sons married Moabite women: Ruth and Orpah. About 10 years after Naomi and her family arrived in Moab, her husband and sons died. Naomi decided to return to Israel, telling Ruth and Orpah that they should stay in Moab with their own people. Read what Ruth said to Naomi in Ruth 1:16–17.

Ruth (continued)

Orpah returned to her home, while Ruth remained committed to Naomi. In Israel, Ruth gathered grain for Naomi and herself. Boaz, the landowner Ruth worked for, made sure that Ruth always had enough grain. Naomi wanted Ruth to be taken care of, and she knew that Boaz would make a good husband.

One day Naomi told Ruth to go to Boaz while he slept and lie down at his feet. Boaz would understand that he was to ask for the right to marry Ruth.

Boaz then found the man who was legally entitled to marry Ruth and to inherit the land of her first husband. Before a court the man surrendered his rights to Boaz. Boaz married Ruth, and God blessed them with a son. This son became the grandfather of King David, the ancestor of Jesus. Ruth's story teaches us that love is the vocation of all human beings and that we are called to recognize all people as brothers and sisters and to accept our responsibility to care for others.

A Right to the Truth

The Bible shows that some of the judges of Israel were authentic faith-filled leaders, while others were flawed people who had to learn from their mistakes. Today, through media such as TV and the Internet, we are presented with many people who can influence us, either positively or negatively. We have a right to information based on truth. Although the media has a responsibility to communicate

information honestly and fairly, sometimes it is not reliable. Because of our commitment to honor the truth, we must question the media, be it music, movies, or the news. We must also think carefully about the messages we receive, asking whether they respect or threaten the life and dignity of the human person. Only then can we learn to live as people of truth, a virtue that shows itself in both words and deeds.

Heroes and Heroines of Tomorrow

People we admire can inspire us to discover the gifts God gave us, so that we may learn how to use them to serve others—especially those who are poor and vulnerable. Then we, too, can inspire others.

Think of someone in your life whom you admire. What about this person do you like the most? How has this person helped you grow in life? What does he or she value as important?

A Moment with Jesus

All of us admire certain people. They may be parents, brothers or sisters, teachers, athletes, performers, or friends. We respect what they do and value their opinions. We try to imitate their actions. These people are our heroes or heroines. In Baptism, you chose to imitate Jesus. That's what it means to be a Christian: to be one who is like Christ. Take a moment now to thank Jesus for the example he has set for you. Ask him for the grace you need to be his disciple. Thank him for the role models he has provided for you. Ask him to help you be a role model for others.

We Remember

Who were the judges?

The judges were people sent by God to lead the Israelites during a time of great change. They often fought battles and encouraged the Israelites to be faithful to the Lord.

What responsibility do we have as Catholics when it comes to the media?

Because of our commitment to honor the truth, we must question the media that we are exposed to. We should think carefully about the messages we receive, asking whether they respect or threaten the life and dignity of the human person.

Word to Know

abstain

We Respond

I am special. God has gifted me in many ways. One of my best qualities is

_____

_____

I can give a good example by

_____

_____

_____

_____

Things to Do at Home

1. Interview an adult about his or her heroes. Ask these questions:
   - Who is someone you really admired?
   - Why did you admire this person?
   - What did you learn from this person about life or about yourself?
   - Do you still admire this person? Why or why not?

2. Read with your family Judges 8:22–23 to find out what Gideon said when the people asked him to rule over them. Talk with your family about why Gideon's response shows that he was a good leader.

3. Imagine that you write for an online news service. Write an article to help people who have made serious mistakes or have failed at something. Include in your article at least two positive things, ideas, or behaviors that might come from each mistake or failure. Share your article with the class.

4. Choose a night of the week that you watch TV or movies with your family. Work with them to list the characters portrayed in the TV shows or movies that you watch. Talk with your family about which characters display strong faith or morality. Discuss qualities that each character has that you and the members of your family might model.

5. Choose a person from the Book of Judges. It can be a judge you read about in this chapter or one from your own reading. Draw a series of pictures that show scenes from the life of that judge. Use the pictures to tell your family the story of that judge. Talk with them about how that judge showed faith in God or learned an important lesson.

Visit **www.christourlife.org/family** for more family resources.

A Whole New World Match the Israelites' old way of living with their new experiences in Canaan.

Old Life

_____ 1. Lived together under Moses and Joshua

_____ 2. Had the Ark of the Covenant in their midst

_____ 3. Had no land to fight over

_____ 4. Were desert travelers

New Life

A. Had unfriendly neighbors

B. Tribes separated and not united under a leader

C. Had to learn to farm

D. Had to make yearly trips to Shiloh where the Ark of the Covenant was

Crossword Puzzle Complete the following crossword puzzle and then follow the final direction.

Across

1. The name of a pagan idol

2. A judge known for his tremendous physical strength

4. Men and women sent by God to defend the Israelites

6. She led the Israelites into battle against the Canaanites.

Down

3. Name of the Promised Land

5. He led a small army and defeated the Midianites.

7. She was an ancestor of the Savior.

8. The period of judges began shortly after his death.

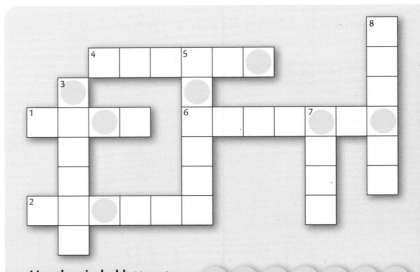

Use the circled letters to write the name of a gift from God that is given for the good of others.

An Acrostic Fill in the following acrostic.

1. The period of judges began after the death of _____.

2. In general, the number of steps in the Israelites' pattern of life presented in the Book of Judges was _____.

3. Baal was the name of the Canaanite false god, or _____.

4. The book that records the struggles of the Israelites after they entered the Promised Land is _____.

5. The judges were tribal _____.

6. When the Israelites entered the Promised Land, they either fought battles with the people there, settled in peacefully, or made _____.

1. J _ _ _ _ _

2. _ _ U _

3. _ D _ _

4. _ _ _ G _ _

5. _ E _ _ _ _ _

6. _ _ _ _ _ _ _ S

^ Claude Lorrain, *David Crowned by Samuel.*

The Kings of Israel

God's Revelation to Samuel

based on 1 Samuel 1—4; 7

The last and greatest judge was Samuel. He was judge over all of Israel, not just a few tribes. The people loved and respected Samuel because they knew that he was a prophet, someone who spoke God's Word to them.

Samuel's mother, Hannah, had prayed a long time for a child. She promised God that if she had a baby, she would give the baby to him. A few years after Samuel was born, Hannah took him to the Temple at Shiloh to be dedicated to the Lord. Samuel was entrusted to the care of Eli, the temple priest. To reward Hannah's faith and devotion, God blessed her with five more children.

As a boy, Samuel heard God's call in his sleep. At first, he thought it was Eli. But after a few times, Eli understood that the Lord was speaking to Samuel. He instructed the boy to answer with a generous "Here I am, Lord" and "speak, Lord, your servant is listening." It was then that God gave Samuel the first of many hard tasks.

God was not pleased with Eli. Eli had failed in his duties as a father. God told Samuel to warn Eli that he and his sons would be punished for their sins. Because Eli was Samuel's teacher, Samuel was afraid to tell him God's message. But he did as God asked. Eli realized that Samuel was speaking for God, and he answered, "He is the Lord. He will do what he judges best."

A short time later, the Philistines attacked the Israelites. Hoping that God would help them defeat the Philistines, the Israelites sent for the Ark of the Covenant. Eli's sons brought the Ark into battle, where they were killed and the Ark was captured. When Eli heard that the sign of God's presence had been taken by the Philistines, he fell off his chair and died of a broken neck.

Samuel then became judge of Israel. The Ark of the Covenant was returned, and once again God's people could pray there. Samuel spent many years leading the Israelites back to God and trying to heal their damaged relationship with him. As a judge, Samuel was a great spiritual leader rather than a military one. Through Samuel, God prepared his people for kings.

The Demand for a King

based on 1 Samuel 8

In his old age, Samuel appointed his sons as judges over Israel. However, they could never be good leaders, for they were not faithful to God. The Israelites needed a strong leader to unite them as they struggled to bring justice to the land and to promote the well-being of all God's people. The countries around them had kings, so the people told Samuel that they also wanted a king.

At first, Samuel objected. Kings in other countries were treated like gods. Samuel warned the Israelites that kings could easily get too powerful and become corrupt. But the people would not listen. So Samuel prayed for guidance. God told him to grant the people's request.

The beginning of the monarchy in Israel is important because it helps us understand Jesus Christ and the concept of God's kingdom. Jesus began the Kingdom of Heaven on earth. Jesus' voluntary entrance into Jerusalem was a sign of the coming of the kingdom because of what he, the Messiah, would accomplish through his death and Resurrection. The Church, under the guidance of the successors of Peter, is a sign of God's kingdom.

The Reign of Saul

based on 1 Samuel 10–16; 2 Samuel 5

God inspired Samuel to anoint Saul as king. Although he was from one of the smallest tribes, Saul was tall, handsome, and courageous. He was also a good soldier. Samuel poured oil over Saul's head as a sign that God had chosen Saul as ruler. God sent Saul his spirit to help Saul rule in God's name.

At the beginning of his rule as king, Saul was a great military

leader. He united the people and led them against other nations. But as time went on, he forgot that he was called to rule in God's name, not in his own. Several times Saul did not listen to the messages of the Lord that Samuel brought him. Instead, he did as he pleased.

Saul was no longer a fit ruler for Israel, and Samuel told him that his kingdom would not last. The Lord had chosen another man to lead his people, a man who would carry out his will.

Saul ruled for about 10 more years. When he was no longer open to the spirit of the Lord, an evil spirit filled him. Saul became moody and difficult to live with. Some of his servants thought that soothing music would help him feel better. They suggested that David, a shepherd boy from Bethlehem, play the harp for Saul whenever he was troubled. That was how David, who was to be the second king of Israel, came to work for Saul. David's music calmed Saul, and Saul became very fond of David. Saul's son Jonathan and David became best friends. Eventually Jonathan prevented Saul from killing David.

The Uses of Oil

Athletes in ancient Greece rubbed their bodies with oil to prepare for their races. The penetrating oil gave them a feeling of new strength and helped them to run better.

Before the development of pain relievers, people treated sore muscles by rubbing them with ointments or oils. Today parents sometimes use baby oil to soften and heal a baby's dry skin.

Oil has many important uses. It strengthens and heals. It gives light and warmth. It powers some of our greatest machines. It is even used to cook many foods.

Anointing with Oil

Because of oil's wonderful effects, people began to use it in religious ceremonies. The words and actions used in a religious ceremony are called *ritual*. One ritual of the Israelites showed their respect for the Ark of the Covenant. They kept a lamp burning before the Ark at all times. Oil made from crushed olives was used in the lamp.

To **anoint** is to pour or rub on oil when performing a ritual. It means that a person or thing has been dedicated to God. For instance, when Jacob poured oil over the stone he used to mark Bethel as a holy place, he anointed it.

Marked with God's Seal

People who had been chosen by God for special work were anointed. The anointing was a sign that God's spirit was with the chosen one. Those who were anointed could count on strength from God to do his work. **Christ,** the title that we give to Jesus, means *anointed one* or **Messiah.** When Jesus was born, he was consecrated as Christ by the anointing of the Holy Spirit. Jesus' first public proclamation in the Gospel of Luke were words taken from the prophet Isaiah: "The Spirit of the Lord is upon me, because he has anointed me to bring glad tidings to the poor."

Moses anointed Aaron when he consecrated him to God as a priest. Among God's anointed ones were those, such as Saul, who were chosen to be kings of the Israelites. The kings were anointed to carry out God's saving plan.

Today a sacred oil used in sacramental anointing is called *chrism*. The word *chrism*, like *Christ*, comes from a Greek word that means "anoint."

Chrism is made by mixing olive or vegetable oil with perfume. Its fragrance reminds us that all who are anointed with it should fill the world around them with the spirit of God. Chrism is used in Baptism, Confirmation, and the ordination of priests and bishops.

On Holy Thursday (or another suitable day), a special Mass, called the Chrism Mass, is celebrated in each diocese. During this Mass, the bishop consecrates chrism and blesses the other oils that will be used by the Church for anointing and healing. Priests from the diocese concelebrate with the bishop. Then representatives from the various parishes carry the holy oils to their parishes, where they will be used for the celebration of the sacraments throughout the year.

Immediately after the waters of Baptism made you a member of the Church, you were anointed with oil as priest, prophet, and king. You were chosen to pray, lead, and proclaim God's Word. During the anointing, everyone prayed that you would always live as a good member of the Body of Christ. When you are confirmed, you are anointed on the forehead with sacred chrism, together with the laying on of the minister's hands, and the words "Be sealed with the gift of the Holy Spirit."

Anointing of the Sick and Holy Orders

In addition to the Sacrament of Confirmation, anointing with oil plays an important role in the sacraments of the Anointing of the Sick and Holy Orders.

The letter of James tells us that the mission to anoint and heal the sick, which Jesus gave his disciples, was continued into the early Church. James wrote, "Is anyone among you sick? He should summon the presbyters of the church, and they should pray over him and anoint [him] with oil in the name of the Lord, and the prayer of faith will save the sick person, and the Lord will raise him up. If he has committed any sins, he will be forgiven." (James 5:13–15) God's care and concern for the seriously ill and aged is shown today through the Sacrament of the Anointing of the Sick. We celebrate this sacrament to confer a special grace on the person who is experiencing the difficulties that come with serious sickness and old age.

The priest anoints the sick person by tracing in oil the Sign of the Cross on the forehead and hands. The sacrament gives the person the grace to be healed spiritually and, at times, physically. It also provides forgiveness of sins, venial as well as mortal, if the person is truly sorry and unable to confess them.

The Sacrament of Holy Orders gives the Church its leaders in worship, education, and governance. For that reason, the Church takes seriously its obligation to choose the right men for the offices of deacon, priest, and bishop. The sacrament can only be conferred by a bishop, who is acting in the name of the Church.

In the ceremony, the bishop lays his hands on the head of the man being ordained. He then says a prayer of consecration, asking God to give the man the graces he will need to perform his duties. Finally, the bishop anoints the palms of the new priest with chrism. The Sacrament of Holy Orders leaves a sacramental character on the man that can never be removed.

A Moment with Jesus

Jesus was anointed by the Holy Spirit to bring glad tidings to the poor. In the Sacrament of Confirmation, you are anointed and called to follow Jesus' example. One way you can do this is by making specific efforts to defend and promote the dignity of the poor and vulnerable and to meet their immediate needs. Take a moment to ask Jesus to help you recognize those who are poor in your community. Ask him for the grace you need to be compassionate and selfless as you seek to serve their needs. Thank Jesus for the gift of his Holy Spirit.

We Remember

What is anointing?
Anointing is pouring or rubbing oil on a person or thing to dedicate that person or thing to God.

Why were kings anointed?
Kings were anointed as a sign that God had chosen them to rule in his name.

In which sacraments is anointing with oil included?
Baptism, Confirmation, Anointing of the Sick, and Holy Orders.

Words to Know
anoint   Christ   Messiah

We Respond
"Living the truth in love, we should grow in every way into him who is the head, Christ."

Ephesians 4:15

The Hill of Ramah, where Saul was anointed. ❯

Things to Do at Home

1. Pray that the leaders of our country will follow God's ways and make wise and just decisions.

2. Read the biography of a great leader, such as Mahatma Gandhi, Mother Theresa, or Martin Luther King, Jr. Be ready to share the following:
   - how that person showed concern for others.
   - what you liked best about the way the leader worked with others.
   - some difficulties the leader faced.

3. Read the story of Samuel's calling by the Lord. (1 Samuel 3:1–10) Think about how God is calling you and to what he may be calling you.

4. Read more about the friendship between David and Jonathan in 1 Samuel 18:1–5; 19:1–7; 20. What qualities of friendship do the two men show?

5. Do an Internet search to identify nations that are ruled by a monarch. See what you can learn about how the people of those nations view their king or queen. Think about what it means for us to think of God as our king.

6. With your parents, do a search of your house for various kinds of oils, for example: cooking oils, oils for lamps, and skin-care oils. Consider the different uses of these oils and talk about what anointing with oil symbolizes in the sacraments.

7. Ask your parents about their favorite colognes and perfumes. Tell them what you learned about why the sacred chrism used in Confirmation is perfumed.

Visit **www.christourlife.org/family** for more family resources.

Who Am I? Match each person with his or her description.

A. Samuel   _E_   1. I was a judge and a priest who anointed Samuel.

B. Saul   _F_   2. I prevented my father from killing my friend David.

C. David   _B_   3. I was the first king of Israel, who lost the throne because of disobedience.

D. Hannah   _D_   4. I longed for a son. When he came, I gave him to the Lord.

E. Eli   _C_   5. I was a shepherd who became king of Israel after Saul.

F. Jonathan   _A_   6. I was the last judge of Israel; I anointed two kings.

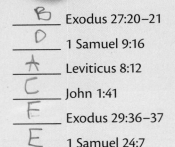

Oil in Scripture Match each fact with the correct verse from the Bible.

_B_ Exodus 27:20–21

_D_ 1 Samuel 9:16

_A_ Leviticus 8:12

_C_ John 1:41

_F_ Exodus 29:36–37

_E_ 1 Samuel 24:7

A. Moses ordained Aaron by pouring oil on his head.

B. Olive oil is to burn perpetually in a light in the Tent of Meeting.

C. The word *Messiah* means "anointed one."

D. God told Samuel to anoint Saul as king of Israel.

E. David would not harm Saul because the anointing had consecrated him to the Lord.

F. An altar is anointed as a sign that it is sacred and consecrated to the worship of God.

Marked for Mission Can you fill in the missing words to complete the acrostic? Use the clues below.

1. The first anointing, which sets people apart as members of the Body of Christ
2. The anointing that seals the Christian with the Gift of the Holy Spirit
3. The anointing that consecrates a man to the service of God and the Church
4. The fragrant oil used in Baptism and Confirmation
5. To set apart as sacred, as being dedicated to God
6. The words and actions used in a religious ceremony

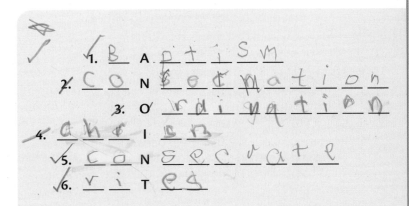

1. B A P T I S M
2. C O N F E C M A T I O N
3. O R D I N A T I O N
4. C H R I S M
5. C O N S E C R A T E
6. R I T E S

↑ *The battle between David and Goliath depicted on a Cassone panel.*

David and Solomon

God Looks at the Heart

based on 1 Samuel 16:1–13

Although presenting ourselves properly to others is important, the story of David reminds us that outward appearances can be deceiving.

Because Saul was no longer open to the spirit of the Lord, God sent Samuel to Bethlehem to anoint a new king from among the sons of a man named Jesse. God warned Samuel not to select the next king based on appearances: "Not as man sees does God see, because man sees the appearance but the Lord looks into the heart." Jesse presented seven sons, but Samuel knew that none of them had been chosen by God. When Samuel asked Jesse whether he had any other sons, Jesse replied that the youngest, David, was tending sheep. Samuel told Jesse to send for the boy. When he came before them, God told Samuel, "There—anoint him, for this is he!" Samuel then anointed David and the spirit of the Lord rushed upon him. After he was anointed, but before he became king, David faced a difficult challenge. Read about David's fight against the Philistine champion, Goliath, in 1 Samuel 17.

David's Leadership

based on 2 Samuel 5–8; 11

After the deaths of Saul and his son Ishbaal, all of the tribes of Israel proclaimed David as their king. David wanted to unite his country and to make it strong. He showed his gift of leadership by obeying God's law, serving his people, and providing protection for those who were vulnerable. He was able to lead the army in conquering new lands for Israel, to unite the people, and to build up their confidence.

David made Jerusalem the capital of his newly united kingdom. With a great celebration, he brought the Ark of the Covenant to the tent he had set aside for it. The presence of the Ark in Jerusalem led the people to travel there often to worship God. This helped unite the people into one great nation.

David's Sin

David was a great king and warrior, but he allowed his feelings to lead him into sin. While David's men were at war, he saw a very beautiful woman named Bathsheba and desired her. David's servants told him that she was the wife of Uriah, one of his soldiers. David got Bathsheba pregnant and wanted her to be his wife. He ordered his army's commander to place Uriah in the front line where he was killed. After Bathsheba had mourned the death of her husband, she became David's wife.

David's Sorrow

based on 2 Samuel 12

God was very displeased by David's sin. So he sent the prophet Nathan to tell David the following story.

In a certain town, there were two men. One was rich, the other poor. The rich man had many animals. The poor man had only one lamb, so that lamb was very important to him. One day the rich man had a visitor. He didn't want to take an animal from his own flocks for a meal, so he took the poor man's lamb instead.

Then Nathan asked David how he would judge this case. David was very angry at the story. He said, "The man who has done this deserves to die. He should give the man he stole from four lambs as repayment."

Nathan replied, "You are that man! You have been given everything from the Lord, and yet you had Uriah killed so that you could have his wife. The Lord God is angry with your sin, and it will bring you suffering." Nathan showed David that he had shown a blatant disregard for the dignity of human life. He reminded David that he had acted freely and deliberately, so he must bear responsibility for his actions.

David realized his sin, but he also knew that God, who is rich in mercy, makes it possible for sinners to return to him. This returning to God is called *conversion* or *repentance*. To truly repent, we must be sorry for our sins and resolve to sin no more. David repented for offending God, for being unjust to Uriah, and for the bad example he gave his people. Nathan told him God had forgiven him, but as punishment the son born to David and Bathsheba would die. Soon after he was born, David's son became very sick. David fasted and prayed, hoping that his child's life would be spared, but on the seventh day the boy died.

David learned well the lesson of God's love and forgiveness. Later in David's life, when his son Absalom rebelled against him, David remained loving and forgiving. He earned one of the greatest compliments given to anyone in the Old Testament. God called David "a man after my own heart and mind."

David—Noble in Failure

Answer the following questions about David.

1. Why was David's sin so serious? _____

2. Why did David repent? _____

3. What harm did his sin cause? _____

4. How should we accept others when they make mistakes? _____

5. How can we make up for our failures? _____

David's Love for God

The Book of Psalms contains prayer-songs, or *psalms*, that are full of praise, love, and gratitude for God's great kindness. Many of the psalms carry a message of sorrow for offenses and ask for God's forgiveness. Although we are not sure who wrote the psalms, or when they were written, many of them are credited to King David.

The psalms are a very important example of prayer in the Old Testament. Because Jesus practiced **Judaism,** he prayed the psalms throughout his life. As he was dying on the cross, Jesus prayed words from Psalm 22, "My God, my God, why have you abandoned me?"

The psalms can be prayed as part of personal or communal prayer. The psalms remind us of how God kept his promises in the past. They also express hope for the future. The psalms are an important part of the prayer of the Church. They help us to unite our prayers and feelings with the prayers of the Church as a whole.

Here is a psalm attributed to David, which many Catholics pray before the Sacrament of Reconciliation.

Psalm 51

Have mercy on me, God, in your
goodness;
in your abundant compassion
blot out my offense.
Wash away all my guilt;
from my sin cleanse me.
A clean heart create for me, God;
renew in me a steadfast spirit.

Psalm 51:3–4,12

▲ *Detail of David and King Solomon, "The Resurrection,"* 11th c.

In the Footsteps of David

based on 1 Kings 1–3

When King David was old, he commanded that his son, Solomon, be anointed as the next king. After his anointing, Solomon took his place on David's throne. Before David died, he instructed his son, "Take courage and be a man. Keep the mandate of the Lord, your God, following his ways . . . that way you may succeed in whatever you do."

David had ruled over Israel for more than 40 years. When David died, he was buried in Jerusalem, which is also known as the City of David.

Solomon, a Wise King

Solomon loved the Lord and followed the commands of his father, David. One night the Lord spoke to him in a dream, "Solomon, ask a favor of me, and I will give it to you."

Solomon answered, "I am a mere youth, not knowing at all how to act. I serve you in the midst of the people whom you have chosen, a people so vast that it cannot be numbered or counted. Give your servant, therefore, an understanding heart to judge your people and to distinguish right from wrong."

The Lord was pleased with Solomon and said, "I do as you requested. I give you a heart so wise and understanding that there has never been anyone like you, and after you there will come no one to equal you."

The Gift of Wisdom

based on 1 Kings 4–8; 10–11

Wisdom is one of the seven Gifts of the Holy Spirit, along with understanding, counsel, fortitude, knowledge, piety, and fear of the Lord. Through the Sacrament of Confirmation, our relationship with Jesus is strengthened. We ask God to send us the Holy Spirit to give us these gifts.

Tradition says that Solomon, in his wisdom, composed 3,000 proverbs (which are wise sayings) as well as many songs. He was regarded as the patron of all wisdom in Israel and has been given credit for most of the Wisdom Literature in the Old Testament.

Solomon brought Israel great wealth and fame. He increased its trade and military power. He had two grand palaces built, one for him and one for his wife, who was the Pharaoh's daughter. Solomon's reputation even led to a visit from the Queen of Sheba, who ruled a wealthy and powerful kingdom in what is now Ethiopia. You can read about this visit in 1 Kings 10:1–10.

A Moment with Jesus

The gift of wisdom is the ability to put God first, to see things from God's point of view, to recognize the sacredness of all people, and to see the real value of things. Take a moment to ask Jesus for the gift of wisdom. Ask him for the grace you need to hear the voice of wisdom within you and to make wise decisions.

Work of Wonder

During his rule, David had wanted to build a great temple to house the Ark of the Covenant. Nathan, speaking for the Lord, replied, "I will make you famous. I will establish a house for you. Your son will build a house for me. I will favor him with many gifts. Your family and your kingdom will last forever, and your throne will stand firm."

Nathan's prophecy came true. God gave David's son, Solomon, the honor of building a permanent dwelling place for the Ark of the Covenant. It took seven years to build the **Temple.** On the day of the dedication, the people of Israel gathered to offer sacrifices and praise to God. The priests brought the Ark of the Covenant in a great procession and placed it in the *Holy of Holies,* a special room in the Temple.

Solomon stood before the people and praised the Lord: "Is it possible for God to dwell among men? If the heavens cannot contain your greatness, how much less can this temple which I have built contain you?"

Then Solomon blessed the whole community of Israel, saying: "May the Lord be with us as he was with our fathers. May this prayer remain always before the Lord that he will defend Israel, and that all peoples of the earth may know that the Lord is God. May he draw our hearts to himself, so that we may faithfully serve him."

The End of Solomon's Reign

Solomon ruled for many years. To keep peace with neighboring countries, he married many foreigners. To please his pagan wives, Solomon built temples for their idols. Eventually he also began to worship foreign idols. God was displeased. He told Solomon that most of the kingdom would not be ruled by his descendants. After Solomon's death, the kingdom was divided. Ten tribes in the north kept the name Israel. The two tribes in the south became known as Judah. A few kings ruled the various tribes of Israel for a short time. But never was there so great a king as David or so wise a king as Solomon.

We Remember

What can we learn from God's selection of David as king?

David's story reminds us not to judge solely by appearances.

What serious sins did David commit?

When David saw Bathsheba, he wanted her to be his wife. He ordered his army's commander to place her husband, Uriah, in the front line, where he was killed. After Bathsheba mourned the death of her husband, she became David's wife.

How was David a great king?

David united the kingdom, made Jerusalem the capital, and repented after he sinned.

What is Solomon known for?

Solomon is known for his wisdom and for building the Temple.

Words to Know

Judaism   Temple

We Respond

Lord God, bless our leaders with wisdom and courage. Keep them faithful to your laws. In their weakness, be their strength.

⌃ The eastern side of the Temple Mount viewed from the Mount of Olives.

Things to Do at Home

1. Go over the Book of Proverbs with your family. Have each family member, including yourself, write a favorite proverb on a card, then cut each card into a shape or symbol. String the proverb shapes onto a hanger to create a "Wisdom Mobile." Display the mobile in a prominent place in your home.

2. Nathan taught David a lesson by telling him a story. Jesus did the same thing when he told parables. Imagine you know someone who hurts others by teasing them too much. Write a parable that you might tell to help that person learn a lesson.

3. Review 1 Samuel, 2 Samuel, and 1 Kings. List examples of how David and Solomon showed, or failed to show, the following qualities:

   obedience   service
   fairness   courage
   wisdom   self-control

4. Go over the Book of Psalms with your family. Choose several psalms and work together to make a chart that identifies different occasions and moods addressed by each psalm. Talk with your family about how you might use the chart to include a psalm during your family prayer time.

5. Search online to find pictures and information about the Western Wall of the Temple in Jerusalem. Note the custom of writing prayer notes on small pieces of paper and placing them in cracks in the wall. Then write your own prayer requests on a small sheet of paper. Put the prayer in a special place to remind yourself that you have placed your prayers in God's hands.

Visit **www.christourlife.org/family** for more family resources.

Being Healed What remedies would you suggest for a person who has been wounded by sin? Write three things he or she should do as soon as possible.

1. _____

2. _____

3. _____

Like Father, Like Son? Complete this chart that compares King David to King Solomon.

1. **David** committed the sins of adultery and murder.	**Solomon** committed the sin of _____.
2. **David** _____ before he died.	**Solomon** died before repenting.
3. **David** wrote _____.	**Solomon** wrote proverbs.
4. **David** wanted to build a temple, but instead became the father of a royal line.	**Solomon** built the _____.
5. Because of his faith and obedience, **David** united the kingdom.	Because of his sins, **Solomon** _____ the Kingdom.

Places What are two other names for Jerusalem? Explain why Jerusalem has these other names.

_____ because _____

_____ because _____

After the division, what was the northern kingdom called? _____

What was the southern kingdom called? _____

Word Hunt

Complete each sentence below. Then find in the puzzle the words that complete each sentence.

```
S  O  L  H  B  K  V  W  J  J  D  F  J  Y  E
O  P  J  Z  V  Y  C  M  J  P  L  R  U  B  T
L  W  H  B  R  U  T  H  Y  N  U  X  D  L  N
O  L  E  O  H  H  T  E  Y  O  A  N  G  B  O
M  P  S  A  L  M  S  A  H  E  S  T  E  T  S
O  J  T  L  R  Y  N  M  L  D  T  N  S  I  M
N  S  I  O  K  A  O  I  E  I  C  I  T  H  A
E  O  Y  Q  K  D  K  F  U  G  R  O  A  M  S
L  A  B  S  T  A  I  N  H  H  R  N  G  B  M
P  A  P  L  W  V  O  K  C  O  B  A  R  F  S
M  O  J  E  Q  I  X  V  I  L  L  E  C  M  I
E  O  X  U  T  D  W  M  P  N  V  I  D  Y  A
T  M  Q  M  L  N  M  A  P  O  G  C  E  M  D
X  T  M  A  D  E  B  O  R  A  H  S  L  S  U
K  X  E  S  B  P  O  P  U  L  Y  Z  I  O  J
```

1. _____ were leaders called by God to free the Israelites from their enemies.

2. The _____ were the anointed leaders of Israel.

3. _____ is the substance used to anoint kings, priests, and prophets.

4. The last and greatest judge of Israel was _____.

5. _____ advised the military leader Barak to march on Mount Tabor.

6. God gave _____ the power to defeat the Midianites.

7. _____ lost his gift of strength when he broke his vow to God.

8. Samson had to _____ from drinking wine, eating unclean meat, and cutting his hair.

9. _____ was the loyal Moabite woman who was an ancestor of Jesus.

10. The first king of Israel was _____.

11. The greatest king of Israel was _____.

12. _____ was the king who asked God for the gift of wisdom.

13. Solomon built a _____ for God.

14. The _____ in the Temple was where the Ark of the Covenant was kept.

15. To dedicate a person or thing to God by pouring or rubbing on oil is to _____.

16. _____, the title we give to Jesus, means *anointed one*.

17. Prayer-songs written to praise and worship God are called _____.

18. Because Jesus practiced _____, he prayed the psalms throughout his life.

19. Wise sayings that are used to teach lessons are called _____.

Opening Lines

Suppose each of the following sentences is the opening line of a book. Which judge or king would the book most likely be about? You will use some names more than once.

One day a poor child would lead the Israelites to victory.

_____

From under a palm tree in the desert, a great woman judged the people.

_____

Jealousy turned the handsome king's face an ugly purple.

_____

The boy awoke with a start; someone had called his name.

_____

He would have the greatest strength the world had ever seen.

_____

A wise prophet knows how to teach a lesson through a good story.

_____

What would you ask for if you could have anything you wished?

_____

His temple would not be of stone, but of flesh—his descendants.

_____

Hebrew Prayers

Read Psalm 21 in your Bible. Pick out your favorite verse and write it here.

_____

_____

_____

_____

_____

_____

_____

_____

Now write in the heart your own prayer-song praising God for the good things he has done for you.

Israelite Leaders

Unscramble the names and put them in the proper column.

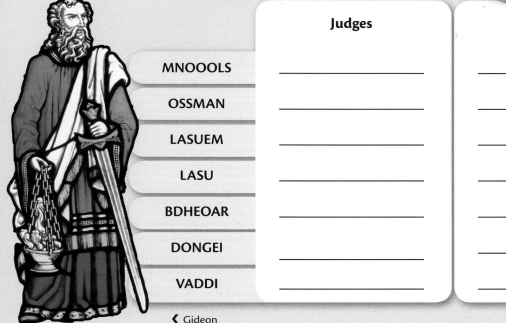

MNOOOLS	**Judges**	**Kings**
OSSMAN	_____	_____
LASUEM	_____	_____
LASU	_____	_____
BDHEOAR	_____	_____
DONGEI	_____	_____
VADDI	_____	_____
	_____	_____

‹ Gideon

Wisdom from Proverbs

Fill in the blanks using the words in the box.

bones	poor	might	virtue
entrust	joyful	succeed	

A _____ heart is the
health of the body, but a depressed spirit
dries up the _____.

Proverbs 17:22

Better a little with _____,
than a large income with injustice.

Proverbs 16:8

[H]appy is he who is kind to the _____!

Proverbs 14:21

A wise man is more powerful than a
strong man, and a man of knowledge
than a man of _____.

Proverbs 24:5

_____ your works
to the LORD, and your plans will
_____.

Proverbs 16:3

Celebrating

God's Name

(Song: Distribute slips of paper to all.)

Leader: We begin our prayer together, in the name of the Father, and of the Son, and of the Holy Spirit. Amen.

The Israelites had many different leaders after they reached the Promised Land. Each leader was chosen by God to help the people follow in his ways. David was the greatest of these leaders. He loved God and tried to serve him faithfully. When he sinned, he was sorry and repented. He was kind and just. He taught his son Solomon to be a good leader and to depend on God for help.

Reader 1: Solomon asked for gifts to help him be a good leader. *(Read 2 Chronicles 1:7–12.)*

The Word of the Lord.

All: Thanks be to God.

Leader: God gave Solomon these gifts to help him rule his people wisely. Even though he stumbled later in life, these gifts helped him lead his people with wisdom and fairness for many years.

God grants each of us with special gifts. Sometimes those gifts help us become good leaders. Describe someone in your life who is a good leader. Tell what special gift you think God has given that person.

(Invite the students to share.)

Leader: God asks us to be leaders. Whether we are leaders in a game, in a family, or in our nation, we all need God's help. In the Sacrament of Confirmation, we are strengthened in a special way with the Gifts of the Holy Spirit that we received in Baptism. The Spirit's gifts help us to lead others to Jesus Christ. Let us pray now that the Gifts of the Holy Spirit will help us to lead others to Jesus. Our response to each prayer is:

℞: Lord, send out your spirit and renew the face of the earth.

Reader 1: We pray for the gift of wisdom that helps us to put God first and to love the things of God. Holy Spirit, help us to see things from God's point of view and to recognize the sacredness of all people and the real value of things. **℞**

Reader 2: We pray for the gift of understanding that helps us to learn more about our Catholic faith. Holy Spirit, help us to gain insights and understanding into the meaning of life and recognize that we are all brothers and sisters called to care for one another. **℞**

Reader 3: We pray for the gift of knowledge that helps us to know God and ourselves. Holy Spirit, help us to read Scripture, participate in religion class, listen closely to homilies at Mass, pray for greater knowledge, and celebrate the Sacraments. **℞**

Reader 4: We pray for the gift of counsel that helps us to know what to do in life, to make good decisions, and to accept our responsibility to care for others. Holy Spirit, help us to seek good advice from others and to advise others when needed. ℞

Reader 5: We pray for the gift of piety that helps us to love and worship God. Holy Spirit, help us to pray regularly and to show respect for the dignity of others. ℞

Reader 6: We pray for the gift of courage that gives us the inner strength to do what is right in the face of difficulties. Holy Spirit, help us to face the challenges of being a follower of Jesus. ℞

Reader 7: We pray for the gift of fear of the Lord that helps us to marvel at God's greatness. Holy Spirit, help us to live in wonder and awe of God, always offering him thanks and praise. ℞

Leader: Let us each think of the gift we need from God to be a good leader and write it on the paper we have received.

(Take time to think and write. Place your papers on the plate near the Bible.)

Leader 4: Let us ask God for the gifts we need.

(Pause)

Reader 2: Please respond: We thank you, God, for good leaders. *(Read Psalm 21:1–7, stopping at every period for the response.)*

(Song)

Looking Back at Unit 4

In this unit, you learned that even in the Promised Land the Israelites did not remain faithful to the Lord. Influenced by their neighbors, they often worshiped false gods. When they turned away from God, the Israelites became weak. Their enemies overcame them, and in their suffering the Israelites recognized their sin. As a people of hope, they knew how to deal with their mistakes. They asked God for help. God sent the judges to deliver them from their enemies.

But judges weren't enough—the people wanted a king. Samuel, the last judge, anointed Saul as the first king of the Israelites. Anointing is a sign of God's choice and gives the person special rights, authority, and duties. However, Saul did not use his rights and authority to fulfill God's will. He disobeyed God and followed his own will.

God told Samuel to anoint David, a young shepherd, as king of Israel. David was chosen by God even before Saul died. David was a great leader and he united the tribes of Israel as one nation. He loved God. When he sinned, he was sorry and did penance. To show his love for God, he wrote psalms that praised God and expressed sorrow for sin.

David's son Solomon was the third king. God gave him wisdom and an understanding heart to help him rule. Solomon built the Temple where all Israelites came to worship God. However, after a time Solomon forgot that he ruled in God's name. The kingdom became weaker and was split into two kingdoms after Solomon's death.

To summarize the characteristics of these three kings: Saul, the warrior, had physical strength. Solomon, the builder, had great wisdom. Both fell because of pride and selfishness. David, the poet and musician, had both physical strength and wisdom. Beyond this, David loved and forgave. He was a balanced human being. When he sinned, he learned from his mistake and grew. He became a fully human being, in the image and likeness of God—a man after God's own heart.

Living the Message

Can you give yourself a check (✓) for each statement?

○ **1.** I know some important facts about each of the first three kings of Israel.

○ **2.** When I make a mistake, I stop to think what I should do.

○ **3.** I know that when I was anointed at Baptism, I became a child of God with certain rights and duties.

○ **4.** When I am a leader, I try to help others do what God wants.

○ **5.** I plan to use my special gifts to serve God and others.

Planning Ahead

We are all called to be leaders in some way. We can learn to be good leaders from Jesus. Ask him to send the Holy Spirit to teach you. Then read some things he tells us about leaders: Matthew 20:24–28, Mark 9:34–37, Luke 17:3–4.

Describe the kind of leader you will try to be.

_____

_____

_____

Lenten Lesson:
Parents Don't Have to Be Perfect

Sara turns out the light, flops into bed, and realizes that she didn't even remember to brush her teeth. With her husband out of town on business, family life has been more difficult than usual. Remembering things—such as the kids needing to bring food-pantry items to their religion classes or the fact that they were almost out of milk—is harder without a copilot. She wishes she were better at asking for help from her extended family and friends.

In a house across town, Jim lies sleepless, replaying in his mind the argument he had with his son during supper. Thoughts of his son's stubbornness and surliness run through Jim's mind. Would his son ever snap out of it? Was his son this way because he was getting involved with drugs? Jim panics for a moment and then prays, "Please, God, don't let it be so!" And then he simply prays for patience.

Jesus said that he came to cure the sick, not the healthy—to give most of his attention to the lost, not the saved. As the season of Lent settles over us, Jesus' saving act can offer "imperfect parents" a great deal of comfort. We can also take comfort that Lent returns relentlessly, year after year, age after age—because we will never be perfect. As parents, it will likely take years before any of us becomes expert at virtues such as patience and mercy—and if not patience and mercy toward our kids, then patience and mercy toward ourselves.

Tom McGrath, author of *Raising Faith-Filled Kids* (Loyola Press, 2000), emphasizes "parents' need for forgiveness. If we can't deal with our own fallibility, we will make it that much more difficult for the kids to deal graciously with theirs." Lent gives us the grace and strength to do something that families need to do all year-round. Our homes need to be a safe place in which parents and children "can do the difficult work of owning up to sin," says McGrath, "learning to become heartily sorry, and doing the repair work necessary to effect reconciliation." This Lenten season, take extra care to not only forgive others for their imperfections but to remember to accept God's forgiveness yourself.

Reconciliation and the Imperfect Parent

In *Raising Faith-Filled Kids*, Tom McGrath identifies a three-part process that Catholics tap whenever we participate in the Penitential Act at Mass, receive the Sacrament of Reconciliation, or examine our ways during the prayerful preparation of Lent.

The way to deal with sinful tendencies is to: (a) tell the truth, (b) accept the consequences, and (c) vow to change your ways. As a child, telling the truth was probably a simple matter for you. But as you grew up and learned to navigate a complex world, you probably discovered that the truth is sometimes harder to see. Here are three truths that aid the imperfect parent:

1. **Truth:** Sometimes our kids are holier than we are. Maybe this is why Jesus said we must become like children to enter the Kingdom of Heaven. In *Good Parents, Tough Times* (Loyola Press, 2006), authors Charlene Giannetti and Margaret Sagarese offer an example: "When your child secludes himself in his bedroom, are you suspicious? Do you assume he's up to no good, or wasting time goofing off? St. Benedict ruled silence and solitude to be a critical part of spiritual life. Rather than nag, shouldn't you be cultivating personal time and space for everyone, including yourself?" Small children also know how to properly greet the splendor of God's creation, by splashing in puddles instead of cursing the rain or break-ing into spontaneous song when the sun is shining. Their pleasure can teach us gratitude. Their sense of wonder can remind us that God is in charge.

2. **Truth:** Our kids can be reminders of our own flaws. In many families, the child who gets on a parent's nerves the most is—iron-ically—the child whose temperament matches that parent. An impatient dad will butt heads with the child who is the most impatient. A mom who is overly concerned about appearances will argue endlessly with the child who believes the same. The problem? The mom's tastes are preppy but the child loves punk. What neither sees is that appearance isn't everything—certainly not worth hating each other over. Like the angry crowd that dispersed after Jesus invited the sinless among them to "cast the first stone," parents would do better to recog-nize children as the mirrors they often are. Rather than always nagging a child for his or her flaws, a good parent's job is to work harder on his or her own flaws, and thus be better able to help the child wrestle with those tendencies.

3. **Truth:** We hurt kids when we let them get away with bad behavior. "Not my kid!" is a refrain that seems to be on the rise. A Wisconsin dad tells of being behind another family as they all moved from teacher to teacher during a parent-teacher conference. The other parents kept insisting that it was the teacher who was to blame for their son's discipline problems. "Those parents sure aren't doing their kid any favors. They're creating a monster!" noted the dad. In a world where ordinary human sinfulness is the norm, chil-dren who aren't compassionately taught to own up to their faults fail to learn a lesson as basic as walking and talking. Such parents may think they are helping, even protecting, their kids, but in reality they're giving them "stones when they ask for bread."

Recognizing Faces and Feelings

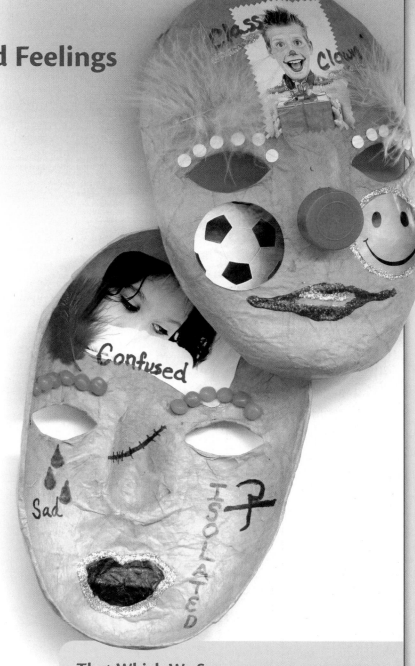

A person who has real integrity doesn't just pay lip service to an idea—he or she walks the talk. But this is easier said than done. Sometimes the face we show the world is the way we'd *like* to be perceived, rather than an accurate reflection of our real feelings.

The masks made in this activity can serve as reminders for your family to try to live with integrity. These masks are not to be worn. Instead, display them in the space reserved for your family prayer sessions, or in a prominent place in your home. Use them to spark discussion with family members during prayer time, or when a particular family member is having difficulty communicating his or her feelings.

Materials

Simple Mardi Gras masks or homemade paper-bag masks, one for each family member

Markers, colored pencils, or paint

Photos or magazine pictures that clearly show different emotions

Decorative items such as glitter, beads, and feathers (optional)

Instruct each member to do the following:

On the inside of the mask, write words, draw pictures, or glue photos that represent how you feel on a normal day—include both good and bad feelings, and don't be afraid to add feelings that you aren't especially proud of.

On the outside of the mask, write words, draw pictures, or glue photos that represent feelings that you think other people see, especially people who don't know your true feelings—who see only the face you show the world. You can also add decorative items.

That Which We See Educators, psychologists, and philosophers have long recognized the importance of art in childhood development. Not only can creating art promote cognitive development and a sensitivity to a child's environment, it can often help kids express feelings or emotions that they cannot express in words or speech. You might use variations of the mask activity when your child is having trouble communicating his or her feelings. Suggest that your child draw, paint, or sculpt how he or she is feeling. The art that your child creates can help open dialogue about why he or she feels a particular way.

You Say *Angry*, I Say *Annoyed*

If you are a fan of reading novels or watching movies, you are probably familiar with the idea of a character having a tragic flaw. For example, in the *Star Wars* films, Anakin Skywalker's tragic flaw is anger—in fact, it consumes him, eventually resulting in his transformation into Darth Vader. The Church has explored the theme of personality traits and tragic flaws for centuries—little wonder, given some of the extreme characters we meet in the Old Testament. One way Catholics have explored this subject is by reflecting on the seven capital sins: anger, gluttony, sloth, envy, greed, covetousness, and pride—seven sinful tendencies that every person must contend with.

The first step to combating sinful tendencies is learning to identify them. Help your child learn to analyze sinful behavior by choosing two characters from a film or a recently read book. Work with your child to identify one sin or tragic flaw that each character is prone to. Talk about ways that the character demonstrates tendencies toward this tragic flaw throughout the story. Then help each other identify ways that the character did or might combat the tragic flaw. Use the chart below to record your answers.

Character Name	Tragic Flaw	Tendencies toward this flaw	How the character did/might combat this flaw

Analyzing for Life Re-create this chart to analyze characters in other books or films to provide your child with additional practice and a deeper understanding of the ways that sins can manifest and how to overcome them. Honing analytical skills will help your child become a better critical thinker as well as sharpening his or her ability to constructively self-reflect on his or her behavior and choices.

Visit **www.christourlife.org/family** for more family resources.

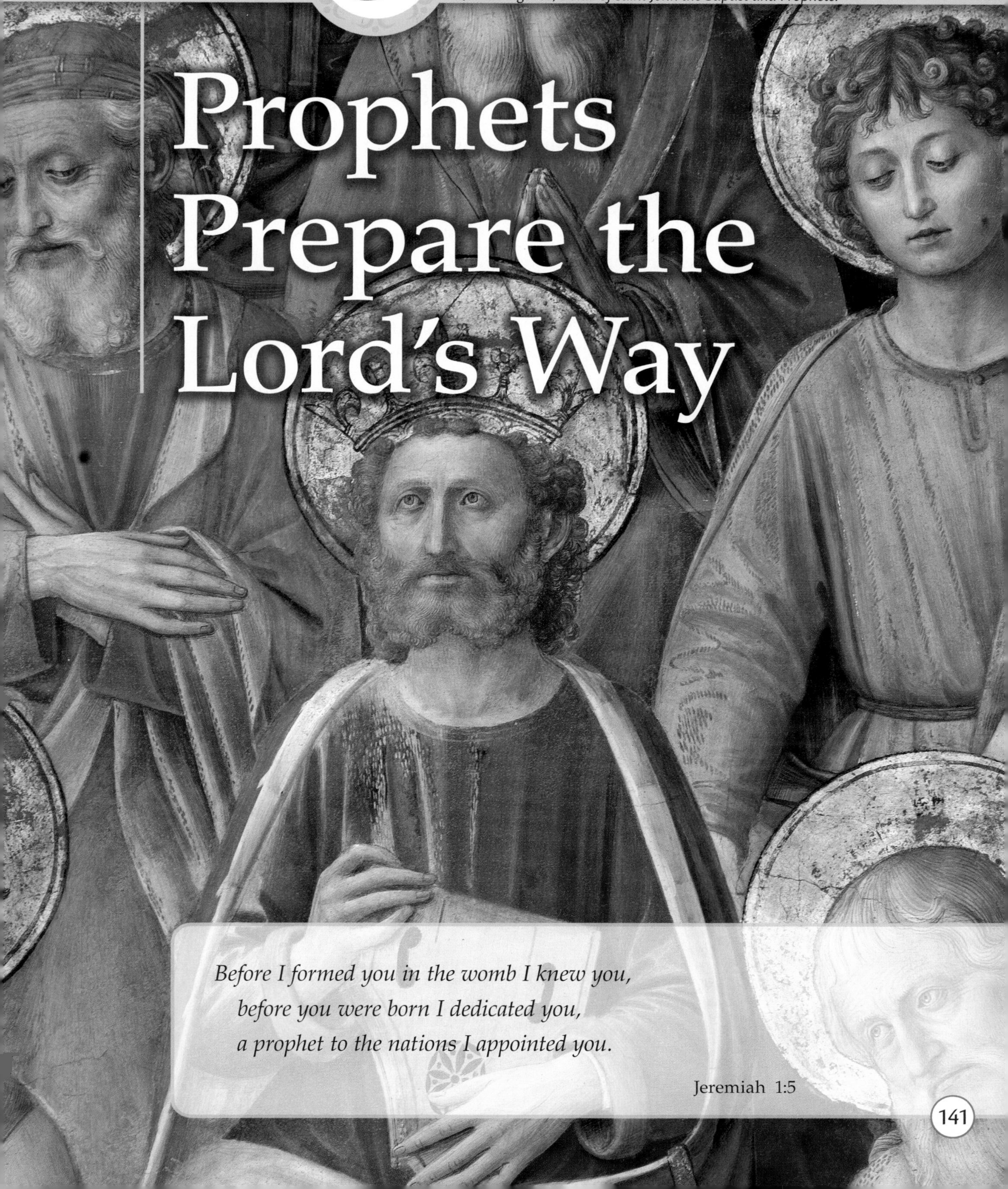

▾ Fra Angelico, *Detail of Saint John the Baptist and Prophets.*

Prophets Prepare the Lord's Way

Before I formed you in the womb I knew you,
before you were born I dedicated you,
a prophet to the nations I appointed you.

Jeremiah 1:5

141

Prophets Prepare the Lord's Way

IN THIS UNIT, you will be learning about how the message of God was delivered to the people of Israel through the prophets.

Elijah and Amos Speak for the Lord

Elijah and Amos had a message that continues to speak to us today. It calls us to show our love for God and for one another by working for social justice. You are called to support the missionary efforts of the Church by recognizing God's love for all people.

Isaiah Proclaims the Promised Messiah

Isaiah tried to reawaken the people's love for and trust in God. He nourished hope with his description of the coming Messiah and the new kingdom. He also foretold the remnant—

a small group within Israel who would remain faithful in spite of misfortune, while others turned away from God. You are challenged to plan and undertake a program for spiritual growth.

Prophet Isaiah

Prophets Proclaim God's Everlasting Love

Jeremiah and Ezekiel were the prophets chosen to speak God's word during the fall of Jerusalem and the Babylonian Exile. You will learn to recognize your obligation to listen to those speaking God's word today and to worship the Lord with a sincere heart.

The Savior Is Jesus, the Son of God

John the Baptist was the last and greatest of the prophets. You will learn to recognize and appreciate the role of John in the fulfillment of earlier prophecies of the coming of the Messiah. You will also consider the Virgin Mary's role, realizing that through her, God's promise was fulfilled. You are encouraged to prepare for the coming of Christ into your life, as John and Mary did.

Giorgio Vasari, *Prophet Elijah, Disputation in the Temple.*

Elijah and Amos Speak for the Lord

Prophet—Called to Speak

Prophets are people God calls to speak his Word to others. God gives prophets the special gift of seeing things as they truly are. They see good as good and evil as evil. They see the goodness and holiness of God, and they see sin pulling people away from God. The prophets' main roles are to point out how people are turning away from God and to energize them with faith. Prophets know that sinners will not want to hear God's Word. They understand that they may be ridiculed and persecuted if they speak out. Still, prophets risk persecution in order to deliver God's message to the people.

Sometimes prophets tell what will happen in the future, but we should not imagine that it is like looking into a crystal ball. Rather, God gives them the grace to understand what will happen if people continue to act in a certain way. Prophets are sent not to foretell, but to tell forth, to call people to repent and to believe.

Old Testament Prophets

After Solomon's death the Chosen People and most of their kings became unfaithful to the Lord. God called prophets to remind the people of the Covenant. The prophets encouraged the people to turn away from sin towards God and to live as his people. The prophets warned the people that the kingdom would suffer and fall if they continued to live only for pleasure. The prophets are often called the conscience of Israel.

The Sacred Scripture gives account of some of the prophets' lives and preachings. Each prophetic book is named for a prophet. The prophets whose names are given to the three longest books are called the major prophets. They are Isaiah, Jeremiah, and Ezekiel. The other prophets are minor prophets. All the prophets spoke God's Word to Israel, and they speak his Word to us today.

A Moment with Jesus

When you were baptized, you were given a share in Jesus' ministry as priest, prophet, and king. Take a moment to ask Jesus to help you to be prophetic in your words and deeds. Ask him for the grace you need to speak his word of truth to others, to recognize good and evil, and to see the goodness and holiness of God.

Elijah the Prophet

based on 1 Kings 18,21; 2 Kings 2

Elijah is a prophet who called his people back to believe in the one true God. He helped the people to hope in God and to love him above all else.

The early prophets were often advisors to kings. During Elijah's time, the northern kingdom was ruled by a wicked king, Ahab, and his equally wicked queen, Jezebel, who worshiped Baal. One day Elijah held a contest between God and Baal. When he proved that Baal was a fake, Jezebel vowed to kill Elijah. Later, when Ahab desired a vineyard that belonged to his neighbor, Naboth, Jezebel arranged to have Naboth falsely accused of a crime. Naboth was stoned to death and Ahab got his vineyard.

Elijah spoke to Ahab about his double-dealing and foretold his punishment. Ahab repented and even ordered that all false idols be destroyed. When Jezebel found out, she became even angrier with Elijah and tried to have him killed. However, Jezebel failed because Elijah was protected by God. He managed to escape Jezebel's wrath and to flee to another country.

When Elijah's work was finished, he passed on his spirit to the prophet Elisha. Then a fiery chariot came down and carried Elijah away. To this day, Jewish people celebrating the Seder meal on Passover leave a large cup and an empty chair for Elijah's return.

Amos the Prophet

based on the Book of Amos

Nearly 800 years before the coming of Jesus, the northern kingdom of Israel was powerful and rich. However, it had serious problems. Worship was being offered from empty hearts. Rites used to worship pagan gods were introduced into the worship of the true God.

Most of the people were poor and weak. But the wealthy and powerful had stopped taking care of them as the Covenant called them to do. Instead, they took all they could from the poor. To remind his people of their responsibilities to care for one another, the Lord called Amos to be his prophet.

Amos raised sheep and took care of sycamore trees in Tekoa, a town in Judah. There God told him, "Go prophesy to my people Israel." So Amos went to the northern kingdom to speak God's Word. It was his mission to tell the people that if they continued with their idol worship and injustices, they would meet with doom and destruction.

Like a lion, Amos verbally attacked the rich city people. He warned them that bad things would happen if they did not return to God. Amos taught that because all human beings have equal dignity, we are all called to eliminate the inequalities that exist in society. He caused so much trouble that the priest got King Jeroboam to banish Amos from the Temple.

Amos was not recognized as a prophet until his prophecy of woe came true: Israel was conquered by Assyria in 722 B.C. Read Amos 5:14–15. What reasons does Amos give for seeking good rather than evil?

Amos

_____

_____

Chosen by God

In his preaching, Amos reminded the people that the LORD had a special love for them. This love came with great responsibilities. One of these was to make the true God known to all people. The Israelites were to spread the knowledge of the LORD by the way they lived, faithfully keeping the Covenant.

Because God had shown such great love for his people, their sins were even more serious. Worst of all, they didn't even recognize their sins. Through Amos, God told the people:

> You alone have I favored,
>   more than all the families of the
>   earth;
>
> Therefore, I will punish you
>   for all your crimes.
>
> Amos 3:2

The Israelites had been looking forward to the Day of the LORD, when God would come to conquer their enemies and make them the world's most powerful nation. Amos told them that the Day of the LORD would indeed come, but it would be a day of darkness for the Israelites, a day when they would suffer for their sins.

The Justice of God

A key verse in the Book of Amos tells us:

> Let justice surge like water,
> and goodness like an unfailing
>   stream.
>
> Amos 5:24

When people think of justice, they are usually thinking of human justice. This justice gives to all people what they have earned or deserve.

However, the justice of the Covenant commands us to model our lives on God's justice, which surges like an unfailing stream. All people are to share the goods of the earth. No one person or group of people is to live in luxury while others are in need. The right to private property does not eliminate our responsibility to share with all people the goods of God's creation. Giving alms to the poor is a way of showing that we are all brothers and sisters. It is an act of charity and a work of justice that is pleasing to God.

When people live according to divine justice, they are concerned about others. They are willing to sacrifice and to practice mercy. God's justice asks that all people have what they need to live a truly human life.

Where Is God's Justice?

Here are some of the evils Amos condemned in Israel. Check (✓) those he would find if he were to prophesy in our country today.

- ○ People were more concerned about themselves and their comfort than about justice.

- ○ Rich people were trying to get richer and were not helping the poor.

- ○ Some rich people looked down on the poor.

- ○ Many people used sex simply for pleasure and amusement rather than as a gift from God.

- ○ People sat in luxurious houses eating and drinking more than enough while the needy had little to eat.

- ○ The poor were not able to protect themselves from the rich, even in the courts.

Jesus and Justice

Jesus was an example of God's justice. His loving kindness was always more than we would ever think of. It was "an unfailing stream." He cured the sick, forgave sinners, gave food and drink to the hungry and thirsty. He instructed the ignorant and comforted the sorrowful. He was patient with those who wronged him and gave his life for those who offended him.

Although we see a lot of evil around us, we know that many people are trying to follow the example of Jesus. They show care and concern for every person. They try to find ways to help people in need. They live simply and share what they have. There are also people who use their money to help people who are in need.

Pedro de Orrente, *Jesus Heals the Paralytic.*

A Modern Prophet

For three years, Archbishop Oscar Romero of El Salvador spoke out against injustice. His country was ruled by a few wealthy families. The rest of the people lived in extreme poverty. People who worked to improve this situation were beaten or killed, or they simply disappeared. The Archbishop condemned the government's violent tactics. He preached justice, love, and peace. He called for change. He broadcast the truth over the Church radio until a bomb destroyed the transmitter.

Romero's enemies started a campaign against him. Aware that he was on the list of those to be killed, Archbishop Romero pardoned those who would murder him. He offered his life for his people. While celebrating Mass on March 24, 1980, Archbishop Romero was shot to death. He was a martyr for the cause of human rights.

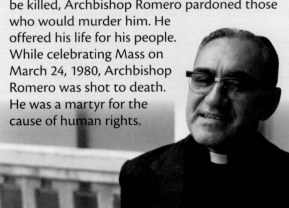

Called to Social Justice

People who help others to live truly human lives are working for social justice. It is social justice because its goal is for all people to live together in love. People who work for social justice in a Christian manner follow Jesus' example. They practice the Works of Mercy listed on page 217. Corporal Works of Mercy are those that help meet the physical needs of people. **Spiritual Works of Mercy** help meet the needs of the spirit.

Change Your Heart

Worship is meaningful only if it is a sign of a person's desire to do what God asks. God asked the Israelites for goodness and justice, but they paid no attention. God did not want their worship unless they changed their hearts and loved one another. Amos told the people that love for God and love for others go together. This means that when we live a moral life, we are offering a spiritual worship to God.

What does God see when he looks into our hearts? Are our prayers and worship signs of our willingness to do what he asks? Are we trying to make justice and goodness flow like an unfailing stream?

No matter how empty or sinful our lives have been, it is never too late to be reconciled with God and to begin again. The Book of Amos ends on a note of hope—although the sinners would die, a day would come when the LORD would restore the fallen house of David.

We Remember

What is a prophet?
A prophet is a person God calls to speak his Word to others.

What is the goal of social justice?
The goal of social justice is having all people live together in love by ensuring that all live truly human lives.

Words to Know

prophet
Spiritual Works of Mercy

We Respond

Decide what you can do this week to help one person live a life of dignity.

Things to Do at Home

1. Share with your family the description of a prophet on page 143. Discuss ways that parents are prophets for their children. Then talk about ways that children may be called as prophets to their families.

2. Read Psalm 72 and pick out the verses that tell about God's justice. Pray the psalm, keeping in mind the needs of the poor.

3. List ways that you can practice social justice. For ideas, look at the works of mercy listed on page 217. Illustrate one of these ways.

4. Collect magazine and newspaper articles about people working for social justice or giving Christlike service to others. Divide the articles into two groups: those working on their own and those working with an organization. Share these stories with your family. Talk about how you might model yourself on these people.

5. Our bishops carry out a prophetic role. Find out what issues they have addressed recently in

documents and letters to the members of the Church.

6. Invite new, lonely, or culturally different students to join you at lunch or during after-school activities.

7. Talk to your family about donating to those in need your outgrown or unwanted clothes.

8. Do not ask for expensive gifts for your birthday or Christmas. Suggest that your family share handmade gifts instead

9. Research some of the things you use every day, such as cosmetics, food, or clothes. Do without or find alternatives to those things made by companies that are unfair to their workers or that abuse or destroy God's creation.

10. Participate in activities for social justice, such as bike-a-thons, marathons, or marches. Write letters and encourage others to promote just laws that will protect the poor and oppressed.

Visit **www.christourlife.org/family** for more family resources.

Pick a Picture   Write the letter of the picture that matches the description.

A.

B.

C.

D.

E.

F.

G.

_____ 1. The one a prophet speaks for

_____ 2. One who wanted to kill Elijah

_____ 3. What Ahab killed Naboth for

_____ 4. How Elijah was taken up into heaven

_____ 5. What Amos was taking care of when God called him

_____ 6. What Amos told people to worship with

_____ 7. What Amos said justice should be like

Men and Their Message   Fill in the missing words in the prophets' messages.

Israelites: The __k__ __i__ ◯ __ __ __ __o__ __ will fall if you continue to sin.

Jezebel: Stop worshiping __B__ __ __ __ __.

Ahab: Repent for your greed and the __ __ __u__ ◯ __d__ __ __ of Naboth or you will be punished.

Northern kingdom: Stop worshiping idols and practicing __ __ __n__ __ __ __ ◯ __i__ __◯ or you will be doomed.

Israelites: Because of your sins, the Day of the Lord will be a day of __d__ __ __ __.

Israelites: Practice __ __ __u__ __ __ __ __c__ ◯ and share the earth's goods with the◯ __o__ __ __.

Unscramble the circled letters to find one way you can heed the words of Elijah and Amos. Write it.

__ __ __ __ __ __

CHAPTER 22

Isaiah Proclaims the Promised Messiah

A Prophet Touched by God

based on the Book of Isaiah

Our experiences affect the way we see things. If you know how to swim, you may enjoy a boat ride. If you are afraid of the water, the same trip may be very unpleasant.

Isaiah was a prophet in Judah around 740 B.C. He was probably a nobleman, living in Jerusalem. From his book, we know that he was an educated, skilled writer and a man of great faith. He was sensitive to God's presence in his life and the events around him. Like Amos, he defended the poor. Isaiah was active for a long time—possibly 50 years. During that time, he advised several kings of Judah.

Isaiah had a special experience that changed his entire life and affected the way he saw things. It was his call.

In a vision, Isaiah saw the Lord surrounded by seraphim. Read Isaiah 6:3.

Write what the angels were saying.

_____

_____

When do we use these words?

_____

_____

When Isaiah saw the beauty and holiness of the Lord, he was filled with wonder. He saw clearly his own sinfulness and that of his people. He recognized how unfaithful they had been while the Lord had always been loving, faithful, and truthful. In Isaiah's vision, an angel touched his lips with a burning coal to purify him.

Then Isaiah heard the Lord ask, "Whom shall I send? Who will be our messenger?"

Isaiah answered, loud and strong, "Here I am! Send me!"

After this experience, life for Isaiah was not the same. Once his heart was touched by the God of truth, he saw everything differently.

Think of a time when you felt close to God. When you think of God, what words come to your mind? Write them.

_____

_____

_____

_____

Trusting in God

Isaiah saw that God ruled the whole world, not just Judah and the Chosen People. He recognized that all people are to live as brothers and sisters and that God works through all events. God is in charge. Other people might trust in their power, their talents, or their armies, but Isaiah knew that only trust in God mattered.

When the Assyrians, Judah's enemies, threatened to attack, Isaiah saw that the king was afraid. Isaiah explained that God used the Assyrians in his plan. Because the people had been so unfaithful, they would be conquered by their enemies. Only a few—a remnant—would be left, but God would continue his promises through this remnant.

The kings of Judah did not listen to Isaiah. The people trusted God when everything was fine, but when the future looked bad, they turned to their armies and war. They found it too hard to trust God.

Isaiah was calm and secure in his trust. He knew God would remain faithful because he had already shown his faithful love to them over and over. Isaiah referred to the Lord as the "God of truth" which can be translated literally as the "God of Amen." (Isaiah 65:16) When we conclude our prayers with the word **Amen,** we are expressing God's faithfulness and our trust in him. Isaiah called on the people to trust in God, to believe in the Covenant God made with them, and to act on what they believed.

The Book of Isaiah

The Book of Isaiah is a collection of some of the prophecies and warnings of Isaiah. Most of these are in chapters 1 through 39.

Chapters 40 through 55 were not written by Isaiah, but by someone who studied him and was like him in thought and talent. The author of these chapters is called Second Isaiah. He wrote these chapters in Babylon, while the remnant of God's people were in exile. Chapters 56 through 66 were written by still

another follower of Isaiah, after the return from Babylon. He offered words of encouragement to the newly returned exiles. He is called Third Isaiah.

Some of the most beautiful lines in Scripture are in the Book of Isaiah. For instance:

> I will never forget you.
> See, upon the palms of my hands I have written your name.
>
> Isaiah 49:15–16

> Say to those whose hearts are frightened:
>   Be strong, fear not!
> Here is your God . . .
>   he comes to save you.
>
> Isaiah 35:4

> Comfort, give comfort to my people.
>
> Isaiah 40:1

> Come now, let us set things right,
>   says the LORD;
> Though your sins be like scarlet,
>   they may become white as snow;
> Though they be crimson red,
>   they may become white as wool
>
> Isaiah 1:18

The Suffering Servant and the Kingdom

The Chosen People dreamed of the kingdom. They thought they had found it when they entered the Promised Land, but they were wrong. The people thought that they would have a perfect kingdom while the kings ruled and Jerusalem was powerful, but they did not.

The prophets tried to tell them that all kingdoms begin in the heart. All peace begins in the heart. All wars begin in the heart.

In Second Isaiah, the prophet speaks of a servant who will take upon himself all the sins and unfaithfulness of the people. This servant would suffer for many, but through his sufferings, the people would be saved. Love would save them. Then the true kingdom would come.

Jesus spoke of this kingdom often. And, like the servant spoken of by Second Isaiah, he suffered for the people to bring them the real kingdom. By his loving obedience to the Father, Jesus fulfilled the mission of the suffering servant. Jesus brought salvation to all by showing the true meaning of love.

The Kingdom of God

Read the Scripture passages about the Kingdom of God. Match them with the summaries.

_____ Matthew 5:19	**A.**	The Father has given the kingdom to his flock.
_____ Luke 12:32	**B.**	The kingdom is not of this world.
_____ John 3:5	**C.**	Those who do God's will belong to the kingdom.
_____ Luke 22:28–30	**D.**	You must be born of water and the spirit.
_____ Matthew 7:21	**E.**	You must become like children.
_____ Matthew 18:3	**F.**	Those who remain faithful will enter the kingdom.
_____ John 18:33–37	**G.**	Those who keep the commandments will be great in the kingdom.

A Moment with Jesus

Jesus taught that in order to be his followers, we must do his will. We cannot be disciples in name alone. Our actions must speak along with our words. Read Matthew 7:21–23. Ask Jesus for the grace you need to do the will of the Father. Ask the Holy Spirit to help you to know what God's will is.

Dreamers and Planners

One of our greatest gifts is our ability to dream, to see a better world. This desire to improve and grow has led to discoveries, new knowledge, and much more.

Some people dream of life's possibilities, but they don't do anything about their dreams. They want to do great things or to be happy, but they do not plan or take steps to make their dreams come true. Other people dream and plan. They take steps to make their dreams come true. They know that achieving their dreams may mean sacrifice and pain along the way. But they also know that life brings joy and peace.

People share many of the same dreams. Many of us dream of doing great things. We dream of being loved. We want our family, friends, and others to look up to us. But if we want true greatness—the kind that is real and will last forever—then we need to be faithful people.

Faithful people love God and embrace their responsibility to love and care for others. They know that God has called them for very special purposes. They not only believe—they act on what they believe. Action is the difference between dreamers and planners.

The Call to Holiness

Isaiah's call began with a vision of God's holiness. According to Scripture, God alone is **holy.** Bible references to God as holy refer to both God's power and his *otherness* ("For I am God and not man,/the Holy One present among you" Hosea 11:9). When the word *holiness* is used in reference to a person, it suggests that this person reflects a divine quality or godliness, made possible because we are created in the image of God. The vocation to holiness is something that all people are called to. Because the Holy Spirit lives within us, we are called to live holy lives. We seek the Kingdom of God by following gospel values in everyday affairs, such as work or school.

We Remember

Who was Isaiah?

Isaiah was a great prophet who urged the people to trust in God. He foretold that God would save a remnant of his people and that a suffering servant would make up for the sins of the world.

Who is the suffering servant?

In Second Isaiah, the prophet speaks of a servant who will take upon himself all the sins and unfaithfulness of the people. This servant would suffer for many, but through his sufferings, the people would be saved. Christians see Jesus as the suffering servant.

Words to Know

Amen   holy

We Respond

Read Isaiah 41:9–10. Write what these words mean to you.

_____

_____

_____

_____

_____

_____

_____

Things to Do at Home

1. Ask two or three people to share with you a time they felt close to God. What advice do they give for staying close to him?

2. Listen to a recording of Handel's *Messiah*. Many of the lines are from Isaiah.

3. Bring to class magazine or newspaper articles about people who trust in God to protect them. Talk about why these people are models of faith.

4. We use many readings from Isaiah during Advent. We use many readings from Second Isaiah during Lent. Ask to borrow a Lectionary. Read one or two selections from Isaiah during Advent and Lent. Then talk with your family about why these readings are appropriate for those times.

5. Read chapter 53 of the Book of Isaiah. List phrases that seem to refer to Jesus.

6. The next time you are at Mass, pay attention to the number of times that the word *Amen* is used. Recall that the prophet Isaiah referred to God as the "God of truth" or the "God of Amen." List ways that you can live life with more trust in God.

7. Ask members of your family to describe people in their lives who are holy. Ask them to explain why they consider those people to be holy. Talk about how all of us are called to be holy and what that means for each family member in your daily lives at work, home, and school.

Visit **www.christourlife.org/family** for more family resources.

Portrait of a Prophet Provide the missing information for a list of vital statistics about Isaiah.

1. Kingdom where he lived _____

2. Time he prophesied _____

3. People he advised _____

4. Aspect of God he saw in a vision _____

5. His words accepting his mission _____

6. People Isaiah foretold would conquer Judah _____

7. Type of person who would fulfill God's promises to the Israelites _____

8. Number of parts of the Book of Isaiah _____

ISAIAH

Jumbled Messages Write the letter of the alphabet that comes before each given letter to spell out the messages of Isaiah.

H P E   J T   I P M Z .

U S V T U   H P E '   O P U   X B S .

B   S F N O B O U   X J M M   Q B T T   P O   H P E T   Q S P N J T F T .

H P E T   L J O H E P N   X J M M   D P N F   U I S P V H I   B   T V G G F S J O H   T F S W B O U .

Prophets Proclaim God's Everlasting Love

The Times of Jeremiah

based on 2 Kings 22–25; Jeremiah 1, 7

Alfredo spent weeks practicing for the football team. He was cut in the first tryouts. Jamie studied all weekend for a test. When she got her paper back, there was a red D at the top.

Trying hard and then failing can happen to anyone. When it does happen, it is very frustrating. The prophet Jeremiah was frustrated in his work with the Israelites. But today he is known as one of the greatest prophets.

Jeremiah lived in the southern kingdom of Judah. He was the son of a priest who lived in a small village near Jerusalem. When Jeremiah first heard God's call, he said, "I am too young." But God didn't think so. He told Jeremiah not to be afraid, but to do whatever he asked. God promised to be with Jeremiah, giving him strength.

When God called Jeremiah, Josiah was king of Judah. He was a good king who wanted to serve God faithfully. During his reign, a great discovery had been made in the Temple. A scroll of the Book of Deuteronomy had been found. When it was read to King Josiah, he knew that changes must be made in the land. The people were not being faithful to the obligations of the Covenant. They were worshiping the false gods of their neighbors. They were treating the one living God as if he were one god among many. Josiah called them back to authentic worship of the one God, which the First Commandment calls for.

King Josiah and the people renewed their promise to obey all that God asked of them. Josiah called upon the people to believe in God, to place their hope in him, and to love him above all else. He ordered his soldiers to destroy every shrine to a false god in the land. He declared that everyone was to worship the LORD in the Temple of Jerusalem.

Rembrandt van Rijn, *Jeremiah Lamenting the Destruction of Jerusalem*, 1630. ❯

Jeremiah's Warnings

The king passed laws to help everyone live as the Covenant demanded. But the laws did not change the hearts of the people. After Josiah died, the people went back to their old ways. Jeremiah warned them that unless they stopped doing evil and worshiping other gods, the Temple would be destroyed and Jerusalem would be burned to the ground.

Jeremiah told the people that God was not pleased with their worship. They came to the Temple and prayed, but they did not treat others in the way he had shown them. They did not try to bring peace and justice to all. They did not protect the poor and vulnerable of society. Jeremiah stood outside the Temple gates and fearlessly preached God's message:

> This is the temple of the LORD!
> Only if you reform your ways,
> if you treat each other fairly,
> and not follow strange gods,
> will I stay with you.

The Message Is Rejected

based on Jeremiah 18, 29–33, 38

Despite Jeremiah's warnings, the people felt secure. They did not believe that God would let an enemy conquer the Holy City. They did not believe that God would let the Temple built to honor him be destroyed. So they continued to ignore the poor and needy. They continued to boast about their wealth. They even continued to adore false gods. They thought God would bless and protect them as long as they continued to worship at the Temple.

Of course, people did not like Jeremiah's message. They cursed him for pointing out their sins. They beat him, accused him of speaking against the king, and finally had him arrested. But Jeremiah wasn't scared. After being released from prison, he continued to preach that the Holy City would be destroyed. The people still refused to repent.

The Fall of Jerusalem

The terrible things Jeremiah foretold came to be. Jerusalem was captured by the Babylonians in 597 B.C. All the treasures of the Temple and the palace were taken to Babylon. The soldiers and craftsmen were sent into exile in Babylon. Only the poor were left in the land.

The king of Babylon appointed a new king to rule the land he had conquered. The new king did not have the courage to do what was right. False prophets told the people to rise up against the Babylonians. But Jeremiah warned the king and the leaders that their situation would get worse if they rebelled. No one wanted to listen to Jeremiah. He was accused of working against his country and was thrown into a deep, muddy well. Jeremiah would have died there, but the king secretly gave permission for him to be pulled out. Jeremiah was kept in prison until Jerusalem was attacked a second time in 587 B.C.

When the Babylonian army again marched into the city, the Temple was burned. More people were sent into exile. Jeremiah, however, was treated with respect. The Babylonian king had heard how he had told the people to surrender. Jeremiah was allowed to choose to stay in conquered Jerusalem or go to Babylon with the exiles. He chose to stay in Jerusalem. He loved his country and his people. Jeremiah knew that the exiles in Babylon needed to be comforted too. He wrote them this message from God:

> When you seek me with all your heart, you will find me and I will help you.
>
> adapted from Jeremiah 29:13

The Promise of a New Covenant

Jeremiah also told the people that God intended to make a new covenant with them. Read Jeremiah 31:31–34. In your own words, explain what God promises.

_____

_____

_____

_____

Jeremiah's whole life proclaimed God's everlasting love. He was faithful to God even when it meant suffering for him.

Jeremiah's Message for Today

Jeremiah's message is just as important today as it was in his time. Each member of society is responsible for promoting the well-being of all, especially those who are poor and vulnerable. We must do all we can to ensure that our society encourages the practice of virtue. Like Jeremiah, we must call society to conversion when sin has won over virtue. When we recognize that God is our Father, we come to see all people as our brothers and sisters. We can learn to accept our responsibility to care for one another.

Exile in Babylon

based on Ezekiel 1, 18

The first people taken from Judah to Babylon did not believe Jeremiah, who said many years would pass before they would see Jerusalem again. They believed that because they were God's Chosen People, he would deliver them from the Babylonians.

God was at work among his people in exile. He called Ezekiel, a young priest, to be his prophet in Babylon. In a famous vision, Ezekiel saw the glory of God. He was told to eat a scroll—the Word of God—which tasted like honey. This

was a sign that the Word of God was within him. Ezekiel started preaching to the first exiles. He helped them worship the only living God with all their hearts. Like Jeremiah, Ezekiel warned that Jerusalem would be destroyed. At first, the people did not accept his message and did not repent.

Ten years passed and the second group of exiles arrived in Babylon in 587 B.C. The period from 587 until 537 B.C. is known as the **Exile.** The people sent into exile brought with them the awful news of the destruction of both Jerusalem and the Temple. From that time on, Ezekiel no longer spoke of punishment for sin. Instead he told how God planned to bring the exiles back to their land and to raise up a new Israel. His message was one of faith and love. Read Psalm 137:1–5 to see how the Israelites felt during their exile.

Our Own Experience of Exile

Because of sin, we too experience a form of exile. Sin spiritually separates us from our home in God's loving embrace. Through God's grace and mercy, we can return to our home. This return to God, called conversion and repentance, requires us to be truly sorry for our sins. With God's grace, we commit ourselves to sinning no more.

A Moment with Jesus

Returning to God is an act of faith. We return because God invites us and we trust in him. Take a moment to speak with Jesus. Tell him that you are sorry for your sins. Ask him to help you to return to God and to live as God wants you to live. Ask him for the grace you need to sin no more.

More Visions

based on Ezekiel 34, 36, 37

God granted Ezekiel several powerful visions. One involved a vast plain covered with hundreds of dry bones. At God's word, the bones came together again and formed skeletons. Flesh covered the skeletons. This vision conveyed a message of hope—God's spirit would give his people new life and bring them back to their land. In another vision, God told Ezekiel that the people did not need to be in Jerusalem to worship him. God was with them in Babylon just as much as he had been in the Temple; every city is his.

▲ Michelangelo Buonarroti, *Sistine Chapel Ceiling: The Prophet Ezekiel*, 1512.

From still another vision, the people learned that their experiences would help them grow. Ezekiel told the people that God wanted to use their exile in Babylon to teach them to look at things in a new way. God wanted them to repent. Through the Exile, God would bring them closer to himself.

Many of the exiles felt sorry for themselves and blamed others for their misfortune. But Ezekiel pointed out that each individual shares in the responsibility for what the group does. He said that it was not right to blame others when things went wrong. Instead, each person should look into his or her own heart and repent.

Good from Evil

Many good things happened during the Exile. The people came to realize their guilt and were ready to repent.

They studied what God had revealed about himself and wrote down the teachings of the prophets. Many books of the Bible were put together during the Exile.

Since the people no longer had the Temple, they built places where they could gather to pray and read the Scriptures. These places were called **synagogues.** Every Sabbath they met in the synagogues to study God's Word and examine how faithful they were to it.

The people understood that their worship was not sincere unless they shared what they could with the weak and the suffering. They knew that they were responsible for their own deeds and for the deeds of the group.

After 50 years, the Israelites were allowed to return home. Eventually the remnant rebuilt the Temple. Then Nehemiah, the governor, began political reforms. One of his projects was to rebuild the city walls. Ezra, a priest, guided the people in being faithful to the Law of Moses. During this time of rebuilding after the Exile, the children of Abraham became known as **Jews,** which means descendants of those who lived in Judah.

▲ A scale model of the second Temple.

We Remember

What did the prophets Jeremiah and Ezekiel proclaim?

Jeremiah and Ezekiel proclaimed that God's everlasting love would be shown through the Exile.

What was the experience of the Exile?

In 597 B.C., the Babylonians conquered Jerusalem and sent a small number of craftsmen and soldiers into exile in Babylon. Ten years later, a larger group was sent into exile, and the Temple was destroyed. The period from 587 to 537 B.C. is known as the Exile.

Words to Know

Exile   Jews   synagogue

We Respond

Help us, God our savior,
   for the glory of your name.
Deliver us, pardon our sins
   for your name's sake.
              Psalm 79:9

Things to Do at Home

1. Ask adults in your family to share a story about a time in their lives when good came from a disappointment or failure. Talk about what lessons they learned from these experiences.

2. Read about someone who courageously spoke out against an injustice. Imagine that you are that person. Write an entry for a diary, telling one significant thing that happened. Then tell how you felt about it.

3. Find out how one of the people below was a prophet in his or her day. Be ready to tell one thing that person did to help those whose rights were not being respected.

4. Who are some prophets that are active in the world today? Make a list with the help of your family and friends.

5. Imagine that you are part of a parish committee searching for guest speakers for an Advent or Lenten program. You have been asked to research the backgrounds of Jeremiah and Ezekiel as potential speakers. Write a report that includes their experience, a summary of their messages, what each prophet might think of your parish, and how you think the parish might react to each prophet's message.

Visit **www.christourlife.org/family** for more family resources.

| Vincent de Paul | Catherine of Siena | Frances Cabrini | Martin de Porres | Damien of Molokai | Katherine Drexel |

Bringing Order Number these events
in the order in which they occurred.

_____ Ezekiel's prophecy of a new Israel

_____ The finding of the Book of
Deuteronomy in the Temple

_____ The exile to Babylon

_____ The destruction
of Jerusalem and
the Temple

_____ Josiah's laws that
called the people
back to the
Covenant

_____ The rebuilding of
the Temple and
the city walls

_____ Jeremiah's
warnings not to
rebel against
Babylon

Crime and Punishment
Answer these questions.

1. For what sins were the
Israelites conquered
and exiled, according to the
prophets?

_____

2. To what country were the Israelites exiled?

_____

3. How long were they in exile?

_____

4. What is one good thing that came
out of the Exile?

_____

_____

Find the Match Write the letter of the term or person that matches each description.

A. Josiah

B. synagogues

C. Jeremiah

D. Ezra

E. Exile

F. New Covenant

G. Ezekiel

H. Jews

I. Nehemiah

J. Temple

_____ 1. Only place where sacrifice was offered

_____ 2. King who tried to reform his country

_____ 3. Prophet who was attacked for his criticism

_____ 4. Prophet who had a vision of bones that came back to life

_____ 5. A good thing that Jeremiah promised for the people

_____ 6. Term for the time the people of Judah were kept in Babylon

_____ 7. Governor who worked for reform after the Exile

_____ 8. Places where the Israelites met to pray and read Scripture

_____ 9. Descendants of those who lived in Judah

_____ 10. Priest who guided the people in keeping the Law of Moses
after the Exile

↑ Sandro Botticelli, *Madonna and Child with Saint John the Baptist.*

The Savior Is Jesus, the Son of God

The Exiles Return

After the return of the exiles to Jerusalem in 537 B.C., Palestine was governed by Persia, Greece, Egypt, and then Syria. In 167 B.C., the King of Syria forbade the practice of Judaism and persecuted the Jewish people. He had a statue of the Greek god Zeus erected in the Temple. The Jewish people rebelled under the leadership of the Maccabees, a father and his five sons. The enemy was defeated, and the Temple was rededicated. The feast of Hanukkah commemorates this event. Palestine was independent until the Romans conquered it in 63 B.C.

A New Testament Prophet

based on Luke 1:5–25,57–80

Luke's Gospel gives the account of the birth of John, who came to be known as John the Baptist. Zechariah and his wife, Elizabeth, were called by God to be the parents of the prophet who would prepare the people for the coming of the Messiah. Elizabeth and Zechariah were quite old at the time. Though they followed God's laws faithfully, Zechariah questioned how this could happen. Because of his doubt, he was told he would be unable to speak until the child was born.

Read the announcement of the good news of John's birth as told in Luke 1:5–25.

Luke tells us that God's promise to Zechariah was fulfilled when the time came for Elizabeth to have her child. A son was born, and that made Elizabeth and Zechariah very happy. Their neighbors and relatives thought the boy should be named after his father, but Elizabeth said his name would be John.

The people could not understand why the child's name would be John. No one in the family had that name. They asked the father, who still could not speak. He made signs for a writing tablet and wrote on it, "John is his name." At that moment, Zechariah was able to speak again. He was filled with the Holy Spirit, and he spoke words that the Church would later include in the Morning Prayer in the Liturgy of the Hours. Read the first part of Zechariah's Canticle in Luke 1:68–75. Write verse 68 here.

_____

_____

_____

_____

Then Zechariah looked upon his son, John, and continued:

> You, my child, shall be called the prophet
>   of the Most High;
> for you will go before the Lord to prepare
>   his way,
> to give his people knowledge of salvation
> by the forgiveness of their sins.
>
> In the tender compassion of our God
> the dawn from on high shall break
>   upon us,
> to shine on those who dwell in darkness
>   and the shadow of death,
> and to guide our feet into the way
>   of peace.
>
> Christian Prayer: The Liturgy of the Hours

John the Baptist's Preparation for the Messiah

Matthew 3:1–7; 11:2–15; 14:3–12

It takes a lot of training to learn a profession. The more difficult the job, the longer and harder the preparation. An athlete must spend hours practicing to be tops in his or her field. A doctor must spend years studying and practicing medicine to become a good doctor. All of this takes *self-discipline*, which is "planned control and training of oneself in order to improve."

John the Baptist had the most important work of all. His mission was to prepare the way for the Savior, the Messiah. Long ago the prophet Isaiah spoke of him, saying:

> A voice cries out:
> In the desert prepare a way for the
>   LORD.
> Make straight a highway for our God!
>
> adapted from Isaiah 40:3

For the entire prophecy, read Isaiah 40:1–5.

John knew he had to prepare himself before he could prepare the people for Christ's coming. So he went to the desert for his training. There he disciplined himself through prayer and penance.

Some Scripture scholars believe John may have belonged to a religious group known as the Essenes. They were people who lived in the desert and tried to live the Covenant perfectly. They studied the scrolls of Scripture and hand-copied the scrolls to help spread the Word. The Essenes had many strict rules and rites, including a bathing or purifying rite. That may be where John got the idea of using bathing, or baptism, as a sign of repentance. The Essene way of life was one of self-discipline—a good preparation for the hard life of a prophet.

Preparing the People

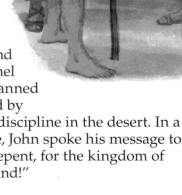

The Gospel of Matthew tells how John prepared the people for the coming of the Messiah. It says the Spirit came to John to tell him it was time to leave the desert. John's first appearance in public must have been startling. He was bearded, long-haired, and dressed in camel skin. He was tanned and toughened by his life of self-discipline in the desert. In a powerful voice, John spoke his message to the people: "Repent, for the kingdom of heaven is at hand!"

John the Baptist in Advent

Throughout the year, the Church celebrates the mystery of Jesus. The Church's liturgical year begins with the season of Advent—a time of hope and joyful anticipation of the coming of Christ. While we prepare to celebrate the birth of Christ, we also anticipate his second coming. During the season of Advent, we often hear Gospel readings that feature John the Baptist, which challenge us to prepare for the coming of the Lord.

John proclaimed a baptism of repentance for the forgiveness of sin. But he also told the people that the one who would come after him would baptize with fire and the Holy Spirit.

Many people listened to John and were baptized by him. They asked him how they should repent of their sins, and he gave them some good suggestions. Finally, Jesus himself came to the Jordan River to be baptized by John. At first, John objected, saying that Jesus should baptize him, but he did what Jesus wished. John then told his disciples to follow Jesus, the Lamb of God.

As Jesus began his public life, John was heard from less and less. He got into trouble for telling King Herod that the king was living in sin. Herod had him arrested. From prison, John sent his followers to Jesus. Though John was later beheaded by Herod's order, his mission was completed and he had done very well.

Read the story of the end of John's life in Matthew 14:1–12.

You Can Be Like John the Baptist

John the Baptist called for people to repent from their sins and to prepare for the coming of Jesus into their lives. You can be like John the Baptist whenever you add your voice to causes that call for repentance from sin. These can be anything that does not respect the dignity of human life or that does not promote the well-being of all people, especially the poor and vulnerable. Think of an example of one way that you can be like John the Baptist today.

_____

_____

_____

_____

_____

_____

_____

A Moment with Jesus

John the Baptist proclaimed a message of hope and anticipation. He teaches us that we can look forward to the coming of Christ into our lives. Take a moment to ask Jesus to help you be a person of hope. Ask him for the grace you need to help others who may be experiencing despair. Thank Jesus for coming into your life and ask him to help you prepare others to welcome him into their lives.

The Promise Fulfilled

God's Chosen People longed for the coming of the Messiah, who had been promised by God again and again. The prophets had announced the signs by which he would be known. On the day planned by God from the beginning of time, an announcement was made to Mary that the promise was about to be fulfilled. Mary, who was full of grace and who had been preserved from sin from the moment of her conception, was told that she was to be the Mother of the Messiah.

Read the story in Luke 1:26–38.

What were the words of the angel Gabriel when he greeted Mary?

_____

What did Mary say when she agreed to be the Mother of the Messiah?

_____

_____

When Mary freely agreed to become the Mother of Jesus, God the Son became man without losing his divine nature. He loved us so much that he became like us in all things except sin. We call this mystery *the Incarnation.* We call Mary the "Mother of God" because she is the mother of Jesus, who is God himself. We call Jesus "the Christ," meaning the "anointed one," because at his birth, he was consecrated as the Messiah by the Holy Spirit.

The angel also told Mary that her relative Elizabeth was to have a son, even though Elizabeth was quite old. The angel assured Mary that nothing is impossible with God.

Peter Paul Rubens, *Annunciation,* 1628.

The Gospel of Luke tells us that Mary went to visit Elizabeth in a little town in Judah. It gives us a prayer in which Mary praises and thanks God for all he has done. Her prayer of praise is called the **Magnificat.** It is a prayer that the Church prays daily during Evening Prayer of the Liturgy of the Hours. Read the story of Mary's visit to Elizabeth in Luke 1:39–56. It is an event that the Church celebrates each year on May 31, the Feast of the Visitation.

Mary's Magnificat

My soul proclaims the greatness of the Lord,
my spirit rejoices in God my Savior;
for he has looked with favor on his lowly servant.

From this day all generations will call me blessed:
the Almighty has done great things for me,
and holy is his Name.

He has mercy on those who fear him
in every generation.

He has shown the strength of his arm,
he has scattered the proud in their conceit.

He has cast down the mighty from their thrones,
and has lifted up the lowly.

He has filled the hungry with good things,
and the rich he has sent away empty.

He has come to the help of his servant Israel
for he has remembered his promise of mercy,
the promise he made to our fathers,
to Abraham and his children for ever.

Christian Prayer: The Liturgy of the Hours

Jesus Christ—the Messiah

based on Luke 2:1–7; 21

Joseph and Mary were both from the family of David. At the time of the census, they had to go to Bethlehem, the city of David, to register. While they were there, Mary gave birth to her Son. They named him Jesus, a name that means "God saves," as the angel had directed. He was the long-awaited one, the Messiah, the Christ. In him, God established a covenant with us forever. Jesus fulfilled what was written in the Scriptures.

Andrea del Sarto, *Holy Family.*

When Jesus began his ministry, he went to the synagogue at Nazareth and proclaimed that a passage in Isaiah was fulfilled in him.

> "The Spirit of the Lord is upon me,
>   because he has anointed me
>   to bring glad tidings to the poor.
> He has sent me to proclaim liberty to captives
>   and recovery of sight to the blind,
>   to let the oppressed go free,
> and to proclaim a year acceptable to the Lord."
>
> Luke 4:18–19

The Center of Mary's Life

Christ's coming marked the start of a new understanding of salvation history. Mary was the first to grasp that new understanding, for she was the first to make Jesus the center of her life.

Mary watched Jesus grow up. She heard him teach during his public life. She knew his friends and his enemies. She knew of his miracles, and she was at the foot of the cross when he was crucified. No one has ever loved Jesus as Mary did.

Mary was with the apostles as they waited for the coming of the Holy Spirit. She was with them when they received the Spirit and began to teach about Jesus.

Mary is with us now, as she was with her people then. She prays that we allow the Holy Spirit to work freely in us, as he worked in her and still works in the Church today. Because of Mary's great faith and trust in the Holy Spirit, we turn to her, in prayer, to offer praise to God with her and to ask for her intercession.

The Center of Our Lives

How much does Jesus mean to you? Is he the center of your life? The questions below can help you determine the part he plays in your everyday living. Answer *yes, no, not sure,* or *sometimes.*

1. Do you realize that Jesus loves you and wants you to be happy? _____

2. Do you try to think, speak, and act as Jesus would? _____

3. Do you believe in Jesus and trust in his power? _____

4. Do you appreciate and thank Jesus for all that he has done for you? _____

5. Do you recognize Jesus in other people, especially in those who are poor and vulnerable? _____

Think what you can do to be able to answer yes to every one of these questions. Then Jesus will truly be the center of your life.

Preparing the Way of the Lord

Through his saving plan of love, God revealed himself and prepared his people for the coming of the Messiah. The people and events were part of salvation history. This timeline shows the order of historical events and how much time passed between them.

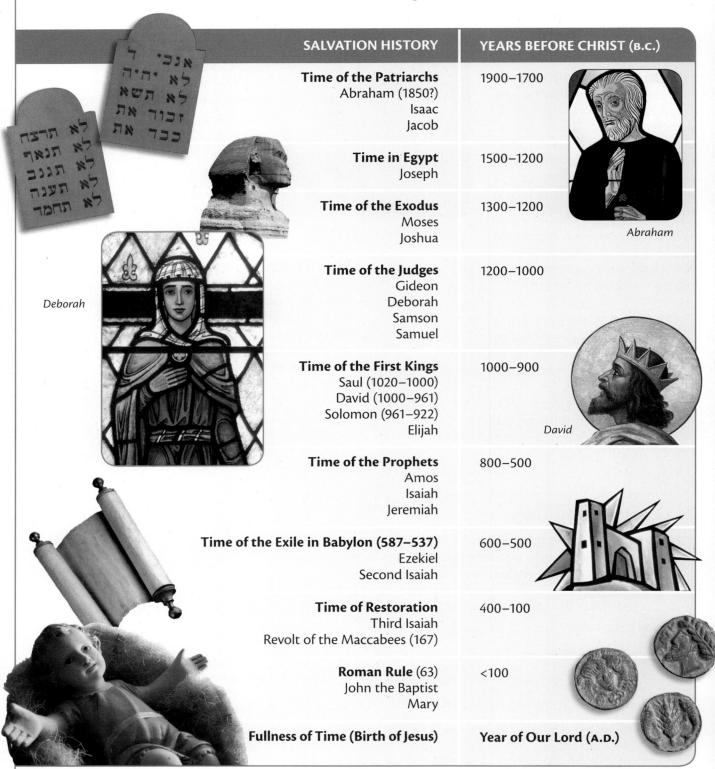

SALVATION HISTORY	YEARS BEFORE CHRIST (B.C.)
Time of the Patriarchs Abraham (1850?) Isaac Jacob	1900–1700
Time in Egypt Joseph	1500–1200
Time of the Exodus Moses Joshua	1300–1200
Time of the Judges Gideon Deborah Samson Samuel	1200–1000
Time of the First Kings Saul (1020–1000) David (1000–961) Solomon (961–922) Elijah	1000–900
Time of the Prophets Amos Isaiah Jeremiah	800–500
Time of the Exile in Babylon (587–537) Ezekiel Second Isaiah	600–500
Time of Restoration Third Isaiah Revolt of the Maccabees (167)	400–100
Roman Rule (63) John the Baptist Mary	<100
Fullness of Time (Birth of Jesus)	**Year of Our Lord (A.D.)**

Abraham

Deborah

David

We Remember

What was John the Baptist's place in salvation history?

John the Baptist was the last and greatest prophet. He prepared the people for the coming of the Messiah by calling them to repent.

Why is Mary important?

Mary is the Mother of God because she is the Mother of Jesus, who is God incarnate.

Word to Know

Magnificat

We Respond

Blessed be the Lord, the God of Israel;
he has come to his people and set them free.

He has raised up
for us a mighty
savior,
born of the
house of his
servant David.

from Zechariah's Canticle

Michelangelo Buonarroti,
The Prophet Zechariah,
1512. ❯

Things to Do at Home

1. Share with your family the timeline on page 166. Then work together to create your own family timeline. Ask adults in your family to recall a significant date, such as the wedding of parents or grandparents, to start your timeline. Talk about which important family events to include. When you have finished, pray together to thank God for his loving care of your family.

2. John the Baptist prepared for his mission in life by prayer, penance, and fasting. How can you prepare for your mission in life? Think about what goals you have for your future and list the steps you will have to take to accomplish those goals. For help and ideas, you might talk to adults in your family about how they prepared for their jobs, or special training they might have received to achieve a specific skill.

3. Watch with your family one or two TV programs. Talk about whether any characters practiced self-discipline. The following questions might help guide your discussion:
   - In what ways did the character(s) display self-discipline? What was the result of this practice? Was it difficult for the character(s) to practice self-discipline? How was it worth the effort?
   - In what ways did these or other characters not practice self-discipline? What was the result of not practicing? What might the character(s) have done differently to achieve more positive results?

4. There is a lot of information about Mary in books or on the Internet. Do research about her privileges, her feast days, her appearances, or her shrines. Write a short report of the topic you choose and share it with your classmates.

Visit **www.christourlife.org/family** for more family resources.

A Promise Passed On Complete this summary of salvation history. Use the timeline on page 166.

God called Abraham, the first patriarch, about 1. _____ B.C.

Nearly 2. _____ years later, Joseph, one of Jacob's sons, was sold

into slavery in Egypt. The Israelites were forced into slavery and lived in Egypt for

about 3. _____ years.

Finally, about 1280 B.C., 4. _____ led the Israelites out of Egypt.

The time of the judges lasted about 5. _____

years. Two of the judges who led the Israelites to victory over their

enemies were 6. _____

and 7. _____ .

Samuel anointed 8. _____ as the first king of Israel. The greatest king

of Israel, King 9. _____ , ruled from 1000 to 10. _____

B.C. David's son, King 11. _____ , died in 922 B.C.

In 587 B.C., the people of the southern kingdom were exiled to 12. _____ .

After the Exile, the Syrians oppressed the Jewish people until

the 13. _____ overthrew them. Eventually the

14. _____ conquered Palestine in 63 B.C.

When Jesus was born, the fullness of time had arrived.
God had become one of us to save us!

CHAPTER 25

Unit 5 Review

Show What You Know

Read each description and question. Then use a word from the word bank to answer each question.

prophets	exiles
holy	Spiritual Works of Mercy
Amen	seraphim
synagogues	Jews
Magnificat	

1. The people of Judah were sent to Babylon after Jerusalem was captured. During this time, Ezekiel began preaching to the people.

What do we call the people of Judah during this time?

_____

2. God gives some people the special gift of seeing things as they truly are. These people see good as good and evil as evil. They tell forth, call people to repent, and help them to believe.

What do we call these special people?

_____

3. After 40 years in exile, the Israelites were allowed to return home. They rebuilt the Temple and were more faithful to the Law of Moses.

What were the children of Abraham called during this time?

_____

4. Works of mercy are practiced by people who work for social justice in a Christian manner.

Which works of mercy help meet the needs of the spirit?

_____

5. When Isaiah was called by God, he saw the Lord surrounded by angels. The angels had a special message for Isaiah.

What do we call angels of this type?

_____

6. When Mary went to visit Elizabeth in a little town in Judah, she said a special prayer. It gave thanks to God for all he had done.

What is this special prayer called?

_____

∧ Sebastiano del Piombo, *Virgin Mary Visits Saint Elisabeth.*

7. During the Exile, the people built places where thy could gather to pray and read the Scriptures. Every Sabbath they met in these places to study God's Word and to examine how faithful they were to it.

What were these special places called?

_____

8. Sometimes the Bible refers to God's power and his "otherness." We can reflect this divine quality because we are created in the image of God.

What is the special word that refers only to God, which we can reflect in our lives and actions?

_____

9. We conclude our prayers by expressing God's faithfulness and our trust in him.

What word do we use to conclude our prayers?

_____

Messages of the Prophets   On the golf course color each flag according to the code.

Prophet of social justice—green flag

Prophet of the one true God—red flag

Prophet of the New Covenant—blue flag

Prophet of repentance—purple flag

Prophet of hope—orange flag

Prophet of the Messiah—yellow flag

1

Elijah
1 Kgs 18:21–40

6

John the Baptist
Lk 1:5–25, 57–80;
3:10–17; Jn 1:33–34

2

Amos
Am 2:6–8, 13–16;
3:1–2; 5:21–24

5

Ezekiel
Ez 34:11–16; 37:4–14;
43:5–9

3

Isaiah
Is 7:14; 9:5–6; 11:1–5;
29:18–21

4

Jeremiah
Jer 1:4–10; 31:31–34

Which Prophet?

Match each prophet to something important that happened in his life.

1. Amos

2. Elijah

3. John the Baptist

4. Ezekiel

5. Jeremiah

6. Isaiah

_____ **A.** He stood up to a wicked king whose greed led to the death of Naboth. He also proved that the god of a wicked queen was false.

_____ **B.** He spoke out against the idol worship and injustices in Israel. Because of the trouble he caused, he was banished from the Temple. It was only after Israel was conquered by Assyria, as he had prophesied, that he was recognized as a prophet.

_____ **C.** God told him that because the people had been unfaithful, they would be conquered by their enemies. He knew that God would continue his promises through a remnant of the people.

_____ **D.** He prophesied that the Temple would be destroyed and that Jerusalem would be burned to the ground. After the Babylonians conquered Jerusalem, he stayed there to help his people.

_____ **E.** He was called as a prophet during the Exile in Babylon. He had many powerful visions about ways the Exile would help the people grow.

_____ **F.** He baptized many people and helped them repent for their sins. He also prepared the way for the Messiah.

❮ *Christ baptized*, Fra Angelico, 1438.

The Last Prophet

Imagine that you are Zechariah and that you have written this description of your son's life. Fill in the blanks to complete the description.

△ Michelangelo Buonarroti,
The Prophet Zechariah,
from The Sistine Chapel, 1512.

My wife, _____ , and I did not expect to have children because we were old. I didn't even believe it and was punished for my lack of faith by being unable to _____ until our son was born.

When he was born, our neighbors were surprised to learn that his name would be _____ . They didn't believe it until I confirmed it in writing. At that moment, I was able to _____ again!

Our son had a special job. It took a lot of preparation. He often went to the _____ for training. There he would discipline himself through _____ and _____ . All of this was done to prepare for the _____ .

His message to the people was "_____ , for the kingdom of God is near!" Many people listened to him and were _____ . He even baptized _____ !

Our son's life ended because of a foolish promise made by _____ . But we know that our son did his job well and that he is with God.

A Message to Remember

In Isaiah 48:17, there is a message from God that is good to remember when things go wrong or we can't understand what's happening around us. Read that verse. Then use this space to write and decorate the words God says.

Celebrating

The Prophets

Song and Procession

(Students carrying Bible and candles lead, followed by those bearing banners and the box of hearts.)

Introduction

Leader 1: We are gathered here today not only to honor God's prophets from the past, but also to encourage one another to accept the challenging role of being prophets today. This means being ready and willing to turn our life over to God completely by resisting evil and doing good. It means helping others return to him in mind and heart. It takes great courage and self-discipline, but we want to serve the Lord and proclaim his Word. Let's stand now and hear it for God!

Leader 1: *(Sing a spirited Amen, Alleluia, or another acclamation.)*

Reader: *(Read Ephesians 4:22–24.)*

All: *Thanks be to God!*

(Song)

Banner Presentations

(One at a time, students with banners step to the front center and stand there while the rally leader reads the message of their prophet. After each message, all sing "We do!" or a similar acclamation.)

Leader 2: Elijah, prophet of the one true God, said, "It is wrong to worship false gods. The Lord is the one true God." Do you promise to love and worship our God?

All: "We do!"

Leader 3: Isaiah, the prophet of the Messiah, said, "Take courage. The Messiah will come to save you. He will be the Son of David, wise and powerful." Do you promise to prepare for the coming of the Messiah to all people by living in peace?

All: "We do!"

Leader 4: Jeremiah, the prophet of the New Covenant, said, "Because of your sin, the enemy will destroy Jerusalem and leave your land empty. But God will establish a new covenant with you." Do you promise to stay away from sin and draw closer to God?

All: "We do!"

Leader 5: Amos, the prophet of social justice, said, "You are cheating others and living dishonestly. See that justice is done, for justice must flow like water." Do you promise to be just and honest in dealing with God and others?

❮ Jeremiah, Daniel, Isaiah, and Ezekiel

All: "We do!"

Leader 6: Ezekiel, the prophet of hope, said, "God will be a shepherd to you, leading you back to your own land." Do you promise to follow the Good Shepherd in loyalty, love, and peace?

All: "We do!"

Leader 7: John the Baptist, the prophet of repentance, said, "You must have a change of heart to obtain forgiveness. Repent, for one greater and more powerful than I is coming, and he will save you from your sin." Do you promise to repent, and to put on the mind and heart of Jesus?

All: "We do!"

Prayer

Leader 8: Let us bow our heads and take a few moments to pray to God in the quiet of our hearts. *(Pause.)*

Reader 2: *(Read Jeremiah 32:38–41.)*

The Word of the Lord.

All: Thanks be to God.

Acceptance of Mission

Leader 9: At this time, we ask those who are willing to accept the role of prophet to come forward, and, one at a time, take a heart from the box. Read the message you have chosen, and then pin on the heart.

(Song: Sung while students process up for their hearts)

Prophet's Pledge

All: I praise and thank you, heavenly Father, for showing me the way to you through your Son.

I promise I will do my best in the role of prophet today.

I will obey your laws, I will work for peace and justice, I will fight evil and warn others of it, and I will do my best to lead others to you by showing them your love.

Help me to do your will. Amen.

(Song)

Looking Back at Unit 5

In this unit, you have read about several prophets whom God sent to speak his Word to his people. These prophets tried to convince the people to change their ways and to live according to God's will. When the people did not listen, their sinful, selfish lives brought them sorrow and suffering.

Elijah was sent to call the king and the people to the worship of the one true God.

Amos is known as the prophet of social justice. He told the people that they must care for the poor and the needy. Amos was the first prophet whose teachings were written down.

Isaiah is the prophet of holiness because he had a vision of the holiness of God. Isaiah spent his life trying to convince the people that they too must be holy. He told them to trust the Lord and to serve him with their whole hearts.

Jeremiah was a young man when he was called to be a prophet. God promised to be with him and to help him. Jeremiah told the people how displeased God was when they came to worship him without repenting. Through Jeremiah, God promised his people a new covenant.

Because of the sinful lives of the people, the kingdom of Judah became weak and was conquered. The people were exiled to Babylon. God called Ezekiel to be his prophet there. Ezekiel's preaching helped the people realize that God was still with them and that he still loved them. During the Exile, the people learned to worship God from their hearts.

John the Baptist was the last and greatest prophet. God called him to prepare the way for Jesus. His message was that the time for the Messiah to come had arrived. He told the people to repent and believe in God's love and forgiveness.

The message of the prophets is for us too. God loves us and wants us to show our love for him by the way we live. He wants us to make his Son, Jesus, the center of our lives, just as Mary made him the center of her life. Only when we do this will we be able to worship God with loving hearts.

Living the Message

Can you give yourself a check (✓) for each statement?

○ 1. I know why God sent prophets to his people. I can tell something about the messages of Elijah, Amos, Isaiah, Jeremiah, Ezekiel, and John the Baptist.

○ 2. I know that God has a special love for the poor and needy and wants me to love them and share what I have with them.

○ 3. I try in any way I can to help those who have less than I have.

○ 4. I am trying to reflect God's holiness every day.

○ 5. When something bad happens, I believe God can use the situation to bring about good.

Planning Ahead

Think about the messages of the prophets. Below, write the message that you think is most important for people to hear today. Write how you want to respond to this message. Write something you can do to spread the prophet's message.

Message _____

_____

Your response _____

_____

Spreading the message _____

_____

The Prophets Speak to Us Today

Prophets played an important role in the history of ancient Israel. Their words ring with truth for us today, even in our own homes. Prophets are individuals called by God to speak his Word to the people. Prophets didn't have supernatural powers. They weren't fortunetellers or magicians; they were people inspired with the understanding of what would happen if the Chosen People didn't change their ways. Their words are meant to awaken us to what's most important in our lives and how we are to treat those around us.

Here's what some of the prophets said and how it matters to you today in your home:

Elijah: "Reject false gods and idols"
What have we made into an idol in our own lives: money, security, self-determination, work, a hobby or pastime?

Amos: "Have a social conscience. Consider the well-being of the poor and needy."
Does our family treat all others with respect and dignity? Do we share what we have with those in need?

Isaiah: "God calls us all to be holy. Here I am, Lord, ready to do your will."
Is our family ready to help with important causes at church and in the community? When others are in need do we respond, "Here I am?"

▲ Titian, *Saint John the Baptist.*

Jeremiah: "Don't engage in empty worship."
Does our family go to church prepared to worship, praise, and thank God? Do we weave prayer into our daily life?

Ezekiel: "Don't use people and love things. Instead, love people and make wise use of material things."
Does our family treat one another with respect? Do we care for people more than for our own ease and comfort?

John the Baptist: "Repent with all your heart. God is near."
As a family are we willing and able to ask for and accept forgiveness from one another? Do we admit when we're wrong and help one another live the right way?

Family Feature

Our Role as Prophet

When we are baptized, we share in Jesus' role as priest, prophet, and king. Here are three ways that families exercise the role of prophet.

1. Saying no when tempted to take the easy way out. We act as prophets when we realize the consequences of actions that may seem acceptable, but might actually harm our children. Parents often have to say no and set limits that are unpopular—curfew, bedtimes, styles of clothing, and types of entertainment are all areas where parents hold the line for the ultimate benefit of their children. It takes the courage of a prophet to take a stand.

   Think of two situations with your children where you have had to say no. Pray for God's wisdom and guidance to know when and how to stand fast for the benefit of your family.

2. Parents have the difficult task of trying to tame an overloaded family calendar. With so many activities and options, there seems to be precious little time for the most important things in life, including prayer, worship, religious formation and practices, and helping those in need. Parents take on the role of prophet when they act with wisdom to balance their children's schedules and make time for spiritual development.

   Take a look at your family calendar. If you were going to take one action to achieve more balance for your family, what would it be? How can you claim more time for God and your family's spiritual development?

3. Parents need to be beacons of hope in troubled times. This is not a naive hope that overlooks the obvious and real challenges in our world. Like the prophets, parents need to ground their hope in the faithfulness of God who sent his Son, Jesus, to save us from sin and death.

   Examine your heart. Where do you find hope in life? How do you share that hope with your family? Ask God to increase the virtue of hope in your life and in the life of your family.

John the Baptist's Message

John the Baptist was "a voice crying out in the wilderness, 'Make straight the paths of the Lord.'" How he lived was a rebuke of the people of his time. They sought places of honor; he lived in the wilderness. They wore fancy clothes; he wore a rough cloak made of camel skins. They ate the finest meals and drank rich wine; he ate the insects and honey he found in the desert. His message was clear, "Change your life to make room for Christ."

To commemorate the life and message of Saint John the Baptist, make these tasty grasshopper cookies and serve them with honey-colored apple juice to represent his meal of grasshoppers and honey.

Grasshopper Cookie Recipe

¼ cup butter

2 tablespoons vegetable shortening

1 ¼ cup powdered sugar

⅛ teaspoon salt

2 tablespoons nonalcoholic mint syrup or crème de menthe (can be substituted with a couple drops of peppermint extract and a few drops of green food coloring)

1 (8 ½ ounce) package of chocolate wafer cookies

In a small bowl, whip the butter and shortening together until combined. Slowly sift in the powdered sugar and salt. Add the crème de menthe or syrup and beat until the mixture is light and fluffy.

Make little sandwiches by spreading one teaspoon of the filling between two of the wafer cookies. There should be enough filling for 20 cookies. When all the cookies are assembled, refrigerate until set.

Time-Saver

Check a grocery store for ready-made chocolate mint sandwich cookies.

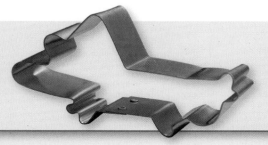

Fancy but Fun

Get a grasshopper shaped cookie cutter (available in specialty stores and on the Internet) to make rollout sugar cookies. Decorate with green and brown royal icing.

Family Feature

Family Justice

The bishops carry on Jesus' role as prophet, often speaking out against injustice and oppression in the world. In *Follow the Way of Love, A Pastoral Message of the U.S. Catholic Bishops to Families*, the bishops pointed out the ways families carry out the mission of the church of the home in ordinary ways, including:

*You welcome the **stranger**, the lonely one, the grieving person into your home. You give drink to the thirsty and food to the hungry. The Gospel assures us that when we do this, they are strangers no more, but Christ.*

At your next family gathering, think of who else you might invite to join in the festivities. Perhaps there's a lonely neighbor, a newcomer to your town, or a family that's down on their luck that would enjoy a chance to join a celebration. Jesus was always extending an invitation to whomever he encountered. We can do likewise.

*You act **justly** in your community when you treat others with respect, stand against discrimination and racism, and work to overcome hunger, poverty, homelessness, illiteracy.*

As a family, decide on a worthy cause that can help improve the lives of others. It might be helping at a homeless shelter, collecting books for a literacy program, or donating funds to a far-away mission or nearby emergency child- care institution. Have your child research possible causes to support at Catholic Charities *www.catholiccharitiesusa.org/*, the bishop's Campaign for Human Development *www.nccbuscc.org/cchd/*, or Catholic Relief Services *www.crs.org/get_involved/at_home/index.cfm*.

*You **affirm life** as a precious gift from God. You oppose whatever destroys life, such as abortion, euthanasia, unjust war, capital punishment, neighborhood and domestic violence, poverty, and racism. Within your family, when you shun violent words and actions and look for peaceful ways to resolve conflict, you become a voice for life, forming peacemakers for the next generation.*

Respect is at the heart of the Golden Rule—to do unto others as we would have them do unto us. Teach your child respect by first creating a climate of respect in your family. Children who grow up treated with respect, learn to respect themselves and others. Teach your child fairness by building on their innate desire to be treated fairly themselves. Practice conflict resolution in your home that maintains the dignity of all involved. Don't allow your children to speak disrespectfully about others.

Visit **www.christourlife.org/family** for more family resources.

Special Seasons and Lessons

Symbols from Other Old Testament Books

	Moses and the Exodus Deuteronomy 7:6–9	God gave Moses the Ten Commandments. When the people broke God's laws, God told them he would plant a new law in their hearts that would not pass away. Christ brought that new law.
	Ruth Ruth 1:1–18	Ruth was not an Israelite, but a Gentile. Ruth became the grandmother of King David. Ruth reminds us that God's love extends to everyone.
	Jesse Isaiah 11:1–10	Isaiah prophesied that the Messiah would be the flower springing from the root of Jesse and that he would sit on the throne of David.
	David 2 Samuel 5–8; 11–13	David was the greatest king of Israel. The Messiah would be born from his family line, and his kingdom would last forever.
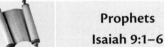	**Solomon** 1 Kings 6	Solomon, son of David, was known for his wisdom and for building the Temple, a place of worship. Christ came to show us how to worship God with our whole heart, soul, and mind.
	Prophets Isaiah 9:1–6	Prophets foretold things about the Messiah and called upon the people to remain faithful to God.

Symbols from the Story of the Birth of Jesus

	John the Baptist Matthew 3:1–12	John the Baptist prepared the way for Jesus and called the people to a baptism of repentance. He was privileged to baptize Jesus himself!
	City of Bethlehem Micah 5:1–4	Saint Joseph was the foster father of Christ and the husband and protector of Mary. He worked as a carpenter and probably taught Jesus the trade.
	Mary Luke 1:26–38	God chose Mary, a young Jewish woman, to be the Mother of his Son. It was because she said yes to God that God's promise was fulfilled.
	Jesus Matthew 2:1–12	A new star appeared in the heavens on the night Jesus was born. He came as the Light of the World to banish the darkness of sin and ignorance forever.

Reflection

Think of what you can do to prepare for the coming of Christ. How can you be more like Jesus? How can you be a light to others? You may want to write your thoughts as a prayer.

Dear Lord, during Advent, I will prepare for your coming by _____ _____

3 | Christmas

Christmas and the Feast of the Holy Family

Think about your favorite Christmas traditions. What do you most look forward to as Christmas approaches? Who are the people with whom you celebrate Christmas?

_____

_____

For many people, the season of Christmas is a time when family members get together and share special time and traditions.

In part, this is because our families are an important part of all of our holiday celebrations. However, something about Christmas leads us to focus particularly on our family. Perhaps this is because families are so important to what it means to be a human person. When God sent his Son to be born among us, he chose for Jesus to be born into a human family.

Families—Jesus' and Mine

Certainly, Jesus' family, called the Holy Family, was unique. However, all families can learn from the Holy Family as each family creates its own unique expression of family life.

Think about the Holy Family and your family. List two ways these families are alike.

1. _____

_____

2. _____

_____

Now list two ways these families are different.

1. _____

_____

2. _____

_____

Think of one thing that makes it easy for your family to love and serve God.

_____

Think of one thing that makes it difficult.

_____

My Family and I

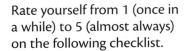

Each family has different gifts and different strong points. That is good! People should look for the strong points of their families and try to make them grow even stronger. Every member of the family is responsible for helping the family grow in happiness.

Rate yourself from 1 (once in a while) to 5 (almost always) on the following checklist.

① ② ③ ❹ ⑤ **1.** I praise the members of my family when they do something well.

① ② ③ ④ ❺ **2.** I thank members of my family when they do things for me.

① ② ③ ❹ ⑤ **3.** I do my share of the work at home.

① ② ③ ❹ ⑤ **4.** I speak respectfully to the members of my family and do not use put downs.

① ② ❸ ④ ⑤ **5.** I pray that the members of my family will love God and one another and help spread God's love to others.

 _____ **Total**

Try to remember these five points every day during the Christmas season.

Praying for Your Family During the Christmas Season

Our celebration of Christmas begins on Christmas Eve and continues until the feast of the baptism of the Lord. Special feasts of the Christmas season call our attention to aspects of Jesus' family life. Here are some ways that we can honor these feasts and use them as opportunities to enhance our family lives.

The feast of the Holy Family is celebrated on the Sunday after Christmas (or on December 30). On that day, pray for each member of your family and plan some fun time together.

The Solemnity of Mary, the Mother of God is celebrated on January 1. Pray for your mother as you honor Mary, the Mother of our faith.

The feast of the Epiphany is celebrated on the Sunday between January 2 and 9. On that day, plan to give gifts of time to members of your family. One example is a coupon that promises to do something special for each family member, such as helping with a household chore or sharing fun time together.

Let's PLAY a bOARD Game Together —mike

On Epiphany Sunday, use the checklist at the left to rate yourself again. If your total is higher, you have probably helped make your family happier. On this day, think of at least one good thing that makes your family special. Thank God for that gift. Pray to the Holy Family, asking Jesus, Mary, and Joseph to help your family grow in love and service of God and one another.

4 | Lent

Lent

The Springtime of the Church Year

Every year we wait for spring. The chirping birds, the fresh shoots of green grass, the gentle and steady rains, and the warm sunshine are signs that tell us new life is coming. We look forward to seeing spring in all its beauty. But new life comes in spring only because other things have died during the winter. Their death was a necessary step in the birth of new life.

Lent is the springtime of the Church year. It is a time of preparation. During Lent, Christians devote themselves to prayer, fasting, and almsgiving to prepare for the joy of Easter. Jesus loves us so much that he was willing to suffer and die for us. Through his sacrifice, he saved us from sin, and through the sacraments, he shares his life with us. Easter celebrates the Paschal Mystery, the mystery of our dying to sin and rising with Christ to the new life of grace.

Preparing for Easter

When we truly love God and others as Jesus has taught us, we are living a life of grace. During Lent, we look closely at how we are taking care of the life of God within us. We follow the Church law to fast and abstain from eating meat on certain days of Lent. Adults fast on Ash Wednesday and Good Friday. People over the age of 14 abstain from eating meat on Ash Wednesday and every Friday of Lent. During Lent, we pray more often and celebrate the Sacrament of Reconciliation. We also give alms to help people who are in need. Through these Lenten practices, we try in a special way to die to sin and to live in God's love.

The Church gives us six weeks of Lent to prepare for Easter. Each of us will experience Easter joy if we use this time to become the person God wants us to be. The life of grace, like all life, is meant to grow. But like other kinds of life, grace needs certain conditions for growth. Our Lenten practices of prayer, fasting, and almsgiving provide the conditions needed for grace to flourish. The more we live in the spirit of Lent, the better we will be able to enjoy the new life Jesus has given us.

Reflection

Are there some bad habits you need to correct or some good ones you want to form? How will you use the season of Lent to prepare for Easter?

_____

_____

_____

_____

_____

_____

_____

_____

_____

Lenten Puzzle

Show what you know about Lent. Fill in the missing words in the article on the right. Then complete the crossword puzzle.

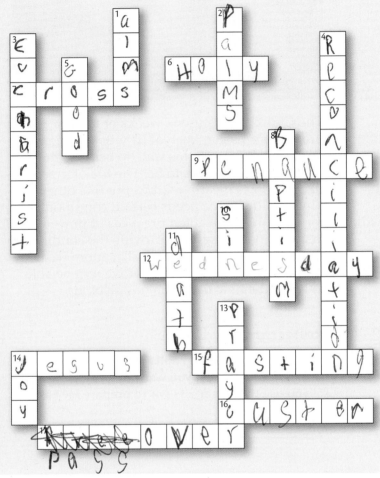

Lent begins on Ash _____. On this
(12 across)
day, the priest or other minister makes the
sign of the _____ on the forehead
(7 across)
with ashes made from burning blessed
_____. The words of the minister
(2 down)
and the ashes remind us that Lent is a time
of _____. Lenten practices help us
(9 across)
live the life we receive at _____. We
(8 down)
open our hearts to God's love by the Lenten
practices of _____, _____,
(13 down)   (15 across)
and giving _____ to those in need.
(1 down)
We think about how _____ was
(14 across)
willing to sacrifice his life for us, and
we celebrate his _____ and
(11 down)
Resurrection. We participate in his Paschal
Mystery by turning from _____
(10 down)
and by celebrating the Sacrament of
_____. The last Sunday of Lent
(4 down)
begins _____ Week. It is a
(6 across)
week when everyone who loves Jesus
tries to participate in the liturgies.
The Holy Thursday liturgy celebrates
Christ's gift of the priesthood and the
Holy _____. No Mass is celebrated
(3 down)
on _____ Friday. During the liturgy
(5 down)
of that day, the passion is read, and we ask
God that the sufferings of Jesus may free
all people from sin. During the solemn
_____ Vigil, we remember that most
(16 across)
holy night when our Lord Jesus Christ passes
from death to life. We celebrate our own
_____ from sin and praise God for
(17 across)
sending us Jesus. Celebrating Lent prepares
us for true Easter _____.
(14 down)

184 Lent

5 | Holy Week

Life Through Death

A mystery is something that we experience but do not fully understand. One mystery is so important to Christians that we spend special days renewing and celebrating it. That mystery is the death and Resurrection of Jesus. Each year we set aside several days—Holy Thursday, Good Friday, and Holy Saturday—to recall Jesus' suffering, death, and Resurrection.

These three days are called the Easter Triduum (also called the Paschal Triduum). These days are the high point of the Church year because our faith is rooted in the mystery of Jesus' death and Resurrection. We call this a mystery because we do not fully understand how death can bring new life. We do not fully understand how pain can lead to joy. Yet we believe this to be the very center of our faith.

We call the mystery of Jesus' suffering, death, and Resurrection the Paschal Mystery. We enter into this mystery through Baptism. By water and the Spirit, marked by the Sign of the Cross, we die to sin and are raised to new life in Christ. We become part of the whole Christian family, the Body of Christ. When people look at how we turn away from sin and live in Christ, they should see the death and rising of Jesus in our lives.

The Easter Triduum

Holy Thursday

Lent ends at sunset on Holy Thursday. The Easter Triduum begins with the Evening Mass of the Lord's Supper. At that Mass, we recall that Jesus Christ gives himself to us in the Eucharist. We also remember that Jesus served others, which is recalled in the story of Jesus washing the feet of his disciples, found in John 13:1–15.

During the Easter Triduum, many symbols remind us of dying and rising. Wheat must be ground and purified to become bread. Grapes must be crushed to become wine. The symbolic washing of feet reminds us that we must "die" to our own needs in order to serve the needs of others.

Good Friday

On Good Friday, we recall the passion and death of Jesus, knowing at all times that he freely gave his life for us. Each year, on this day, we hear the story of Jesus' passion from John 18:1—19:42. Because of the Resurrection,

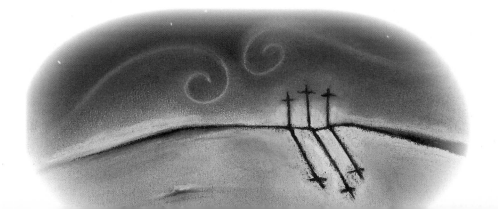

we are able to see the cross—the instrument of Jesus' death—as a sign of victory. Selfless love and forgiveness triumph over hatred. Through Jesus' death and Resurrection, the Church is born, and the hopes of all the ages are fulfilled.

The cross was originally a sign of defeat and shame. But Jesus turned it into a sign of victory and hope. Good Friday invites us to die with Christ to all that is not life-giving in our hearts. It is a time to appreciate the tremendous love Jesus has for us.

Celebrating Reconciliation

The Easter Triduum is a celebration of life, of dying and rising. It is the celebration of our passing from the death of sin to new life in Jesus. It is a sign that not even death can separate us from the life of Christ. It is a reminder that God the Father loves us so much that he gave his only Son so that we may find our way home to him.

Complete the acrostic below.

Holy Saturday

Holy Saturday begins as a quiet day of waiting as we prepare to celebrate the Resurrection. On this night, we celebrate the Easter Vigil, the high point of the Easter Triduum. We wait in vigil to celebrate the glory of Jesus' Resurrection—his triumph over death. We use symbols of fire, water, and oil to represent the light of Christ, new life in Baptism, and the presence of the Holy Spirit.

R	We recall Christ's passion and death on Good _____.	F R I d a y
E	Jesus freely gave his _____ for us.	l i f E
S	_____ is the sacrament of our dying and rising.	B a b t i S m
U	The Easter Triduum begins with the Evening Mass of the Lord's Supper on Holy _____.	T h U r S d a y
R	The Paschal _____ is the passion, death, and Resurrection of Jesus.	m y S t e R y
R	The Easter _____ is lit at the beginning of the Easter Vigil service.	f i R e
E	The high point of the Church year is the _____ Triduum.	E a s t e r
C	The paschal _____ is the symbol of Christ our Light.	C a n d l e
T	_____ means "three days."	T i r d v u m
I	_____ is the evening before a great feast.	v I g i l
O	The _____ is our sign of victory.	C r O s s
N	The Easter Triduum is a celebration of dying and _____.	r i s i N g

6 | Easter

Easter Vigil

Our celebration of Easter begins at the Easter Vigil. The Easter Vigil service begins after sundown on Holy Saturday, starting with the lighting and blessing of the new Easter fire. The large paschal candle, the symbol of Christ our Light, is lit from this fire. Each person lights a taper candle from this new light and new fire. The baptismal waters, sign of our birth and life in Christ, are blessed. The readings during the liturgy are about salvation history and the saving acts of God. The Resurrection of Christ is proclaimed. Our new life in him is also proclaimed, as we celebrate and receive Jesus in the Eucharist.

The Easter Vigil is a special time  for the elect, the former catechumens who have been preparing for Baptism. On this night, they will be baptized, confirmed, and share in the Eucharist for the first time. They will become members of the community of believers. Throughout the Easter season, all Catholics share the joy of the newly baptized and renew the promises of their own Baptisms.

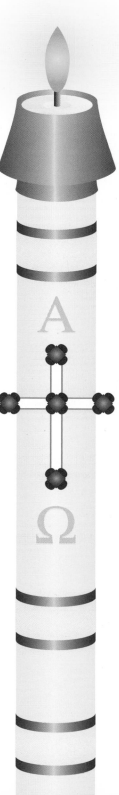

Easter Sunday

On Easter Sunday, we gather at church to sing our Easter praise to God. Our prayer for this day, and for the next 50 days, is filled with exclamations of "Alleluia!" Many people wear their finest clothes for Easter Sunday, which recalls the new white garment given at their Baptisms.

The Easter Season

Easter is so important that we celebrate it for 50 days. We remember the ways in which Jesus appeared to his disciples after his Resurrection. On the 40th day of the Easter season (or on the seventh Sunday of Easter), we celebrate the feast of the Ascension, when Jesus was taken up to be with God in heaven. We remember that Jesus promised to be with us always. The season of Easter concludes with the feast of Pentecost, when the Holy Spirit filled the apostles.

Symbols of Life

Read the explanations for each Easter symbol. Add your own thoughts about each explanation or drawings that represent each. At the bottom of the page, design your own symbol of life and write an explanation of it.

Water

Water can be deadly. Human beings cannot breathe underwater. At the same time, without water, we could not survive. Plants need it, animals need it, and we need it. Through the waters of Baptism, we die to sin and rise to new life.

Easter Lily

Jesus taught that his dying and rising is like the seed that dies to give a plant new life. The flowers and plants of springtime remind us of this, the Paschal Mystery. The beauty of the Easter lily represents the glorified new life of Jesus and the new life he promised to us.

Candles, Fire, Light

The Easter Vigil begins with the lighting and blessing of the Easter fire. Light and fire are powerful symbols that remind us that Christ is our Light. The paschal candle is lowered into the water three times in blessing during the Easter Vigil service. The paschal candle remains in the sanctuary at Church throughout the Easter season.

Lamb

John the Baptist called Jesus the Lamb of God. When God freed the Israelites from slavery in Egypt, he told them to sacrifice an unblemished lamb and to mark their homes with its blood. By doing this, they were saved. By dying for us, Jesus is our sacrificial lamb, saving us from sin and death.

Your Symbol of Life

_____

_____

_____

_____

7 | Pentecost

The Spirit Forms the People of God

God began shaping a people thousands of years ago. With the coming of Jesus, God fulfilled the promise he had made to the Chosen People that he would send a Savior. On Pentecost, the spirit of God came to the disciples of Jesus and filled them with his gifts, helping them to form the Church, the new people of God.

Jesus promised that God would send the Spirit to help the disciples. At the Last Supper, Jesus said, "[H]e will teach you everything and remind you of all that [I] told you." (John 14:26) Forty days after Jesus rose from the dead, he returned to the Father. As he was taken to heaven, Jesus again promised his followers the gift of the Spirit.

At Jesus' directions, his followers prayed and waited in Jerusalem. Nine days after the Ascension, a noise like a strong, driving wind filled the house

where they were. They saw what looked like tongues of fire resting on each one of them. They were given the courage to spread the Word of God. They began to speak in different languages.

Because it was the Jewish feast of Pentecost, a harvest feast, people from all nations were gathered in Jerusalem. When the disciples came out and proclaimed the Good News, everyone heard them in their own language. In the story of the Tower of Babel (Genesis 11:1–9), sin had caused people to speak many languages, so they were divided. Now in Jerusalem, the Spirit used the gift of languages to unite people in the knowledge of God's love.

❮ El Greco, *The Pentecost.*

Symbols of the Holy Spirit

In the Old Testament, God's presence is often associated with fire. God first spoke to Moses in the form of a burning bush (Exodus 3). Later, God guided the Chosen People to the Promised Land as a column of fire at night (Exodus 13:21). At Pentecost, God again used the symbol of fire as he gifted us with his loving presence in the Holy Spirit.

God is also often associated with wind or breath. Read the following Scripture verses and identify whether God is associated with wind or breath:

Passage	Wind	Breath
Genesis 1:1–2	●	○
Genesis 2:7	○	○
Exodus 14:21–22	○	○
1 Kings 19:12–13	○	○
Psalm 33:6	○	○
John 20:21–23	○	○

The Holy Spirit in the Early Christian Church

Read the following passages from the Acts of the Apostles. Describe how the Holy Spirit was working in the early Christian Church.

Acts 2:4,11: _____
_____
_____
_____

Acts 2:14: _____
_____
_____
_____

Masolino da Panicale, *St. Peter Preaching to the Multitudes.* ❯

Acts 2:41: _____
_____
_____
_____

Acts 2:43: _____
_____
_____
_____

Acts 2:44–45: _____
_____
_____
_____

Feast Day—December 12
8 | Our Lady of Guadalupe

A Beautiful Lady

Juan Diego

Juan Diego was an Aztec in Mexico and a convert to the Catholic faith. On Saturday, December 9, 1531, he was walking to church for Mass when a beautiful lady appeared to him, surrounded by light. She told him she was the Immaculate Virgin Mary, the Mother of the true God. She wanted to have a shrine built at Tepeyac Hill so that she could show her love for the people. She said,

> "Ask for my help. Here I will listen to people's prayers, and I will help them."

Mary then asked Juan to tell the bishop her wishes. Juan did so, but the bishop didn't believe him. Juan returned to the lady and suggested she send to the bishop someone who spoke better. But Mary told Juan she had chosen him for this work, and she would bless him for helping her.

The second time Juan visited the bishop, the bishop told him to ask "his Lady" for a sign that proved she was the Mother of God. When Juan did so, Mary told him to return on Monday for the sign.

Her Miraculous Image

In the meantime, Juan's uncle became very ill, and Juan had to stay home to care for him. He was unable to return on Monday for Mary's sign. By Tuesday, his uncle was dying, so Juan set off to get a priest. On the way, he met the Holy Virgin. Embarrassed, he apologized for not meeting her. Mary replied,

> "Do not let anything bother you, and do not be afraid of any illness, pain, or accident. Am I, your mother, not here? Are you not under my shadow and protection? What more could you want? Don't worry about your uncle. He is well already."

Mary told Juan to go to the top of a hill and gather the flowers he would find growing there. Juan knew that nothing ever grew on that rock hill, let alone in the middle of winter. However, he did as the Virgin told him and climbed the hill. At the top, he found gorgeous roses. He picked them and brought them to Mary, who arranged the roses in his tilma. She told Juan to take them to the bishop.

When the bishop saw Juan, he wanted to know what he had in his tilma. Juan opened it, letting the fragrant roses fall in a shower to the floor. You can imagine the bishop's surprise at

Jose Guadalupe Posada, *Saint Juan Diego and the Virgin image.*

Our Lady Today

The picture of Our Lady of Guadalupe has meaningful symbols. Its main message is that Mary loves us and wants to help us. The cloak itself is made from the rough fibers of a cactus plant. If this type of material is painted on, it will not last more than 20 years. Yet the picture remains fresh and beautiful on the cloak after almost 500 years! It can be seen above the main altar in the Shrine of Our Lady of Guadalupe in Mexico.

seeing roses in winter. As he looked, however, the bishop saw an even greater miracle. There on Juan's tilma, a beautifully painted image began to appear. It was the Lady who had appeared to Juan!

The bishop cried out, "The Immaculate!" and knelt and with tears, asking the Blessed Mother's pardon for not believing Juan.

On that same day, Mary appeared to Juan's uncle and cured him. Uncle Bernadino went to the bishop and told how he had been cured. He also gave the bishop a message from the Virgin, saying that she would "crush the serpent's head." The bishop did not understand the Aztec language. He heard the Aztec words for "crush the serpent" which sounded like "Guadalupe," the name of Mary's shrine in Spain. Thinking that the Virgin wanted the new shrine to have the same name, the bishop called her Our Lady of Guadalupe.

︿ *Our Lady of Guadalupe*

The feast of Our Lady of Guadalupe is celebrated by the Church on December 12. Do you know why that date was chosen?

1. How can we dedicate—give ourselves wholeheartedly—to Mary?

2. What hidden and silent sacrifice can we perform?

3. How can we walk the way of complete faithfulness to Jesus and the Church?

❮ Outdoor altar of Guadalupe Basilica in Mexico City

9 | March: The Month of Saint Joseph

A Good Father

Joseph, the husband of Mary, was a descendant of King David. In the first chapter of Matthew, we learn that an angel came to Joseph in a dream. The angel told him to take Mary as his wife, for her child was of the Holy Spirit. The child, Jesus, would save the people from their sins. Joseph obeyed the angel and became Mary's husband. The marriage bond also made him the legal father of Jesus.

Though Scripture tells us very little about Joseph directly, we can learn much from what we read there. We recognize the virtues he practiced in the events of his life.

Saint Joseph probably died some time before Jesus began his public life of teaching. Imagine what a beautiful death he had, with Jesus and Mary at his side. This is why we honor Joseph as the patron of a happy death.

Just as Saint Joseph took care of the Holy Family, so he cares for the Church, the family of God. In 1870, Pope Pius IX named Joseph Patron and Protector of the Universal Church.

Because Saint Joseph sanctified labor by doing it for Jesus and Mary, Pope Pius XII proclaimed him Patron of Workers. May 1 is celebrated as the feast of Saint Joseph the Worker, to emphasize the dignity of the worker and the value of honest work.

Saint Joseph is willing to help us in any way he can. All we have to do is ask. During March, we honor Saint Joseph in a special way. We can show our love for him especially by praying to him and by imitating his holy life. He is honored as the Guardian of the Holy Family, next in holiness and dignity to Mary. He is honored on March 19, and the whole month of March is dedicated to him.

Faith Joseph accepted God's Word to take Mary as his wife. (Matthew 1:18–25)

Obedience to Civil Law He went to Bethlehem to register for the census. (Luke 2:1–5)

Obedience to Religious Law He and Mary took Jesus to the Temple 40 days after his birth to present him to God and to offer sacrifice. (Luke 2:22–24)

Obedience to God's Word He took Mary and Jesus on a hurried journey to Egypt in the middle of the night to save Jesus' life. (Matthew 2:13–15)

Faithfulness to Duty He worked hard as a carpenter to support Jesus and Mary. (Matthew 13:55)

Love He provided love, comfort, and security for his family at Nazareth. (Luke 2:39–40)

Trust He trusted in God in all the events of his life. (Matthew 2:19–21)

10 | May: The Month of Mary

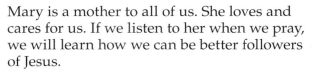

We honor Mary with many titles, such as Queen of the Universe, Star of the Sea, Seat of Wisdom, and Mother of the Church. However, the greatest title of all is Mother of God. Mary is truly the Mother of God, for she gave birth to Jesus, the Son of God.

We honor Mary in many ways, such as praying the Rosary, celebrating her feast days, and placing a wreath of flowers on a Mary statue at a May crowning. Through these prayers, devotions, and celebrations, we thank Mary for giving us Jesus our Savior, and we ask her to help us follow her Son faithfully.

Mary is a mother to all of us. She loves and cares for us. If we listen to her when we pray, we will learn how we can be better followers of Jesus.

One title of Mary is Mother of Perpetual Help. She has this title because she is always interceding for us, asking her Son to help us follow him more closely. Mary will always help us when we call on her.

Pictures of Our Lady have different titles. The picture on this page is called Mother of Perpetual Help. Whenever we look at it, we can pray,

The Memorare

Remember, most loving Virgin Mary,
never was it heard
that anyone who turned to you for help
    was left unaided.
Inspired by this confidence,
though burdened by my sins,
I run to your protection
for you are my mother.
Mother of the Word of God,
do not despise my words of pleading
but be merciful and hear my prayer.
Amen.

11 | Jonah: A Fish Story

Read in your Bible the Book of Jonah. Then complete this summary.

The Lord called Jonah to preach to the people of the city of _____ , who were a traditional enemy of the people of Israel.

Frightened, Jonah boarded a ship and sailed in another direction. The Lord hurled a violent _____ upon the sea. First, the sailors began to pray to their own gods. Then they _____ the cargo overboard in the hopes of lightening the ship. Finally, the sailors cast _____ to find out whose fault the storm was. They discovered that Jonah was to blame, for he was fleeing from his God.

Jonah said, "Throw me into the _____ . I know that it is because of me that this storm has come upon you." The men did as he said and then prayed to Jonah's God. The storm stopped.

The Lord sent a large _____ that _____ Jonah. From the belly of the fish, Jonah said a psalm of _____ . _____ days later, he was spewed out on the shore.

Jonah then went to Nineveh as God had directed. He predicted that the city would be destroyed in _____ days for its wickedness.

As a result, all the people fasted and did penance. Even the _____ covered himself in sackcloth and ashes. He also proclaimed that all the people of Nineveh must

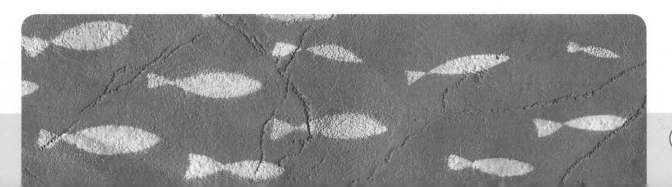

repent. When God saw that they had turned from their _____ ways, he did not punish them.

Jonah, however, was disappointed that God did not destroy the city. He complained to God and then sat outside the city to watch what would happen.

God had a _____ grow up over Jonah's head to shade him. The next morning a _____ killed it and Jonah suffered from the heat. He asked for death, saying "I would be better off dead than _____."

God said, "You are concerned about a plant, which you did not work for. Should I not be concerned over 120,000 persons who can't tell their right hand from their left, not to mention the many _____?"

List the lessons that God taught Jonah in this story. Then tell how those lessons apply to us today.

_____

_____

_____

_____

_____

This prayer is in many ways similar to the prayer that Jonah said while he was in the belly of the fish. It is a good prayer to remember when you feel yourself turning away from God.

Psalm 130

I

Out of the depths I call to you, LORD;
   Lord, hear my cry!
May your ears be attentive
   to my cry for mercy.
If you, LORD, mark our sins,
   Lord, who can stand?
But with you is forgiveness
   and so you are revered.

II

I wait with longing for the LORD,
   my soul waits for his word.
My soul looks for the Lord
   more than sentinels for daybreak.
More than sentinels for daybreak,
   let Israel look for the LORD,
For with the LORD is kindness,
   with him is full redemption,
And God will redeem Israel
   from all their sins.

Annie Lykes Lucas, *Jonah and the Whale*; 1985-1988. ❯

12 | Judith: A Brave Woman

The Book of Judith tells the story of a very brave woman. Imagine that the following letters are from Judith's maid Anna to her friend Sarah. The letters tell Judith's story.

Dear Sarah,

I have just begun a new job as maid to the widow Judith. Ever since her husband died three years ago, Judith, who is a very beautiful woman, has lived a life of prayer and fasting. Everyone respects her for her goodness and wisdom. I think my life will be pretty uneventful from now on.

How are things at home?

Your friend,
Anna

Dear Sarah,

Things here are very tense. Everyone here in Bethulia is preparing for an attack. We hear that Nebuchadnezzar, king of Assyria, plans to conquer the world with his armies. His general, Holofernes, has captured city after city. He is forcing all people to worship his king as a god. We are all fasting and praying to God in the hopes that he will help defend us from these invaders.

I hope things are well with you.

Yours under God,
Anna

Dear Sarah,

Holofernes has reached us. His men have seized our water sources. We have been without water for several days. People are fainting in the streets. Some are begging our leaders to surrender. Uzziah declared that if God doesn't help us within five days, we will surrender.

Please ask your family to pray for us. I hope to see you someday soon!

Yours in hope,
Anna

Dear Sarah,

You will never believe this! My lady Judith actually scolded Uzziah for putting time limits on God. Then she said to our leaders, "Let me pass through the gate tonight with my maid. The Lord will rescue Israel by my hand." The rulers agreed. Judith prayed for a long time. Then she dressed in beautiful garments and jewelry and packed some food. She and I will now walk out of the city toward the Assyrians. I intend to hand this letter to someone at the gate, in the hopes that it will reach you. This might be the last time you hear from me. If so, thank you for always being such a good friend.

Anna

Dear Sarah,

You will never believe what has happened! What an amazing woman Judith is! As soon as we left Bethulia, the Assyrians arrested us. Judith explained that we were fleeing from the town because we knew it was going to be destroyed. She offered to show Holofernes a route to capture the city easily.

The soldiers were obviously impressed by Judith's beauty. They took us straight to Holofernes. Judith told him that the Israelites were to die because they had sinned against God. We stayed in the camp for three days. Each night we went out to pray. On the fourth night, Holofernes asked Judith to dine with him. I could tell he was attracted to Judith.

At that meal, Holofernes drank so much that he lay on his bed in a stupor. Judith took his sword, grasped his hair, and cut off his head! She gave it to me to carry in our food pouch. Then we went out, pretending that we were going to pray, as we usually did. Instead, we returned to Bethulia. The town rejoiced, praising God and Judith.

Thank you for your last letter and all of your prayers. See how God has listened to his people!

Rejoicing in God,
Anna

Dear Sarah,

It is the day after our safe return. This morning our men acted as though they were going to attack. The Assyrians ran to awake Holofernes and found his headless body. Because of their confusion, we overwhelmed them. Judith led everyone in a song of thanksgiving to God.

And I thought my life was going to be uneventful!

Your friend,
Anna

13 | Job: A Man of Suffering

The Book of Job makes us think about the mystery of suffering. Read this play about Job's story.

Cast

Narrator	God
Job	Satan
Job's Wife	Young Man
Herdsman	Friend 1
Shepherd	Friend 2
Camel Keeper	Friend 3
Servant	

Narrator: Job was a good man. He owned more livestock than any other man in the East. He was very wealthy, and he used his money to help those who were poor and suffering. He was happy in his family life, with seven sons and three daughters. He followed God's Law faithfully. One day Satan and God had a conversation about Job.

God: Where have you come from?

Satan: From roaming the earth.

God: Have you noticed my servant Job? There is no one as good as he is on earth.

Satan: No wonder Job respects you. You have protected him and his family. You have made him wealthy. Take these things away and he will turn from you.

God: Alright, let us see. I put all that he has in your power.

Narrator: Suddenly, Job's luck turned.

Herdsman: (to Job) Your oxen and donkeys were grazing and the Sabeans carried them off and killed your herdsmen. I alone escaped to tell you.

Shepherd: Lightning struck and killed your sheep and their shepherds. I barely escaped with my life!

Camel Keeper: The Chaldeans seized your camels and killed their keepers. I am the only one who escaped.

Servant: Your sons and daughters were eating and drinking at the house of your oldest son. A great wind shook the house and it collapsed, killing all the young people. I don't know how I survived.

Job: (wailing and falling to the ground) Naked I came forth from my mother's womb, and naked shall I go back again. The Lord gave and the Lord has taken away; blessed be the name of the Lord.

Narrator: God and Satan discussed what happened.

God: Have you noticed Job is still good and God-fearing, although evil fell on him without cause?

Satan: Threaten his life and he will surely turn against you.

God: You believe so? He is in your power.

Narrator: Things became even worse for Job. He became covered with boils from head to toe.

Job's Wife: Why don't you just curse God and die?

Job: We accept good things from God. Should we not accept evil?

Narrator: Three friends of Job heard of his suffering and came to comfort him.

Job: Why was I born?

Friend 1: You must have done something wrong to deserve this.

Job: God, why are you attacking me?

Friend 2: Pray. God might help you.

Job: I will complain to God.

Friend 3: Confess your sin to the Lord.

Job: What are my sins?

Young Man: Job, God is just. We should not challenge him.

God: Job, face your suffering like a man. I will question you, and you tell me the answers. Where were you when I founded the earth? Who determined its size? And who shut within doors the sea and said, "Thus far shall you come but no farther?" Have you ever commanded the morning? Have you entered the storehouse of the snow? Do you give the horse his strength? Let you who argues with me answer.

Job: I have dealt with great things I do not understand. I take back what I said and repent.

Narrator: The Lord gave to Job twice as much as he had before. He again had seven sons and three daughters, and he lived to be 140. Suffering remains a mystery, but we trust Divine Providence to direct everything for good.

James Jacques Joseph Tissot,
Job Joins His Family in Happiness, c. 1896-1902 ❯

Esther
Queen of Courage and Faith

Ahasuerus, king of Persia, gave a six-month feast to display his country's riches. All went well until the seventh day. A banquet was held at the capital city, Susa.

Esther   Ahasuerus   Mordecai   Haman

Tell Queen Vashti to join us, so everyone can see her beauty.

The servant returns.

My Lord, the queen will not come.

How dare she refuse!

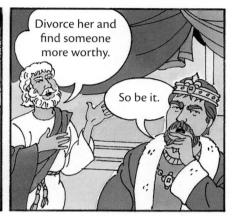

Divorce her and find someone more worthy.

So be it.

Hear ye. Hear ye. Vashti is no longer queen. Let all young women be brought to the palace. She who most pleases the king will be queen.

Mordecai, a Jewish man in Susa, had adopted his cousin Esther. Like the other young women, she had to go before the king. Mordecai warned her not to reveal that she was Jewish.

I choose Esther for my wife. She is beautiful and I love her more than all the others.

Not long after . . .

Haman, for your loyalty I make you the highest official in the land.

Good. Everyone must bow to me.

Every day that Jew Mordecai refuses to bow to you.

I bow to God alone.

Your majesty, there is a people who do not obey your laws. We must destroy them.

Do as you please. Here is my official seal.

Hear ye. Hear ye. The king orders all Jews put to the sword on the fourteenth day of the twelfth month, Adar.

Your Highness, Mordecai is in sackcloth and ashes, and he is crying loudly.

Find out why.

What's wrong?

Haman convinced the king that all Jews are dangerous. We are to be killed. Tell Esther to plead with the king for us.

How can I do that? Anyone who tries to see the king without being summoned is killed, unless the king extends his scepter. Tell Mordecai that.

Mordecai says that you will be killed with the rest. He believes that you are queen just for this crisis.

Tell Mordecai to have the Jews fast for three days. Then I will go to the king.

Esther and the Jews prayed and fasted. Then Esther put on her most beautiful robes and went to the king. The king looked angrily at Esther. But when she started to faint, the king took pity on her.

What is it, Esther? You can have anything you want, up to half my kingdom.

I want to invite you and Haman to a banquet.

At Haman's house.

The queen invites me to dinner, but Mordecai spoils my joy. He still refuses to bow to me.

Why not build a gallows 75 feet high and have him hanged?

Good idea.

That night the king couldn't sleep. He went over some old records.

Look at this. A man named Mordecai once saved my life, and I never rewarded him.

The next morning . . .

Haman, what should be done for a man the king wishes to reward?

He must mean me.

He should wear the king's robe and crown and ride the king's horse. The noblest officials should clothe him and go before him crying his praise.

You are my noblest official. Do this for the Jew Mordecai.

As you wish.

At Esther's banquet . . .

What would you like me to do for you, Esther?

Please save my life and the lives of my people.

What do you mean?

Haman has threatened us.

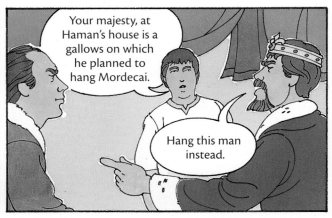

Your majesty, at Haman's house is a gallows on which he planned to hang Mordecai.

Hang this man instead.

Esther, I give you Haman's house.

I will give it to Mordecai. He is my cousin, who adopted me when I was young.

I will give Mordecai my seal. You and he can write whatever you see fit concerning the Jews.

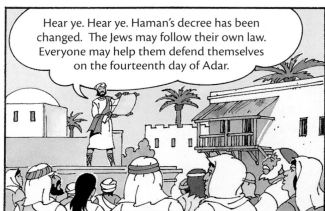

Hear ye. Hear ye. Haman's decree has been changed. The Jews may follow their own law. Everyone may help them defend themselves on the fourteenth day of Adar.

That day has been celebrated ever since. It is the feast of Purim.

What Catholics Should Know

(continued next page)

(continued from previous page)

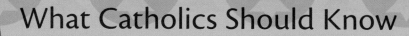

Prayer and How We Pray

God is always with us. He wants us to talk to him and listen to him. In prayer we raise our hearts and minds to God. We are able to speak and listen to God because through the Holy Spirit, God teaches us how to pray.

What Is Prayer?

Being a Christian requires that we believe all that God has revealed to us, that we celebrate it in the liturgy and the sacraments, and that we live what we believe. All this depends on a vital and personal relationship with the living and true God. This relationship is rooted in prayer. Prayer is a gift from God. We can pray because God seeks us out first and calls us to meet him. We become aware of our thirst for God because God thirsts for us. Prayer arises from our heart, beyond the grasp of reason. Only the Spirit of God can understand the human heart and know it fully. Prayer is the habit of being with God—Father, Son and Holy Spirit. This communion with God is always possible because through our Baptism we are united with Christ. By being united with Christ, we are united with others. Christian prayer is communion with Christ that branches out to all the members of his body, the Church.

The Five Basic Forms of Christian Prayer

The Holy Spirit, who teaches us to pray, leads us to pray in a number of ways. This conversation with God can take the form of blessing, petition, intercession, thanksgiving, or praise.

Blessing

To bless someone is to acknowledge the goodness of that person. The prayer of blessing or adoration is our response to God's goodness because of all the gifts he has given us. In the prayer of blessing, God's gifts and our acceptance of them come together. Because God blesses the human heart, the human heart can in return bless him, who is the source of every blessing.

Petition

Petition is much more than asking God for things we want or need. By prayers of petition we express our relationship with God as our Creator. We depend on him, and we ask him for something for ourselves. Sometimes we sin and turn away from God. The first step in the prayer of petition is turning back toward him and asking for forgiveness. We can then ask God for what we need, confident that he knows what we need before we ask.

Intercession

In prayers of intercession we ask something on behalf of another. As a prayer form, intercession is a prayer of petition that leads us to pray as Jesus did. Throughout his life on earth, Jesus interceded with the Father on behalf of all people. To pray in this way means that our hearts are turned outward, focused on the needs around us.

Thanksgiving

Thanksgiving is characteristic of Christian prayer, especially in the Eucharist. The word *Eucharist* means "thanksgiving." Through his death and Resurrection, Christ has reconciled us to God. His sacrifice is made present in every Eucharist. Every joy we experience, as well as our every need, can become an offering of thanksgiving in the Eucharist. In celebrating the Eucharist, the Church reveals itself as and becomes more fully a people of thanksgiving.

Praise

Praise is the form of prayer that recognizes that God is God and gives him glory. Praise goes beyond thanking God for what he has done for us. Praise gives him glory simply because he is. Praise embraces the other forms of prayer and carries them to God, who is the source of all that is.

We Meditate and Contemplate

One way to pray is to meditate. To meditate is to think about God. We try to keep our attention and focus on God. In meditation we may use Scripture, prayer books, or icons to help us concentrate and spark our imagination. Another way to pray is to contemplate. This means that we rest quietly in God's presence.

We Get Ready to Pray

We live in a busy, noisy, and fast-paced world. Because of this, we have difficulty concentrating. In order to meditate or reflect, we need to prepare ourselves.

We can get ready for meditation by resting our bodies in a comfortable position, sitting with our backs straight and both feet on the floor. We can close our eyes, fold our hands in front of us, take a deep breath, and then slowly let it out. We can establish a rhythm by slowly counting to three while breathing in and slowly counting to three while breathing out. Concentrating on our breathing helps us quiet our thoughts.

We Avoid Distractions

If we become distracted by thinking about something, such as the day at school or a sporting event, we can go back to thinking about our breathing. After a little practice, we will be able to avoid distractions, pray with our imagination, and spend time with God or Jesus in our hearts.

An Ancient Language of Prayer

From the beginning of the Church until the Second Vatican Council in the 1960s, the Church in the West used Latin as its common language. The Latin language was used in prayer, worship, documents, administration and all areas of Church life. We have a rich and long tradition of hymns and prayers in Latin.

Even today there are parts of the Mass such as the Holy, Holy, Holy (*Sanctus*) and the Lamb of God (*Agnus Dei*) that are occasionally sung in Latin. Benedict XVI, when he was pope, identified four prayers that are shared by the Church. If learned in Latin, they can be prayed as a sign of the universal nature of the Church.

Signum Crucis (Sign of the Cross)

In nomine Patris,
et Filii,
et Spiritus Sancti.
Amen.

Gloria Patri* (Glory Be to the Father)

Gloria Patri,
et Filio,
et Spiritui Sancto.
Sicut erat in principio,
et nunc, et semper,
et in saecula saeculorum.
Amen.

Pater Noster* (Our Father)

Pater noster, qui es in caelis,
sanctificetur nomen tuum.
Adveniat regnum tuum.
Fiat voluntas tua,
sicut in caelo et in terra.
Panem nostrum quotidianum da nobis hodie,
et dimitte nobis debita nostra
sicut et nos dimittimus debitoribus nostris.
Et ne nos inducas in tentationem,
sed libera nos a malo.
Amen.

Ave Maria* (Hail Mary)

Ave Maria, gratia plena,
Dominus tecum.
Benedicta tu in mulieribus,
et benedictus fructus ventris tui, Iesus.
Sancta Maria, Mater Dei, ora pro nobis
    peccatoribus,
nunc, et in hora mortis nostrae.
Amen.

Agnus Dei (Lamb of God)

Agnus Dei, qui tollis peccáta mundi: miserére nobis. (Lamb of God, you take away the sins of the world: have mercy on us.)

Agnus Dei, qui tollis peccáta mundi: miserére nobis. (Lamb of God, you take away the sins of the world: have mercy on us.)

Agnus Dei, qui tollis peccáta mundi: dona nobis pacem. (Lamb of God, you take away the sins of the world: Grant us peace.)

Sanctus (Holy, Holy, Holy)

Sanctus, sanctus, sanctus, Dominus Deus sabaoth. (Holy, holy, holy Lord, God of hosts.)

Pleni sunt caeli et terra Gloria tua. (Heaven and earth are full of your glory.)

Hosanna in excelsis. (Hosanna in the highest.)

Benedictus qui venit in nomine Domini. (Blessed is he who comes in the name of the Lord.)
Hosanna in excelsis. (Hosanna in the highest.)

*The English versions of these prayers are found on the inside front cover of this book.

The Rosary

The Rosary helps us pray to Jesus through Mary. When we pray the Rosary, we think about the special events, or mysteries, in the lives of Jesus and Mary.

The Rosary is made up of a string of beads and a crucifix. We hold the crucifix in our hands as we pray the Sign of the Cross. Then we pray the Apostles' Creed. Next to the crucifix, there is a single bead, followed by a set of three beads and another single bead. We pray the Lord's Prayer as we hold the first single bead and a Hail Mary at each bead in the set of three that follows. Then we pray the Glory Be to the Father. On the next single bead we think about the first mystery and pray the Lord's Prayer.

There are five sets of 10 beads; each set is called a decade. We pray a Hail Mary on each bead of a decade as we reflect on a particular mystery in the lives of Jesus and Mary. The Glory Be to the Father is prayed at the end of each set. Between sets is a single bead on which we think about one of the mysteries and pray the Lord's Prayer.

In his apostolic letter *Rosary of the Virgin Mary,* Pope John Paul II wrote that the Rosary could take on a variety of legitimate forms as it adapts to different spiritual traditions and different Christian communities. "What is really important," he said, "is that the Rosary should always be seen and experienced as a path of contemplation." It is traditional in some places to pray the Hail, Holy Queen after the last decade.

We end by holding the crucifix in our hands as we pray the Sign of the Cross.

Hail, Holy Queen

Hail, holy Queen, Mother of mercy,
our life, our sweetness, and our hope.
To you we cry, the children of Eve;
to you we send up our sighs,
mourning and weeping in this land of exile.
Turn, then, most gracious advocate,
your eyes of mercy toward us;
lead us home at last
and show us the blessed fruit of your
    womb, Jesus:
O clement, O loving, O sweet Virgin Mary.

PRAYING THE ROSARY

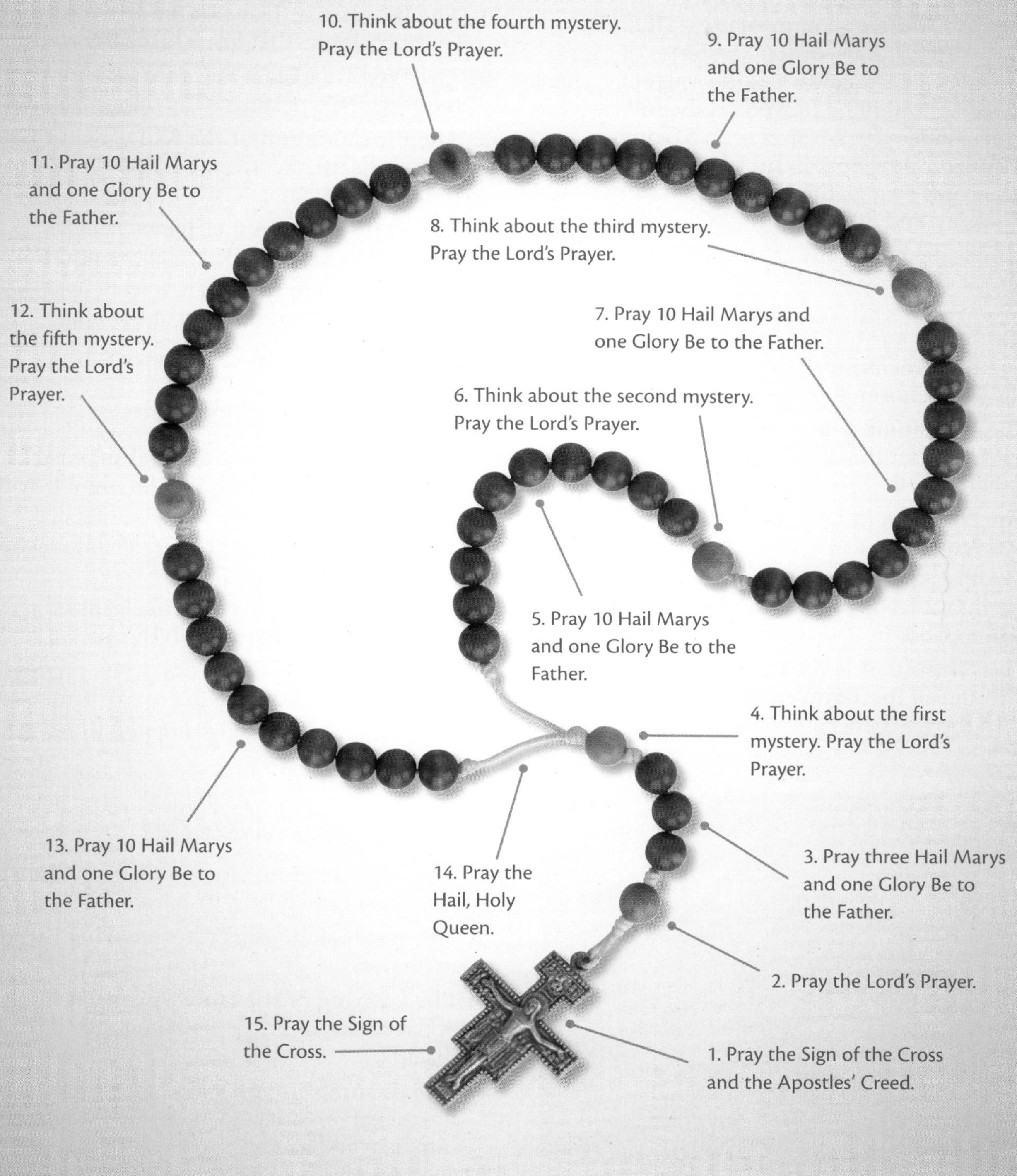

10. Think about the fourth mystery. Pray the Lord's Prayer.

9. Pray 10 Hail Marys and one Glory Be to the Father.

11. Pray 10 Hail Marys and one Glory Be to the Father.

8. Think about the third mystery. Pray the Lord's Prayer.

12. Think about the fifth mystery. Pray the Lord's Prayer.

7. Pray 10 Hail Marys and one Glory Be to the Father.

6. Think about the second mystery. Pray the Lord's Prayer.

5. Pray 10 Hail Marys and one Glory Be to the Father.

4. Think about the first mystery. Pray the Lord's Prayer.

13. Pray 10 Hail Marys and one Glory Be to the Father.

14. Pray the Hail, Holy Queen.

3. Pray three Hail Marys and one Glory Be to the Father.

2. Pray the Lord's Prayer.

15. Pray the Sign of the Cross.

1. Pray the Sign of the Cross and the Apostles' Creed.

Mysteries of the Rosary

The Church had three sets of mysteries for many centuries. In 2002 Pope John Paul II proposed a fourth set of mysteries—the Luminous Mysteries, or the Mysteries of Light. According to his suggestion, the four sets of mysteries might be prayed on the following days: the Joyful Mysteries on Monday and Saturday, the Sorrowful Mysteries on Tuesday and Friday, the Glorious Mysteries on Wednesday and Sunday, and the Luminous Mysteries on Thursday.

The Joyful Mysteries

1. **The Annunciation.** Mary learns that she has been chosen to be the mother of Jesus.
2. **The Visitation.** Mary visits Elizabeth, who tells her that she will always be remembered.
3. **The Nativity.** Jesus is born in a stable in Bethlehem.
4. **The Presentation.** Mary and Joseph take the infant Jesus to the Temple to present him to God.
5. **The Finding of Jesus in the Temple.** Jesus is found in the Temple, discussing his faith with the teachers.

The Luminous Mysteries

1. **The Baptism of Jesus in the River Jordan.** God proclaims that Jesus is his beloved Son.
2. **The Wedding Feast at Cana.** At Mary's request, Jesus performs his first miracle.
3. **The Proclamation of the Kingdom of God.** Jesus calls all to conversion and service to the kingdom.
4. **The Transfiguration of Jesus.** Jesus is revealed in glory to Peter, James, and John.
5. **The Institution of the Eucharist.** Jesus offers his Body and Blood at the Last Supper.

The Sorrowful Mysteries

1. **The Agony in the Garden.** Jesus prays in the garden of Gethsemane the night before he dies.
2. **The Scourging at the Pillar.** Jesus is lashed with whips.
3. **The Crowning with Thorns.** Jesus is mocked and crowned with thorns.
4. **The Carrying of the Cross.** Jesus carries the cross that will be used to crucify him.
5. **The Crucifixion.** Jesus is nailed to the cross and dies.

The Glorious Mysteries

1. **The Resurrection.** God the Father raises Jesus from the dead.
2. **The Ascension.** Jesus returns to his Father in heaven.
3. **The Coming of the Holy Spirit.** The Holy Spirit comes to bring new life to the disciples.
4. **The Assumption of Mary.** At the end of her life on earth, Mary is taken body and soul into heaven.
5. **The Coronation of Mary.** Mary is crowned as queen of heaven and earth.

Stations of the Cross

The 14 Stations of the Cross represent events from Jesus' passion and death. Even before the Gospels were written down, the followers of Jesus told the story of his passion, death, and Resurrection. When people went on pilgrimage to Jerusalem, they were anxious to see the sites where Jesus lived and died. Eventually, following in the footsteps of the Lord on the way to his death became an important part of the pilgrimage.

The stations, as we know them today, came about when it was no longer easy or even possible to visit the holy sites in Palestine. In the 1500s, villages all over Europe started creating replicas of the way of the cross, with small shrines commemorating the places along the route in Jerusalem. Eventually, these shrines became the set of 14 stations we now know.

The important point to remember about the stations is that they are a prayer. They are not an exercise in remembering events from the past. They are an invitation to make present the final hours of Jesus' life and experience who Jesus is. It becomes a prayer when we open our hearts to be touched, and it leads us to express our response in prayer. Jesus wants to use any means available to move our hearts so that we know his love for us.

At each station we use our senses and our imagination to reflect prayerfully upon Jesus' suffering, death, and Resurrection. The stations can allow us to visualize the meaning of his passion and death and lead us to gratitude. They can also lead us to a sense of solidarity with all our brothers and sisters, especially those who suffer, who are unjustly accused or victimized, who are on death row, who carry difficult burdens, or who face terminal illnesses.

1. Jesus Is Condemned to Death.
Pontius Pilate condemns Jesus to death.

2. Jesus Takes Up His Cross.
Jesus willingly accepts and patiently bears his cross.

3. Jesus Falls the First Time.
Weakened by torments and loss of blood, Jesus falls beneath his cross.

4. Jesus Meets His Sorrowful Mother.
Jesus meets his mother, Mary, who is filled with grief.

5. Simon of Cyrene Helps Jesus Carry the Cross.
Soldiers force Simon of Cyrene to carry the cross.

6. Veronica Wipes the Face of Jesus.
Veronica steps through the crowd to wipe the face of Jesus.

7. Jesus Falls a Second Time.
Jesus falls beneath the weight of the cross a second time.

8. Jesus Meets the Women of Jerusalem.
Jesus tells the women to weep not for him, but for themselves and for their children.

9. Jesus Falls the Third Time.
Weakened almost to the point of death, Jesus falls a third time.

10. Jesus Is Stripped of His Garments.
The soldiers strip Jesus of his garments, treating him as a common criminal.

11. Jesus Is Nailed to the Cross.
Jesus' hands and feet are nailed to the cross.

12. Jesus Dies on the Cross.
After suffering greatly on the cross, Jesus bows his head and dies.

13. Jesus Is Taken Down from the Cross.
The lifeless body of Jesus is tenderly placed in the arms of Mary, his mother.

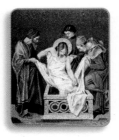

14. Jesus Is Laid in the Tomb.
Jesus' disciples place his body in the tomb.

The closing prayer—sometimes included as a 15th station—reflects on the Resurrection of Jesus.

Formulas of Catholic Doctrine

The following formulas present the basic teachings of the Catholic Church. Benedict XVI, when he was pope, emphasized that these are core teachings every Catholic should know.

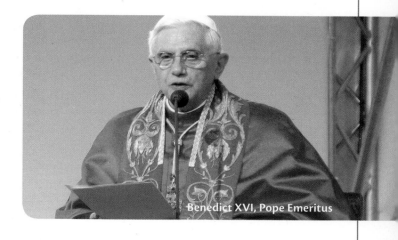

Benedict XVI, Pope Emeritus

The Great Commandment

The Ten Commandments are fulfilled in Jesus' Great Commandment: "You shall love God with all your heart, with all your soul, with all your mind, and with all your strength. You shall love your neighbor as yourself." (adapted from Mark 12:30–31)

The New Commandment

Before his death on the cross, Jesus gave his disciples a new commandment: "I give you a new commandment: love one another. As I have loved you, so you also should love one another." (John 13:34)

The Golden Rule

"Do to others whatever you would have them do to you." (Matthew 7:12)

The Beatitudes

The Beatitudes are the teachings of Jesus in the Sermon on the Mount. They can be found in Matthew 5:1–10. Jesus teaches us that if we live according to the Beatitudes, we will live a happy Christian life. The Beatitudes fulfill God's promises made to Abraham and to his descendants and describe the rewards that will be ours as loyal followers of Christ.

Blessed are the poor in spirit,
for theirs is the kingdom of heaven.
Blessed are they who mourn,
for they will be comforted.
Blessed are the meek,
for they will inherit the land.
Blessed are they who hunger and thirst
    for righteousness,
for they will be satisfied.
Blessed are the merciful,
for they will be shown mercy.
Blessed are the clean in heart,
for they will see God.
Blessed are the peacemakers,
for they will be called children of God.
Blessed are they who are persecuted
    for the sake of righteousness,
for theirs is the kingdom of heaven.

The Ten Commandments

As believers in Jesus Christ, we are called to a new life and are asked to make moral choices that keep us united with God. With the help and grace of the Holy Spirit, we can choose ways to act that keep us close to God, help other people, and be witnesses to Jesus.

The Ten Commandments guide us in making choices that help us live as God wants us to live. The first three commandments tell us how to love God; the other seven tell us how to love our neighbor.

1. I am the Lord your God: you shall not have strange gods before me.
2. You shall not take the name of the Lord your God in vain.
3. Remember to keep holy the Lord's Day.
4. Honor your father and your mother.
5. You shall not kill.
6. You shall not commit adultery.
7. You shall not steal.
8. You shall not bear false witness against your neighbor.
9. You shall not covet your neighbor's wife.
10. You shall not covet your neighbor's goods.

Precepts of the Church

The Precepts of the Church describe the minimum effort we must make in prayer and in living a moral life. All Catholics are called to move beyond the minimum by growing in love of God and love of neighbor. The Precepts are as follows:

1. To keep holy the day of the Lord's Resurrection. To worship God by participating in Mass every Sunday and every Holy Day of Obligation. To avoid those activities (like needless work) that would hinder worship, joy, or relaxation.
2. To lead a sacramental life. To receive Holy Communion frequently and the Sacrament of Reconciliation regularly.
3. To confess one's sins once a year.
4. To observe the marriage laws of the Church. To give religious training, by word and example, to one's children. To use parish schools and catechetical programs.
5. To strengthen and support the Church— one's own parish and parish priests, the worldwide Church, and the pope.
6. To do penance, including abstaining from meat and fasting from food on the appointed days.
7. To prepare to receive the Eucharist and continue a life of conversion.

The Four Last Things

There are four things that describe the end of all human life.

death   judgment   heaven   hell

First is the death of the individual. Then immediately after death is the judgment by Christ. The result of this judgment is either heaven (perhaps with a time in purgatory) or hell.

Virtues

Virtues are gifts from God that lead us to live in a close relationship with him. Virtues are like habits. They need to be practiced; they can be lost if they are neglected.

Theological Virtues

The three most important virtues are called *Theological Virtues* because they come from God and lead to God.

faith   hope   charity

Cardinal Virtues

The *cardinal virtues* are human virtues, acquired by education and good actions. *Cardinal* comes from *cardo,* the Latin word for "hinge," meaning "that on which other things depend."

prudence   justice   fortitude   temperance

Gifts and Fruits of the Holy Spirit

The Holy Spirit makes it possible for us to do what God asks by giving us these gifts.

wisdom   understanding   counsel   piety

fortitude   knowledge   fear of the Lord

The Fruits of the Holy Spirit are signs of the Holy Spirit's action in our lives.

love   joy   peace

patience   kindness   generosity

goodness   chastity

faithfulness   gentleness

self-control   modesty

Works of Mercy

The Corporal and Spiritual Works of Mercy are actions we can perform that extend God's compassion and mercy to those in need.

Corporal Works of Mercy

The corporal works of mercy are the kind acts by which we help our neighbors with their material and physical needs:

- Feed the hungry.
- Give drink to the thirsty.
- Clothe the naked.
- Shelter the homeless.
- Visit the sick.
- Visit the imprisoned.
- Bury the dead.

Spiritual Works of Mercy

The Spiritual Works of Mercy are acts of compassion by which we help our neighbors with their emotional and spiritual needs:

- Counsel the doubtful.
- Instruct the ignorant.
- Admonish sinners.
- Comfort the afflicted.
- Forgive offenses.
- Bear wrongs patiently.
- Pray for the living and the dead.

When we help others, we are performing works of mercy.

Celebrating and Living Our Catholic Faith

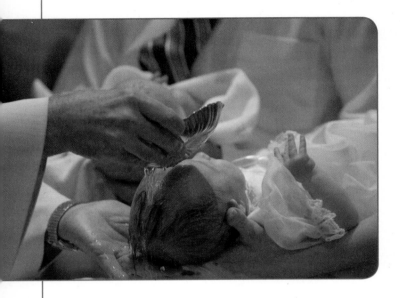

The Mystery of Faith Made Present

The Church was revealed to the world with the coming of the Spirit on Pentecost. This gift of the Spirit ushered in a new era in the history of salvation. This era is the age of the Church in which Christ makes present and communicates his work of salvation through the liturgy. The Church, as Christ's Body, is the first sacrament, the sign and instrument through which the Holy Spirit dispenses the mystery of salvation. In this age of the Church, Christ lives and acts through the sacraments.

The Seven Sacraments

Jesus touches our lives through the sacraments. In the sacraments physical objects such as water, bread and wine, and oil are the signs of Jesus' presence.

Sacraments of Initiation

These sacraments lay the foundation of Christian life.

Baptism

In Baptism, we are born into new life in Christ. Baptism takes away original sin and makes us members of the Church. Its sign is the pouring of water.

Confirmation

Confirmation seals our life of faith in Jesus. The signs of Confirmation are the laying on of hands and the anointing with oil on a person's head, most often done by a bishop. Confirmation and Baptism are received only once.

Eucharist

The Eucharist nourishes our life of faith. We receive the Body and Blood of Christ under the appearance of bread and wine.

Sacraments of Healing

These sacraments celebrate the healing power of Jesus.

Reconciliation

Through Reconciliation we receive God's forgiveness. Forgiveness requires being sorry for our sins. In Reconciliation we receive Jesus' healing grace through absolution by the priest. The signs of this sacrament are the confession of sins, repentance and satisfaction, and the words of absolution.

Anointing of the Sick

This sacrament unites a sick person's sufferings with those of Jesus. Oil, a symbol of strength, is the sign of this sacrament. A person is anointed with oil and receives the laying on of hands by a priest.

Sacraments at the Service of Communion

These sacraments help members serve the community.

Matrimony

In Matrimony, a baptized man and woman are united with each other as a sign of the unity between Jesus and his Church. Matrimony requires the consent of the couple as expressed in the marriage promises. The couple is the sign of this sacrament.

Holy Orders

In Holy Orders, men are ordained priests to serve as leaders of the community or as deacons to be reminders of our baptismal call to serve others. The signs of this sacrament are the laying on of hands and the prayer by the bishop asking God for the outpouring of the Holy Spirit.

Holy Days of Obligation

The Holy Days of Obligation are the days other than Sundays on which we celebrate the great things God has done for us through Jesus and the saints. On Holy Days of Obligation, Catholics attend Mass.

Six Holy Days of Obligation are celebrated in the United States.

January 1—Mary, Mother of God

40 days after Easter—Ascension (in many U.S. dioceses the Seventh Sunday of Easter)

August 15—Assumption of the Blessed Virgin Mary

November 1—All Saints

December 8—Immaculate Conception

December 25—Nativity of Our Lord Jesus Christ

Order of the Mass

The Sabbath, the day on which God rested after creating the world, represents the completion of creation. Saturday has been replaced by Sunday as the Sabbath for Christians because it recalls the beginning of the new creation through the Resurrection of Christ. Since it is the day of the Resurrection, Sunday is called the Lord's Day. The Sunday celebration of the Lord's Day is at the heart of the Church's life. That is why we are required to participate in the Mass on Sundays and other Holy Days of Obligation. We also rest from work, take time to enjoy our families, enrich our cultural and social lives, and perform works of mercy. On Sunday, people from all over the world gather at God's eucharistic table.

The Mass is the high point of Christian life, and it follows a set order.

Introductory Rites

We prepare to celebrate the Eucharist.

Entrance Chant
We gather as a community, praising God in song.

Greeting
We pray the Sign of the Cross, recognizing the presence of Christ in the community.

Penitential Act
We remember our sins and ask God for mercy.

Gloria
We praise God in song.

Collect
This prayer focuses the attention of all gathered.

The Liturgy of the Word
We hear the story of God's plan for salvation.

First Reading
We listen to God's Word, usually from the Old Testament.

Responsorial Psalm
We respond to God's Word in song.

Second Reading
We listen to God's Word from the New Testament.

Gospel Acclamation
We sing "Alleluia!" to praise God for the Good News. During Lent, we sing other acclamations.

Gospel Reading
We stand to acclaim Christ present in the Gospel.

Homily
The priest or deacon explains God's Word.

Profession of Faith
We proclaim our faith through the Nicene Creed.

Prayer of the Faithful
We pray for our needs and the needs of others.

The Liturgy of the Eucharist
We celebrate the meal Jesus instituted at the Last Supper and remember the sacrifice he made for us.

Presentation and Preparation of the Gifts
We bring gifts of bread and wine to the altar.

Prayer over the Offerings
The priest prays that God will accept our sacrifice.

Eucharistic Prayer
This prayer of thanksgiving is the center and high point of the entire celebration.

- *Preface*—We give thanks and praise to God.

- *Holy, Holy, Holy*—We sing an acclamation of praise.

- *Consecration*—The bread and wine become the Body and Blood of Jesus Christ.

- *The Mystery of Faith*—We proclaim Jesus' death and Resurrection.

- *Amen*—We affirm the words and actions of the Eucharistic prayer.

Communion Rite
We prepare to receive the Body and Blood of Jesus.

- *Lord's Prayer*—We pray the Lord's Prayer.

- *Sign of Peace*—We offer one another Christ's peace.

- *Lamb of God*—We pray for forgiveness, mercy, and peace.

- *Communion*—We receive the Body and Blood of Jesus Christ.

- *Prayer after Communion*—We pray that the Eucharist will strengthen us to live as Jesus did.

Concluding Rites
We go forth to glorify the Lord in our homes, our schools, and the world.

Final Blessing
We receive God's blessing.

Dismissal
We go forth to glorify the Lord in our homes, our schools, and the world.

Making Good Choices

Our conscience is the inner voice that helps us know the law God has placed in our hearts. Our conscience helps us judge the moral qualities of our actions. It guides us to do good and avoid evil.

The Holy Spirit can help us form our conscience. We form our conscience by studying the teachings of the Church and following the guidance of our parents and pastoral leaders.

God has given every human being freedom of choice. This does not mean that we have the right to do whatever we please. We can live in true freedom if we cooperate with the Holy Spirit, who gives us the virtue of prudence. This virtue helps us recognize what is good in every situation and make the correct choice. The Holy Spirit gives us the gifts of wisdom and understanding to help us make the right choices in life in relationship to God and others. The gift of counsel helps us reflect on making correct choices in life.

The Ten Commandments help us make moral choices that are pleasing to God. We have the grace of the sacraments, the teachings of the Church, and the good example of saints and fellow Christians to help us make good choices.

Making moral choices involves the following steps:

1. Ask the Holy Spirit for help.

2. Think about God's law and the teachings of the Church.

3. Think about what will happen as a result of your choice. Ask yourself, will the consequences be pleasing to God? Will my choice hurt someone else?

4. Seek advice from someone you respect, and remember that Jesus is with you.

5. Ask yourself how your choice will affect your relationships with God and others.

In making moral choices, we must take into consideration the object of the choice, our intention in making the choice, and the circumstances in which the choice is made. It is never right to make an evil choice in the hope of gaining something good.

The Morality of Human Acts

Human beings are able to act morally only because we are free. If we were not free to decide what to do, our acts could not be good or evil. Human acts that are freely chosen after a judgment of conscience can be morally evaluated. They are either good or evil.

The morality of human acts depends on

- the object chosen;

- the end in view or the intention;

- the circumstances of the action.

For an act to be good, what you choose to do must be good in itself. If the choice is not good, the intention or the circumstances cannot make it good. You cannot steal a digital camera because it is your father's birthday and it would make him happy to have one. But a good act done with a bad intention is not necessarily good either. Participating in a hunger walk, not out of concern for the poor but to impress a teacher from whom you want a good grade, is not necessarily a good act. Circumstances can affect the morality of an

A priest performs a blessing following confession.

act. They can increase or lessen the goodness of an act. Acting out of fear of harm lessens a person's responsibility for an act.

An Examination of Conscience

An examination of conscience is the act of looking prayerfully into our hearts to ask how we have hurt our relationships with God and with other people through our thoughts, words, and actions. We reflect on the Ten Commandments and the teachings of the Church.

My Relationship with God

• What steps am I taking to help me grow closer to God and to others? Do I turn to God often during the day, especially when I am tempted?

• Do I participate at Mass with attention and devotion on Sundays and holy days? Do I pray often and read the Bible?

• Do I use God's name and the names of Jesus, Mary, and the saints with love and reverence?

My Relationships with Family, Friends, and Neighbors

• Have I set a bad example through my words or actions? Do I treat others fairly? Do I spread stories that hurt other people?

• Am I loving toward those in my family? Am I respectful of my neighbors, my friends, and those in authority?

• Do I value human life? Do I do what I can to promote peace and to end violence? Do I avoid talking about others in ways that could harm them?

• Do I show respect for my body and for the bodies of others? Do I keep away from forms of entertainment that do not respect God's gift of sexuality?

• Have I taken or damaged anything that did not belong to me? Do I show concern for the poor and offer assistance to them in the ways I am able? Do I show concern for the environment and care for it as God has asked?

• Have I cheated or copied homework? Have I told the truth even when it was difficult?

• Do I quarrel with others just so I can get my own way? Do I insult others to try to make them think they are less than I am? Do I hold grudges and try to hurt people who I think have hurt me?

How to Make a Good Confession

An examination of conscience is an important part of preparing for the Sacrament of Reconciliation. The Sacrament of Reconciliation includes the following steps:

• The priest greets us, and we pray the Sign of the Cross. He invites us to trust in God. He may read God's Word with us.

• We confess our sins. The priest may help and counsel us.

• The priest gives us a penance to perform. Penance is an act of kindness, prayers to pray, or both.

• The priest asks us to express our sorrow, usually by reciting the Act of Contrition.

• We receive absolution. The priest says, "I absolve you from your sins in the name of the Father, and of the Son, and of the Holy Spirit." We respond, "Amen."

• The priest dismisses us by saying, "Go in peace." We go forth to perform the act of penance he has given us.

The Bible

God speaks to us in many ways. One way God speaks to us is through the Bible. The Bible is the most important book in Christian life because it is God's message, or Revelation. The Bible is the story of God's promise to care for us, especially through his Son, Jesus. At Mass, we hear stories from the Bible. We can also read the Bible on our own.

The Bible is not just one book; it is a collection of many books. The writings in the Bible were inspired by the Holy Spirit and written by different authors using different styles.

The Bible is made up of two parts: The Old Testament and the New Testament. The Old Testament contains 46 books that tell stories about the Jewish people and their faith in God before Jesus was born.

The first five books of the Old Testament—Genesis, Exodus, Leviticus, Numbers, and Deuteronomy—are referred to as the *Torah,* meaning "instruction" or "law." The central story in the Torah is the Exodus, the liberation of the Hebrew slaves as Moses led them out of Egypt and to the Promised Land. During the journey, God gave the Ten Commandments to Moses and the people.

A beautiful part of the Old Testament is the Book of Psalms. A psalm is a prayer in the form of a poem. Each psalm expresses an aspect or feature of the depth of human emotion. Over several centuries, 150 psalms were gathered to form the Book of Psalms. They were once sung at the Temple in Jerusalem, and they have been used in the public worship of the Church since its beginning. Catholics also pray the psalms as part of their private prayer and reflection.

The prophets were called by God to speak for him and to urge the Jewish people to be faithful to the Covenant. A large part of the Old Testament (18 books) presents the messages and actions of the prophets.

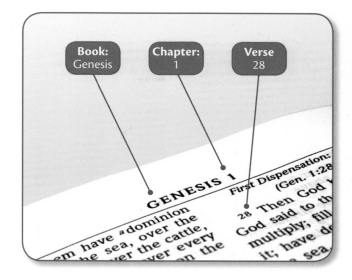

The New Testament contains 27 books that tell the story of Jesus' life, death, and Resurrection, and the experience of the early Christians. For Christians, the most important books of the New Testament are the four Gospels—Matthew, Mark, Luke, and John. Many of the 27 books are letters written by leaders such as Paul.

How can you find a passage in the Bible? Bible passages are identified by book, chapter, and verse—for example, Genesis 1:28. The name of the book comes first. Sometimes it is abbreviated. Your Bible's table of contents will help you determine what the abbreviation means. For example, *Gn* stands for *Genesis.* After the name of the book, there are two numbers. The first one identifies the chapter, which in our example is chapter 1; it is followed by a colon. The second number identifies the verse or verses. Our example shows verse 28.

How the Old Testament and the New Testament Were Put Together

The Old and New Testaments developed in oral cultures, and much of the material was passed on by word of mouth before ever being written down. Stories from the prehistory of Israel were probably the first part of the Old Testament to be written down. These can be

King David.

found in parts of the 2nd through 11th chapters of Genesis. They would have been written by the court historian of King David around 1000 B.C. This writer always referred to God as Yahweh and spoke of God in human terms. It was this writer who wrote the story of God walking in the garden with Adam and Eve. Other stories developed in the northern kingdom of Israel and favor the religious sites of that region, such as Bethel.

The Old Testament as we know it today did not begin to take shape until the Babylonian Exile (587–537 B.C.). There members of the priestly class took many of the oral and written accounts of God's saving work and put them together in what we know as the Torah, the first five books of the bible—Genesis, Exodus, Leviticus, Numbers, and Deuteronomy.

The writers in Babylon also wrote the opening chapter of Genesis that tells of God's orderly creation of the world in six days and his rest on the seventh day.

The historical books were put together from the court accounts of various kings of Israel and Judah. The psalms were gathered from collections of prayers, and new psalms were written for the temple that was rebuilt after 537 B.C. Other Wisdom Literature was also gathered. Finally, the writings of the prophets were gathered together and collected by

their followers. They included prophets who preached and wrote from 150 years before the exile, such as the first Isaiah and Amos, to the second part of the book of Zechariah which was probably written after 330 B.C. In the middle of the third century B.C., these books were translated from Hebrew into Greek in Alexandria, Egypt. In time a number of other books, such as First and Second Maccabees, were added to the Bible in Greek. By the end of the first century A.D., religious leaders in Israel decided which books would be in their Bible. They included only the Old Testament books written in Hebrew.

In about year 50, Paul wrote his first letter to the Thessalonians, followed by a second one later that year. This was more than 20 years after the death and Resurrection of Jesus. Over the next 13 years, Paul wrote letters to other Christian communities as well as to the Christians of Rome, a city he hoped to visit. Meanwhile, Christians were passing on stories about Jesus—his message, his miracles, and others things he did. Probably the first stories to come together centered on his final days— his passion, death, and Resurrection. This is why all four Gospels tell similar stories about Jesus' last days.

Mark.

The first Gospel to be written was the Gospel of Mark. It was written in Rome during and after Nero's persecution in the second half of the 60s. In the 80s, the authors of the Gospels of Matthew and Luke, using Mark's Gospel as a starting point, wrote their own Gospels for their specific Christian communities. Matthew, Mark, and Luke, though writing about Jesus in different ways, tell stories that are similar enough to be read side by side. Because of their similarities, we call them the *Synoptic Gospels*. They also made use of a collection of Jesus' sayings. The Gospel of John was written in the mid-to-late 90s. It is very different in tone and theology. The last book of the New Testament to be written was Second Peter, shortly after the year 100.

Showing Our Love for the World

The Catholic Church has developed a large body of teaching on social justice issues, because action on behalf of justice and work to create a more just world are essential parts of preaching the Gospel. In the story of the Good Samaritan (Luke 10:29–37), Jesus makes clear our responsibility to care for those in need.

The major development of the social doctrine of the Church began in the 19th century, when the Gospel encountered modern industrial society. There were new structures for the production of consumer goods, new concepts of society, new types of states and authorities, and new forms of labor and ownership.

Since that time the Church has been making judgments about economic and social matters that relate to the basic rights of individuals and communities. The Church's social teaching is a rich treasure of wisdom about how to build a just society and how to live holy lives amid the challenges of the modern world.

All human life is sacred, and all people must be respected and valued over material goods. We are called to ask whether our actions as a society respect or threaten the life and dignity of the human person. The Catholic Church teaches this responsibility in the following themes of Catholic Social Teaching.

Call to Family, Community, and Participation

Participation in family and community is central to our faith and to a healthy society. Families must be supported so that people can participate in society, build a community spirit, and promote the well-being of all, especially the poor and vulnerable.

Volunteers distribute free bottled water to survivors of Hurricane Jeanne, Florida.

Rights and Responsibilities

Every person has a right to life as well as a right to those things required for human decency. As Catholics, we have a responsibility to protect these basic human rights in order to achieve a healthy society.

Option for the Poor and Vulnerable

In our world, many people are rich while others are poor. As Catholics, we are called to pay special attention to the needs of the poor by defending and promoting their dignity and meeting their immediate material needs.

The Dignity of Work and the Rights of Workers

The basic rights of workers must be respected: the right to productive work, fair wages, and private property; the right to organize, join unions, and pursue economic opportunity. Catholics believe that the economy is meant to serve people and that work is not merely a way to make a living, but an important way in which we participate in God's creation.

Solidarity

Because God is our Father, we are all brothers and sisters with the responsibility to care for one another. Solidarity is the attitude that leads Christians to share spiritual and material goods. Solidarity unites rich and poor, weak and strong, and helps create a society that recognizes that we depend on one another.

Care for God's Creation

God is the Creator of all people and all things, and he wants us to enjoy his creation. The responsibility to care for everything God has made is a requirement of our faith.

A teen weeds a native habitat restoration site, California.

Glossary

A

Abba an informal word for *father* in Aramaic, the language Jesus spoke. It is like the word *dad* in English. When Jesus spoke to God the Father, he called him "Abba."

abortion the deliberate ending of a pregnancy that results in the death of the unborn child. The Church teaches that since life begins at conception, abortion is a serious crime against life and is gravely against the moral law.

Abraham the model of faith in God in the Old Testament. Because of his faith, he left his home and traveled to Canaan, where God made a covenant with him that promised him land and many descendants. He became the father of the Chosen People.

absolution the forgiveness we receive from God through the priest in the Sacrament of Penance and Reconciliation

abstain the practice of denying oneself food, drink, or other pleasures. Catholics over age 14 abstain from eating meat on Ash Wednesday and on Fridays during Lent.

adore to worship God above all else because he is our Creator. The First Commandment requires us to adore God alone.

adultery an injury to the marriage bond covenant. It occurs when two people have sexual relations while one of them is married to another person. The Sixth Commandment forbids adultery. It undermines the institution of marriage and is harmful to children, who need the stability of their parents' marriage commitment.

Advocate Jesus' name for the Holy Spirit. The Holy Spirit comforts us, speaks for us in difficult times, and makes Jesus present to us.

Alleluia an acclamation meaning "praise God." Alleluia is sung before the proclamation of the Gospel, except during Lent.

altar the table in the church on which the priest celebrates Mass, where the sacrifice of Christ on the cross is made present in the Sacrament of the Eucharist. The altar represents two aspects of the mystery of the Eucharist. It is the place where Jesus Christ offers himself for our sins and where he gives us himself as our food for eternal life.

ambo a raised stand from which a person reads the Word of God during Mass

Amen A Hebrew word meaning "it is so" or "let it be done." It signifies agreement with what has just been said. Prayers in the New Testament, in the Church's liturgies, and the Creed end with *Amen*. In the Gospels, Jesus uses *Amen* to reinforce the seriousness of what he is about to say.

angel a spiritual creature who worships God in heaven. Angels serve God as messengers. They tell us of his plans for our salvation.

Angelus a prayer honoring the Incarnation of Jesus. The Angelus is prayed in the morning, at noon, and in the evening.

Annunciation the announcement to Mary by the angel Gabriel that God had chosen her to be the Mother of Jesus. When Mary agreed, the Son of God became human in her. The feast of the Annunciation is celebrated on March 25, nine months before Christmas.

anoint to put oil on things or people to dedicate them to the service of God. The anointing of the kings of Israel was a sign that they were chosen to rule God's people.

Anointing of the Sick one of the seven sacraments. In this sacrament, a person who is sick has holy oil applied and receives the strength, peace, and courage to overcome the difficulties associated with illness. Through this sacrament, Jesus brings the person spiritual healing and forgiveness of sins. If it is God's will, healing of the body is given as well.

apostle one of twelve men who accompanied Jesus in his ministry and were witnesses to the Resurrection. *Apostle* means "one sent." These were the people sent to preach the Gospel to the whole world.

Apostles' Creed a statement of Christian belief that developed out of a creed used in Baptism in Rome. The Apostles' Creed lists simple statements of belief in God the Father, Jesus Christ the Son, and the Holy Spirit. The profession of faith used in Baptism today is based on the Apostles' Creed.

Ark of the Covenant a portable box in which were placed the tablets of the Ten Commandments. The Ark was the most important item in the shrine that was carried through the desert and then placed in the holiest part of the Temple in Jerusalem. Two angels are depicted on the cover of the Ark of the Covenant. The wings of the angels curve upward, representing the place where God came close to Israel and revealed his will.

Ascension the entry of Jesus into God's presence in heaven. In the Acts of the Apostles, it is written that Jesus, after his Resurrection, spent 40 days on earth, instructing his followers. He then returned to his Father in heaven.

Assumption Mary's being taken, body and soul, into heaven. Mary had a special relationship with her Son, Jesus, from the very beginning, when she conceived him. Catholics believe that because of this relationship, she enjoys a special participation in Jesus' Resurrection and has been taken into heaven where she now lives with him. We celebrate this event in the Feast of the Assumption on August 15.

B

Baptism the first of the seven sacraments. Baptism frees us from original sin and is necessary for salvation. Baptism gives us new life in Jesus Christ through the Holy Spirit. The celebration of Baptism consists of immersing a person in water while declaring that the person is baptized in the name of the Father, the Son, and the Holy Spirit.

Beatitudes the teachings of Jesus in the Sermon on the Mount in Matthew's Gospel. The Beatitudes are eight ways of living the Christian life. They are the fulfillment of the commandments given to Moses. These teachings present the way to true happiness.

benediction a prayer service in which we honor Jesus in the Blessed Sacrament and receive his blessing

Bible the collection of books containing the truths of God's Revelation to us. These writings were inspired by the Holy Spirit and written by human beings. The Bible is made up of the 46 books in the Old Testament and 27 books in the New Testament.

bishop a man who has received the fullness of Holy Orders. As a successor to the original apostles, he takes care of the Church and is a principal teacher in it.

blasphemy mocking or hateful speech concerning God. Blasphemy can also include insulting or making fun of sacred people or things.

Blessed Sacrament the Body of Christ. It is kept in the tabernacle to adore and to be taken to those who are sick.

blessing a prayer that calls for God's power and care upon some person, place, thing, or activity

Body and Blood of Christ consecrated by the priest at Mass. In the Sacrament of the Eucharist, all of the risen Lord Jesus Christ—body, blood, soul, and divinity— is present under the appearances of Bread and Wine.

C

catechumen a person being formed in the Christian life through instruction and by the example of the parish community. Through conversion and maturity of faith, a catechumen is preparing to be welcomed into the Church at Easter through the Sacraments of Baptism, Confirmation, and the Eucharist.

catholic one of the four Marks of the Church. The Church is catholic because Jesus is fully present in it and because Jesus has given the Church to the whole world. It is universal.

charity a virtue given to us by God that helps us love God above all things and our neighbor as ourselves

chastity the integration of our physical sexuality with our spiritual nature. Chastity helps us be completely human, able to give to others our whole life and love. All people, married or single, are called to practice chastity.

chrism a perfumed oil, consecrated by a bishop, that is used in the Sacraments of Baptism, Confirmation, and Holy Orders. Anointing with chrism signifies the call of the baptized to the threefold ministry of priest, prophet, and king.

Christ a title that means "anointed with oil." It is from a Greek word that means the same thing as the Hebrew word *Messiah,* or "anointed." It is the name given to Jesus after the Resurrection when he completed his mission as priest, prophet, and king.

Christian the name given to all those who have been anointed through the Gift of the Holy Spirit in Baptism and have become followers of Jesus Christ

Christmas the feast of the birth of Jesus (December 25)

Church the People of God throughout the whole world, or diocese (the local Church), or the assembly of those called together to worship God. The Church is one, holy, catholic, and apostolic.

clergy those men who are set apart as sacred ministers to serve the Church through Holy Orders

commandment a standard, or rule, for living as God wants us to live. Jesus summarized all the commandments into two: love God and love your neighbor.

Communion of Saints the unity of all, dead or living, who have been saved in Jesus Christ. The Communion of Saints is based on our one faith, and it is nourished by our participation in the Eucharist.

confession the act of telling our sins to a priest in the Sacrament of Penance and Reconciliation. The sacrament itself is sometimes referred to as "confession."

Confirmation the sacrament that completes the grace we receive in Baptism. It seals, or confirms, this grace through the seven Gifts of the Holy Spirit that we receive as part of Confirmation. This sacrament also makes us better able to participate in the worship and apostolic life of the Church.

conscience the inner voice that helps each of us judge the morality of our own actions. It guides us to follow God's law by doing good and avoiding evil.

consecration the making of a thing or a person special to God through a prayer or blessing. At Mass, the words of the priest are a consecration that makes Jesus Christ's Body and Blood present under the appearance of the bread and wine. People or objects set apart for God in a special way are also consecrated. For example, churches and altars are consecrated for use in liturgy, and bishops are consecrated as they receive the fullness of the Sacrament of Holy Orders.

contrition the sorrow we feel when we know that we have sinned, followed by the decision not to sin again. Perfect contrition arises from a love that loves God above all else. Imperfect contrition arises from other motives. Contrition is the most important act of the penitent preparing to celebrate the Sacrament of Penance and Reconciliation.

Corporal Works of Mercy kind acts by which we help our neighbors with their everyday material needs. Corporal Works of Mercy include feeding the hungry, giving drink to the thirsty, clothing the naked, sheltering the homeless, visiting the sick and the imprisoned, and burying the dead.

covenant a solemn agreement between people or between people and God. God made covenants with humanity through agreements with Noah, Abraham, and Moses. These covenants offered salvation. God's new and final covenant was established through Jesus' life, death, and Resurrection. *Testament* is another word for *covenant.*

covet to want to take what belongs to someone else. The Ninth and Tenth Commandments tell us it is sinful to covet.

creation God's act of making everything that exists outside himself. Creation is everything that exists. God said that all creation is good.

Creator God, who made everything that is and whom we can come to know through everything he created

creed a brief summary of what people believe. The word *creed* comes from the Latin *credo,* which means "I believe." The Nicene Creed is the most important summary of Christian beliefs.

D

deacon a man ordained through the Sacrament of Holy Orders to the ministry of service in the Church. Deacons help the bishop and priests by serving in the various charitable practices of the Church. They also help by proclaiming the Gospel and preaching and by assisting at the Liturgy of the Eucharist. Deacons celebrate Baptism, bless marriages, and preside at funerals.

devil a spirit created good by God who became evil through disobedience. The devil tempted Adam and Eve to sin and still tempts us today. God's grace is stronger than the works of the devil.

diocese the members of the Church in a particular area, united in faith and the sacraments, and gathered under the leadership of a bishop

disciple a person who has accepted Jesus' message and tries to live as he did, sharing his mission, his suffering, and his joys

Divine Providence the guidance of God over all he has created. Divine Providence exercises care for all creation and guides it toward its final perfection.

E

Easter the celebration of the bodily raising of Jesus Christ from the dead. Easter is the festival of our redemption and the central Christian feast, the one from which other feasts arise.

Eastern Catholic Church a group of churches that developed in the East (in countries such as Lebanon) that are in union with the Roman Catholic Church but have their own liturgical, theological, and administrative traditions. They show the truly catholic nature of the Church, which takes root in many cultures.

Emmanuel a Hebrew name from the Old Testament that means "God with us." In Matthew's Gospel, Jesus is called Emmanuel.

epistle a letter written by Saint Paul or another leader to a group of Christians in the early Church. Of the 27 books of the New Testament, 21 are epistles. The second reading at Mass on Sundays and holy days is always from one of these books.

Eucharist the sacrament in which we give thanks to God for giving us the Body and Blood of Jesus Christ. This sacrament brings us into union with Jesus Christ and his saving Death and Resurrection.

Eucharistic Liturgy the public worship, held by the Church, in which bread and wine are consecrated and become the Body and Blood of Jesus Christ. The Sunday celebration of the Eucharistic Liturgy is at the heart of Church life.

examination of conscience the act of prayerfully thinking about what we have said or done in light of what the Gospel asks of us. We also think about how our actions may have hurt our relationship with God or with others. An examination of conscience is an important part of our preparing to celebrate the Sacrament of Penance and Reconciliation.

Exile the period in the history of Israel between the destruction of Jerusalem in 587 B.C. and the return to Jerusalem in 537 B.C. During this time, many of the Jewish people were forced to live in Babylon, far from home.

Exodus God's liberation of the Hebrew people from slavery in Egypt and his leading them to the Promised Land

F

faith a gift of God that helps us believe in him. We profess our faith in the Creed, celebrate it in the sacraments, live by it through our good conduct of loving God and our neighbor, and express it in prayer.

fasting limiting the amount we eat for a period of time to express sorrow for sin and to make ourselves more aware of God's action in our lives. Adults 18 years old and older fast on Ash Wednesday and Good Friday. The practice is also encouraged as a private devotion at other times of penitence.

free will the ability to choose to do good because God has made us like him. Our free will is what makes us truly human. Our exercise of free will to do good increases our freedom. Using free will to choose sin makes us slaves to sin.

G

Gifts of the Holy Spirit the permanent willingness, given to us by the Holy Spirit that makes it possible for us to do what God asks of us. The Gifts of the Holy Spirit are drawn from Isaiah 11:1–3. They include wisdom, understanding, counsel, fortitude, knowledge, and fear of the Lord. Church Tradition has added piety to make a total of seven.

Gospel the good news of God's mercy and love that we experience by hearing the story of Jesus' life, death, and Resurrection. The story is passed on in the teaching ministry of the Church as the source of all truth and right living. It is presented to us in four books in the New Testament—the Gospels of Matthew, Mark, Luke, and John.

grace the gift of God, given to us without our meriting it. Sanctifying grace fills us with God's life and makes it possible for us to always be his friends. Grace is the Holy Spirit alive in us, helping us live out our Christian vocation. Grace helps us live as God wants us to.

Great Commandment Jesus' commandment that we are to love both God and our neighbor as we love ourselves. Jesus tells us that this commandment sums up everything taught in the Old Testament.

H

heaven union with God the Father, Son, and Holy Spirit in life and love that never ends. Heaven is a state of complete happiness and the goal of the deepest wishes of the human heart.

Hebrews the descendants of Abraham, Isaac, and Jacob, who were enslaved in Egypt. God helped Moses lead these people out of slavery.

hell a life of total separation from God forever. In his infinite love for us, God can only desire our salvation. Hell is the result of the free choice of a person to reject God's love and forgiveness once and for all.

holiness the fullness of Christian life and love. All people are called to holiness, which is made possible by cooperating with God's grace to do his will. As we do God's will, we are transformed more and more into the image of the Son, Jesus Christ.

holy one of the four Marks of the Church. It is the kind of life we live when we share in the life of God, who is all holiness. The Church is holy because it is united with Jesus Christ.

Holy Communion the reception of the Body and Blood of Jesus Christ. It brings us into union with Jesus Christ and his saving Death and Resurrection.

Holy Days of Obligation the principal feast days, other than Sundays, of the Church. On Holy Days of Obligation, we celebrate the great things that God has done for us through Jesus and the saints. Catholics are obliged to participate in the Eucharist on these days, just as we are on Sundays.

Holy Family the family of Jesus as he grew up in Nazareth. It included Jesus; his Mother, Mary; and his foster father, Joseph.

Holy Orders the sacrament through which the mission given by Jesus to his apostles continues in the Church. The sacrament has three degrees: deacon, priest, and bishop. Through the laying on of hands in the Sacrament of Holy Orders, men receive a permanent sacramental mark that calls them to minister to the Church.

Holy Spirit the third Person of the Trinity, who is sent to us as our helper and, through Baptism and Confirmation, fills us with God's life. Together with the Father and the Son, the Holy Spirit brings the divine plan of salvation to completion.

homily the explanation by a bishop, a priest, or a deacon of the Word of God in the liturgy. The homily relates the Word of God to our life as Christians today.

hope the confidence that God will always be with us, make us happy now and forever, and help us live so that we will be with him forever

I

idolatry the worship of false gods in place of worshiping God. Idolatry is worshiping a creature, person, or thing, such as power, pleasure, or money, in place of the Creator. Idolatry is a sin against the First Commandment.

Incarnation the Son of God, Jesus, being born as a full human being in order to save us. The Son of God, the second Person of the Trinity, is both true God and true man.

inspired influenced by the Holy Spirit. The human authors of Scripture were influenced by the Holy Spirit. The creative inspiration of the Holy Spirit makes sure that the Scripture is taught according to the truth God wants us to know for our salvation.

intercession prayer or petition on behalf of another. Through prayers of intercession, we pray as Christ, our intercessor, prayed for us.

interpretation explanation of the words of Scripture, combining human knowledge and the teaching office of the Church under the guidance of the Holy Spirit

Israelites the descendants of Abraham, Isaac, and Jacob. God changed Jacob's name to "Israel," and Jacob's 12 sons and their children became the leaders of the 12 tribes of Israel. (*See* Hebrews.)

J

Jesus the Son of God, who was born of the Virgin Mary and who died and was raised from the dead for our salvation. He returned to God and will come again to judge the living and the dead. His name means "God saves."

Jews the name given to the Hebrew people, from the time of the Exile to the present. The name means "the people who live in the territory of Judah," the area of Palestine surrounding Jerusalem.

Joseph the foster father of Jesus, who was engaged to Mary when the angel announced that Mary would have a child through the power of the Holy Spirit. In the Old Testament, Joseph was the son of Jacob, who was sold into slavery in Egypt by his brothers and then saved them from starvation when famine came.

Judaism the name of the religion of Jesus and all the people of Israel after they returned from exile in Babylon and built the second Temple

justice the virtue that guides us to give to God and others what is due them. Justice is one of the four central human virtues by which we guide our Christian life.

K

Kingdom of God God's rule over us, announced in the Gospel and present in the Eucharist. The beginning of the kingdom here on earth is mysteriously present in the Church, and it will come in completeness at the end of time.

L

laity those who have been made members of Christ in Baptism and who participate in the priestly, prophetic, and kingly functions of Christ in his mission to the whole world. The laity is distinct from the clergy, whose members are set apart as ministers to serve the Church.

Last Supper the last meal Jesus ate with his disciples on the night before he died. At the Last Supper, Jesus took bread and wine, blessed them, and said that they were his Body and Blood. Jesus' death and Resurrection, which we celebrate in the Eucharist, were anticipated in this meal.

Law the first five books of the Old Testament. The Hebrew word for *law* is *Torah*. The ancient law is summarized in the Ten Commandments.

Lectionary for Mass the official book that contains all the Scripture readings used in the Liturgy of the Word

liturgical year the celebrations throughout the year of all the mysteries of Jesus' birth, life, death, and Resurrection. The celebration of Easter is at the heart of the liturgical year. The other feasts celebrated throughout the year make up the basic rhythm of the Christian's life of prayer.

liturgy the public prayer of the Church that celebrates the wonderful things God has done for us in Jesus Christ, our high priest, and the way in which he continues the work of our salvation. The original meaning of *liturgy* was "a public work or service done for the people."

Liturgy of the Eucharist the second main part of the Mass, in which the bread and wine are consecrated and become the Body and Blood of Jesus Christ, which we then receive in Holy Communion

Liturgy of the Hours the public prayer of the Church to praise God and to sanctify the day. It includes an office of readings before sunrise, morning prayer at dawn, evening prayer at sunset, and prayer before going to bed. The chanting of psalms makes up a major portion of each of these services.

Liturgy of the Word the first main part of the Mass, in which we listen to God's Word from the Bible and consider what it means for us today. The Liturgy of the Word can also be a public prayer and proclamation of God's Word that is not followed by the Liturgy of the Eucharist.

Lord the name used for God to replace the name he revealed to Moses, Yahweh, which was considered too sacred to pronounce. It indicates the divinity of Israel's God. The New Testament uses the title *Lord* for both the Father and for Jesus, recognizing him as God himself. (*See* Yahweh.)

Lord's Day the day Christians set aside for special worship of God. Each Sunday Mass commemorates the Resurrection of Jesus of Easter Sunday. Besides requiring us to offer God the worship owed him, the Third Commandment tells us Sunday is a day for relaxation of mind and body and to perform works of mercy.

M

Magnificat Mary's song of praise to God for the great things he has done for her and planned for us through Jesus

martyrs those who have given their lives for the faith. *Martyr* comes from the Greek word for "witness." A martyr is the supreme witness to the truth of the faith and to Christ to whom he or she is united. The seventh chapter of the Acts of the Apostles recounts the death of the first martyr, the deacon Stephen.

Mary the Mother of Jesus. She is called blessed and "full of grace" because God chose her to be the Mother of the Son of God, the second Person of the Trinity.

Mass the most important sacramental celebration of the Church, established by Jesus at the Last Supper as a remembrance of his death and Resurrection. At Mass, we listen to God's Word from the Bible and receive Jesus Christ in the bread and wine that have been consecrated to become his Body and Blood.

Matrimony a solemn agreement between a woman and a man to be partners for life, both for their own good and for bringing up children. Matrimony is a sacrament when the agreement is properly made between baptized Christians.

Messiah a title that means "anointed with oil." It is from a Hebrew word that means the same thing as the Greek word *Christ*. "Messiah" is the title that was given to Jesus after the Resurrection, when he had completed his mission as priest, prophet, and king.

miracles signs or acts of wonder that cannot be explained by natural causes but are works of God. In the Gospels, Jesus works miracles as a sign that the Kingdom of God is present in his ministry.

mission the work of Jesus Christ that is continued in the Church through the Holy Spirit. The mission of the Church is to proclaim salvation in Jesus' life, death, and Resurrection.

missionary one who proclaims the Gospel to others and leads them to know Christ. Missionaries are lay, ordained, and religious people engaged in mission.

moral choice a choice to do what is right or not do what is wrong. We make moral choices because they are what we believe God wants and because we have the freedom to choose what is right and to avoid what is wrong.

moral law a rule for living that has been established by God and people in authority who are concerned about the good of all. Moral laws are based on God's direction to us to do what is right and to avoid what is wrong. Some moral laws are "written" in the human heart and can be known through our own reasoning. Other moral laws have been revealed to us by God in the Old Testament and in the new law given by Jesus.

mortal sin a serious decision to turn away from God by doing something that we know is wrong. For a sin to be mortal, it must be a very serious offense. The person must know how serious the sin is and freely choose to do it anyway.

mystery a religious truth that we can know only through God's Revelation and that we cannot fully understand. Our faith is a mystery that we profess in the Creed and celebrate in the liturgy and the sacraments.

N

natural law the moral law that is "written" in the human heart. We can know natural law through our own reasoning because the Creator has placed the knowledge of it in our hearts. It can provide the solid foundation on which we can make rules to guide our choices in life. Natural law forms the basis of our fundamental rights and duties and is the foundation for the work of the Holy Spirit in guiding our moral choices.

New Testament the 27 books of the second part of the Bible that tell of the teaching, ministry, and saving events of the life of Jesus. The four Gospels present Jesus' life, death, and Resurrection. The Acts of the Apostles tells the story of the message of salvation as it spread through the growth of the Church. Various letters instruct us in how to live as followers of Jesus Christ. The Book of Revelation offers encouragement to Christians living through persecution.

Nicene Creed the summary of Christian beliefs developed by the bishops at the first two councils of the Church, held in A.D. 325 and 381. It is the Creed shared by most Christians in the East and in the West.

O

obedience the act of willingly following what God asks us to do for our salvation. The Fourth Commandment requires children to obey their parents, and all people are required to obey civil authority when it acts for the good of all. To imitate the obedience of Jesus, members of religious communities make a vow of obedience.

Old Testament the first 46 books of the Bible, which tell of God's Covenant with the people of Israel and his plan for the salvation of all people. The first five books are known as the Torah. The Old Testament is fulfilled in the New Testament, but God's covenant presented in the Old Testament has permanent value and has never been revoked.

Ordinary Time the part of the liturgical year outside of the seasons and feasts and the preparation for them. *Ordinary* does not mean "common." It means "counted time," as in ordinal numbers. It is time devoted to growing in understanding the mystery of Christ in its fullness. The color of Ordinary Time is green to symbolize growth.

ordination the rite of the Sacrament of Holy Orders, by which a bishop gives to men, through the laying on of hands, the ability to minister to the Church as bishops, priests, and deacons

original sin the consequence of the disobedience of the first human beings. They disobeyed God and chose to follow their own will rather than God's will. As a result, human beings lost the original blessing God had intended and became subject to sin and death. In Baptism, we are restored to life with God through Jesus Christ, although we still experience the effects of original sin.

P

parable one of the simple stories that Jesus told to show us what the Kingdom of God is like. Parables present images drawn from everyday life. These images show us the radical choice we make when we respond to the invitation to enter the Kingdom of God.

parish a stable community of believers in Jesus Christ who meet regularly in a specific area to worship God under the leadership of a pastor

Paschal Mystery the work of salvation accomplished by Jesus Christ through his passion, death, Resurrection, and Ascension. The Paschal Mystery is celebrated in the liturgy of the Church, and its saving effects are experienced by us in the sacraments.

Passover the Jewish festival that commemorates the delivery of the Hebrew people from slavery in Egypt. In the Eucharist, we celebrate our passover from death to life through Jesus' death and Resurrection.

penance the turning away from sin with a desire to change our life and to more closely live the way God wants us to live. We express our penance externally by praying, fasting, and helping those in need. This is also the name of the action that the priest asks us to take or the prayers that he asks us to pray after he absolves us in the Sacrament of Penance and Reconciliation. (*See* Sacrament of Penance and Reconciliation.)

Penitential Act the part of the Mass before the Liturgy of the Word in which we ask God's forgiveness for our sins. The Penitential Act prepares us to celebrate the Eucharist.

Pentateuch the first five books of the Bible: Genesis, Exodus, Leviticus, Numbers, and Deuteronomy. *Pentateuch* is Greek for "five books." The Pentateuch tells of Creation, the beginning of God's special people, and the Covenant. It is called *Torah* in Hebrew, which means "law."

Pentecost the 50th day after Jesus was raised from the dead. On this day, the Holy Spirit was sent from heaven, and the Church was born. It is also the Jewish feast that celebrated the giving of the Ten Commandments on Mount Sinai 50 days after the Exodus.

perjury lying while under oath or making a promise under oath without planning to keep it. Perjury is both a sin and a crime. It is a violation of the Second and Eighth Commandments.

personal sin a sin we choose to commit, whether serious (mortal) or less serious (venial). Although the consequences of original sin leave us with a tendency to sin, God's grace, especially through the sacraments, helps us choose good over sin.

pope the Bishop of Rome, successor of Saint Peter, and leader of the Roman Catholic Church. Because he has the authority to act in the name of Christ, the pope is called the Vicar of Christ. The pope and all the bishops together make up the living, teaching office of the Church.

prayer the raising of our hearts and minds to God. We are able to speak to and listen to God in prayer because he teaches us how to pray.

prayer of petition a request addressed to God arising out of our positions as creatures who depend on God our Creator. As sinners, we know we turn away from God. Through prayers of petition, we turn back to him.

Precepts of the Church those positive requirements that the pastoral authority of the Church has determined are necessary to provide a minimum effort in prayer and the moral life. The Precepts of the Church ensure that all Catholics move beyond the minimum by growing in love of God and love of neighbor.

priest a man who has accepted God's special call to serve the Church by guiding it and building it up through the ministry of the Word and the celebration of the sacraments

prophet one called to speak for God and to call the people to be faithful to the covenant. A major section of the Old Testament presents the messages and actions of the prophets.

psalm a prayer in the form of a poem, written to be sung in public worship. Each psalm expresses an aspect of the depth of human prayer. Over several centuries, 150 psalms were assembled into the Book of Psalms in the Old Testament. Psalms were used in worship in the Temple in Jerusalem, and they have been used in the public worship of the Church since its beginning.

purgatory a state of final cleansing after death of all our human imperfections to prepare us to enter into the joy of God's presence in heaven

R

Real Presence the way in which the risen Jesus Christ is present in the Eucharist under the form of bread and wine. Jesus Christ's presence is called real because in the Eucharist, his Body and Blood, soul and divinity, are wholly and entirely present.

reconciliation the renewal of friendship after that friendship has been broken by some action or lack of action. In the Sacrament of Penance and Reconciliation, through God's mercy and forgiveness, we are reconciled with God, the Church, and others.

Redeemer Jesus Christ, whose life, sacrificial death on the cross, and Resurrection from the dead set us free from the slavery of sin and bring us redemption

religious life a state of life recognized by the Church. In the religious life, men and women freely respond to a call to follow Jesus by living the vows of poverty, chastity, and obedience in community with others.

Resurrection the bodily raising of Jesus Christ from the dead on the third day after his death on the cross. The Resurrection is the crowning truth of our faith.

Revelation God's communication of himself to us through the words and deeds he has used throughout history to show us the mystery of his plan for our salvation. This Revelation reaches its completion in his sending of his Son, Jesus Christ.

rite one of the many forms followed in celebrating liturgy in the Church. A rite may differ according to the culture or country where it is celebrated. A rite is also the special form for celebrating each sacrament.

Rite of Christian Initiation of Adults (RCIA) a program of religious instruction and a series of rituals through which a person, called a catechumen, is formed in the Christian life. Through conversion and maturity of faith, a catechumen is welcomed into the Church at Easter through the Sacraments of Baptism, Confirmation, and the Eucharist. Baptized Christians who are preparing to be received into full communion with the Roman Catholic Church may also take part in the RCIA.

Roman Missal the book containing the prayers used for the celebration of the Eucharist. It is placed on the altar for the celebrant to use during Mass.

Rosary a prayer in honor of the Blessed Virgin Mary. When we pray the Rosary, we meditate on the mysteries of Jesus Christ's life while praying the Hail Mary on 5 sets of 10 beads and the Lord's Prayer on the beads in between. In the Latin Church, praying the Rosary became a way for ordinary people to reflect on the mysteries of Christ's life.

S

Sabbath the seventh day, when God rested after finishing the work of creation. The Third Commandment requires us to keep the Sabbath holy. For Christians, the Sabbath became Sunday because it was the day Jesus rose from the dead and the new creation in Jesus Christ began.

sacrament one of seven ways through which God's life enters our lives through the work of the Holy Spirit. Jesus gave us three sacraments that bring us into the Church: Baptism, Confirmation, and the Eucharist. He gave us two sacraments that bring us healing: Reconciliation and Anointing of the Sick. He also gave us two sacraments that help members serve the community: Matrimony and Holy Orders.

Sacrament of Penance and Reconciliation the sacrament in which we celebrate God's forgiveness of sin and our reconciliation with God and the Church. Reconciliation includes sorrow for the sins we have committed, confession of sins, absolution by the priest, and doing the penance that shows our willingness to amend our ways.

sacramental an object, a prayer, or a blessing given by the Church to help us grow in our spiritual life

Sacraments at the Service of Communion the Sacraments of Holy Orders and Matrimony. These two sacraments contribute to the personal salvation of individuals by giving them a way to serve others.

Sacraments of Healing the Sacraments of Reconciliation and Anointing of the Sick, by which the Church continues the healing ministry of Jesus for soul and body

Sacraments of Initiation the sacraments that are the foundation of our Christian life. We are born anew in Baptism, strengthened by Confirmation, and receive in the Eucharist the food of eternal life. By means of these sacraments, we receive an increasing measure of divine life and advance toward the perfection of charity.

sacrifice a ritual offering of animals or produce made to God by the priest in the Temple in Jerusalem. Sacrifice was a sign of the people's adoration of God, giving thanks to God, or asking for his forgiveness. Sacrifice also showed union with God. The great high priest, Christ, accomplished our redemption through the perfect sacrifice of his death on the cross.

Sacrifice of the Mass the sacrifice of Jesus on the cross, which is remembered and mysteriously made present in the Eucharist. It is offered in reparation for the sins of the living and the dead and to obtain spiritual or temporal blessings from God.

saint a holy person who has died united with God. The Church has said that this person is now with God forever in heaven.

salvation the gift, which God alone can give, of forgiveness of sin and the restoration of friendship with him

sanctifying grace the gift of God, given to us without our earning it, that unites us with the life of the Trinity and heals our human nature, wounded by sin. Sanctifying grace continues the work of making us holy that began at our Baptism.

Satan the leader of the evil spirits or devils whom he led in revolt against God. His name means "adversary." God allows Satan to tempt us but gives us the grace to overcome him.

Savior Jesus, the Son of God, who became human to forgive our sins and to restore our friendship with God. *Jesus* means "God saves."

Scriptures the holy writings of Jews and Christians collected in the Old and New Testaments of the Bible

Sermon on the Mount the words of Jesus, written in Chapters 5 through 7 of the Gospel of Matthew, in which Jesus reveals how he has fulfilled God's law given to Moses. The Sermon on the Mount begins with the eight Beatitudes and includes the Lord's Prayer.

sin a deliberate thought, word, deed, or failure to act that offends God and hurts our relationships with other people. Some sin is mortal and needs to be confessed in the Sacrament of Penance and Reconciliation. Other sin is venial, or less serious.

social justice the fair and equal treatment of every member of society. It is required by the dignity and freedom of every person. The Catholic Church has developed a body of social principles and moral teachings described in papal and other official documents issued since the late 19th century. This teaching deals with the economic, political, and social order of the world. It is rooted in the Bible as well as in the traditional theological teachings of the Church.

Son of God the title revealed by Jesus that indicates his unique relationship to God the Father. The revelation of Jesus' divine sonship is the main dramatic development of the story of Jesus of Nazareth as it unfolds in the Gospels.

soul the part of us that makes us human and an image of God. Body and soul together form one unique human nature. The soul is responsible for our consciousness and for our freedom. The soul does not die and is reunited with the body in the final resurrection.

Spiritual Works of Mercy the kind acts through which we help our neighbors meet the needs that are more than material. The Spiritual Works of Mercy include counseling the doubtful, instructing the ignorant, admonishing sinners, comforting the afflicted, forgiving offenses, bearing wrongs patiently, and praying for the living and the dead.

suicide the act of deliberately and intentionally taking one's own life. It is a sin against the Fifth Commandment because we are stewards, not owners, of the life God has given us. Serious psychological disturbances, fears, and suffering can lessen the responsibility of a person who committed suicide. Only God can offer salvation to people who have taken their own life. The Church encourages us to pray for such people.

synagogue the Jewish place of assembly for prayer, instruction, and study of the Law. After the destruction of the Temple in 587 B.C., synagogues were organized as places to maintain Jewish faith and worship. Jesus attended the synagogue regularly to pray and to teach. In every city Paul visited, he went to the synagogue first. The synagogue played an important role in the development of Christian worship and in the structure of Christian communities.

T

tabernacle the container in which the Blessed Sacrament is kept so that Holy Communion can be taken to the sick and the dying. *Tabernacle* is also the name of the tent sanctuary in which the Israelites kept the Ark of the Covenant from the time of the Exodus to the construction of Solomon's Temple.

Temple the house of worship of God, first built by Solomon. The Temple provided a place for the priests to offer sacrifice, to adore and give thanks to God, and to ask for forgiveness. It was destroyed and rebuilt. The second Temple was also destroyed, this time by the Romans in A.D. 70, and was never rebuilt. Part of the outer wall of the Temple mount remains to this day in Jerusalem.

temptation an attraction, from outside us or inside us, that can lead us to disobey God's commands. Everyone is tempted, but the Holy Spirit helps us to resist temptation and choose to do good.

Ten Commandments the 10 rules given by God to Moses on Mount Sinai that sum up God's law and show us what is required to love God and our neighbor. By following the Ten Commandments, the Hebrews accepted their Covenant with God.

Torah the Hebrew word for "instruction" or "law." It is also the name of the first five books of the Old Testament: Genesis, Exodus, Leviticus, Numbers, and Deuteronomy.

Tradition the beliefs and practices of the Church that are passed down from one generation to the next under the guidance of the Holy Spirit. What Christ entrusted to the apostles was handed on to others both orally and in writing. Tradition and Scripture together make up the single deposit of the Word of God, which remains present and active in the Church.

transubstantiation the unique change of the bread and wine in the Eucharist into the Body and Blood of the risen Jesus Christ, while retaining its physical appearance as bread and wine

Trinity the mystery of the existence of God in three Persons—the Father, the Son, and the Holy Spirit. Each is God, whole and entire. Each is distinct only in the relationship of each to the others.

V

venial sin a choice we make that weakens our relationship with God or with other people. Venial sin wounds and lessens the divine life in us. If we make no effort to do better, venial sin can lead to more serious sin. Through our participation in the Eucharist, venial sin is forgiven, strengthening our relationship with God and with others.

viaticum the Eucharist that a dying person receives. It is spiritual food for the last journey we make as Christians, the journey through death to eternal life.

virtue an attitude or way of acting that helps us do good. A virtue is a habit of doing good.

vocation the call each of us has in life to be the person God wants each to be and the way we each serve the Church and the Kingdom of God. Each of us can live out his or her vocation as a layperson, as a member of a religious community, or as a member of the clergy.

vow a deliberate and free promise made to God by people who want especially to dedicate their lives to God. The vows give witness now to the kingdom that is to come.

W

witness the passing on to others, by our words and by our actions, the faith that we have been given. Every Christian has the duty to give witness to the good news about Jesus Christ that he or she has come to know.

worship the adoration and honor given to God in public prayer

Y

Yahweh the name of God in Hebrew, which God told Moses from the burning bush. *Yahweh* means "I am who am" or "I cause to be all that is."

Index

RCIA. *See* Rite of Christian Initiation of Adults (RCIA)
Real Presence, 235
Rebekah, 44, 47, 48, 50
reconciliation, 99, 101, 235. *See also* Penance and Reconciliation, Sacrament of
Red Sea (crossing), 73
Redeemer, 235
relationship conflicts, 25
religious life, 235
respect, 174d
Resurrection, 186, 235
Reuel, 69
Revelation, 10, 15, 235
rite, 236
Rite of Christian Initiation of Adults (RCIA), 236
rituals, 114a, 114b, 114c, 114d, 125. *See also specific rituals*
Roman Missal, 236
Romero, Archbishop Oscar, 146
Rosary, 210, 211, 212, 236
Ruth, 119–20

S

Sabbath, 87, 236. *See also* Lord's Day
sacramentals, 236
sacraments, 50, 218, 236. *See also specific sacraments*
Sacraments at the Service of Communion, 236
Sacraments of Healing, 236
Sacraments of Initiation, 236
sacred deposit, 6
sacrifice, 43, 61, 236
Sacrifice of the Mass, 236. *See also* Mass

saint, 236. *See also specific saints*
Salvation, 236
Salvation History timeline, 166
Samson, 119
Samuel, 123, 124, 129, 140
sanctifying grace, 236
Sanctus, 209
Sarah, 41
Satan, 42, 236. *See also* devil
Saul, King, 124, 129
Savior, 236. *See also* Jesus
Scriptures, 237. *See also* Bible
  God reveals himself through, 9
  inspired, 10
  Jesus, path to knowing, 5
  locating passages, 14
  sacredness, 6, 11
Second Isaiah, 150, 151
seder, 73
self-discipline, 162
seraphim, 149
Sermon on the Mount, 93, 237
serpent, 24
seven deadly sins. *See* sin
Shiloh, 105
Sign of the Cross, 86, 209
  Rosary, as part of praying, 210, 211
Signum Crucis, 209. *See also* Sign of the Cross
sin, 237
  choosing, 27
  definition, 29
  effects of, 25, 26
  exile, as form of, 157
  God's reaction to, 29
  mortal (*see* mortal sin)
  original (*see* original sin)
  separation from God, 25
  seven deadly, 54

tendencies toward, recognizing, 140d
  venial (*see* venial sin)
Sinai, 79
Sisera, 118
social justice, 85, 147, 237
solidarity, 55
Solomon, King
  end of reign, 132, 140
  followed father's commands,131
  God's pleasure with, 131
  proverbs by, 132
  wisdom of, 116, 132
Son of God, 237. *See also* Jesus
Sorrowful Mysteries, 212. *See also* Rosary
soul, 19, 21, 237
Spiritual Works of Mercy, 146, 217, 237
Stations of the Cross, 213, 214
stewardship, 20
suicide, 237
Suscipe, 178
symbols
  Christian *(see specific symbols)*
  Genesis, from book of, 179
  of faith, 36a
  of life, 188
synagogue, 158, 237

T

tabernacle, 237
temperance, 217
Temple, 132, 237
temptation, 237
Ten Commandments. *See* Commandments, Ten
theological virtues, 217
Third Isaiah, 150

Torah, 12, 237. *See also* Pentateuch
Tower of Babel, 26
Tradition, 10, 237
transubstantiation, 238
tree of knowledge of good and evil, 24
Triduum, 185, 186
Trinity, 238
truth, 140b

U

understanding, 217
Uriah, 129

V

venial sin, 100, 238. *See also* sin
viaticum, 238
Vicar of Christ, 106
virtues, 100, 217, 238
vocation, 238
Votive Mass, 74
vow, 238

W

wisdom, 217
Wisdom literature, 12
witness, 238
worship, 238

Y

Yahweh, 238
YHWH, 70

Z

Zechariah, 161, 162
ziggurats, 26

Scripture Index

Art Credits

When there is more than one picture on a page, credits are supplied in sequence, left to right, top to bottom. Page positions are abbreviated as follows: (t) top, (c) center, (b) bottom, (l) left, (r) right.

FRONT MATTER:
iii(cr) © Roy Gumpel/Getty
iii(bl) © The Crosiers/Gene Plaisted OSC
iv(t) Michael Muir
iv(b) © The Crosiers/Gene Plaisted OSC
vi(br) © The Crosiers/Gene Plaisted OSC

UNIT 1:
5(tr) John Brandi Co., Inc.
8 © Franck Fotos/Alamy
9 The Bridgeman Art Library/Getty
10(bc) © The Crosiers/Gene Plaisted OSC
11(tr) www.colonialarts.com
12 William Gorman
14 (bl) © Eric and David Hosking/Corbis
14(br) © Dr. John C. Trever, Ph. D./Corbis
15 www.AgnusImages.com
16 Phil Martin Photography
17 © The Crosiers/Gene Plaisted OSC
18(tr) Scala/Art Resource, NY
22 © The Crosiers/Gene Plaisted OSC
23(tr) Smithsonian American Art Museum, Washington, DC/ Art Resource, NY
23(br) © Getty Images
24(t) Robert Voigts
24(c) © Images.com/Corbis
24(b) © The Crosiers/Gene Plaisted OSC
25(b) © William Hart McNichols
26(tl) The Jewish Museum, NY/Art Resource, NY
26(tr) Robert Voigts
27(t) William Gorman
27(b) © Tim McGuire/Corbis
29 Erich Lessing/Art Resource, NY
30 Alinari/Art Resource, NY
32 © The Crosiers/Gene Plaisted OSC
33(tr) © The Crosiers/Gene Plaisted OSC
34 (t) www.unitedcaribbean.com/lettersofencouragement
34-35(b) Theo Allofs /Getty
35(t) © The Crosiers/Gene Plaisted OSC
36 © Visions of America, LLC/Alamy
36a(bl) © San Bernardino Public Library
36b(br) Erich Lessing/Art Resource, NY
36c(t) Roger Roth

UNIT 2:
39(b) © The Crosiers/Gene Plaisted OSC
41(t) William Gorman
42(t) © William Hart McNichols
42(c) Phil Martin Photography
43(t) © The Crosiers/Gene Plaisted OSC
44 The Jewish Museum, NY/Art Resource, NY
45 © Corbis Corp.
46 Erich Lessing/Art Resource, NY
47(b) The Jewish Museum, NY/Art Resource, NY
48(t) William Gorman
48(b) Scala/Art Resource, NY
49 © The Crosiers/Gene Plaisted OSC
50(b) © The Crosiers/Gene Plaisted OSC
51(t) Erich Lessing/Art Resource, NY
51 Phil Martin Photography

52(t) Bill Wood
52(b) © The Crosiers/Gene Plaisted OSC
55 William Gorman
56(bl) © The Crosiers/Gene Plaisted OSC
57(t) © The Crosiers/Gene Plaisted OSC
57(b) Vera Siffner/Veer
59 Joseph recognised by his brothers, Cornelius, Peter von (1783-1867)/ Staatliche Museen, Berlin, Germany,/The Bridgeman Art Library
61(c) © The Crosiers/Gene Plaisted OSC
62(b) © The Crosiers/Gene Plaisted OSC
63(b) © The Crosiers/Gene Plaisted OSC
65(t) © W.P. Wittman Limited
66(t) © Jim Craigmyle/Corbis
66b(tr) Julie Lonneman/SpiritSource.com
66b(tl) StockFood
66b(bc) © St. James Cathedral, Seattle
66b Bob Daemmrich
66c Julie Lonneman/SpiritSource.com

UNIT 3:
67-68 Scala/Art Resource, NY
69-70(t) Ray App
72(t) Proof Positive/Farrowlyne Assoc., Inc.
72(b) www.AgnusImages.com
73(t) © Shelley Gazin/Corbis
73(c) Ray App
75(b) © Galleria Borghese, Rome/Canali Photo Bank, Milan/SuperStock, Inc.
76(bc) © The Crosiers/Gene Plaisted OSC
77(t) Scala/Art Resource, NY
78(tl) Ray App
78(c) © Myrleen Ferguson Cate/PhotoEdit
79(c) Michael Muir
80(c) © Digital Stock Corp.
81(b) © The Crosiers/Gene Plaisted OSC
84(b) © The Crosiers/Gene Plaisted OSC
86(tr) © The Crosiers/Gene Plaisted OSC
87(tr) Scala/Art Resource, NY
88(br) Scala/Art Resource, NY
90(t) © The Crosiers/Gene Plaisted OSC
91(b) Ray App
92(t) © Sadao Watanabe
93(b) © The Crosiers/Gene Plaisted OSC
94(c) © Images.com/Corbis
94(b) Roy Gumpel/Getty
95 The Sermon on the Mount (figures possibly by Hans Jordeans), Momper, Joos or Josse de, The Younger (1564-1635)/Johnny van Haeften Gallery, London, UK, /The Bridgeman Art Library
97(b) Ray App
98(t) Scala/Art Resource, NY
100(t) © Myrleen Ferguson Cate/PhotoEdit
103(t) Scala/Art Resource, NY
103(b) Erich Lessing/Art Resource, NY
104 Ray App
105(t) © The Crosiers/Gene Plaisted OSC
106(t) © Alessandra Benedetti/Corbis
107 The Fall of Jericho, 1996, Galambos, Tamas (Contemporary Artist)/ Private Collection, /The Bridgeman Art Library
108(b) Erich Lessing/Art Resource, NY

UNIT 4:
109(t) © The Crosiers/Gene Plaisted OSC
109(b) © Myrleen Ferguson Cate/PhotoEdit
110-111 Bill Wood Illustration

Continued on page 262

Lesson Pullouts

- **Map of Palestine**

- **With Christ We Die and Rise**

- **Reconciliation Booklet**

- **Prayer Leaflets**

- **Scripture Prayer Booklet**

- **Timeline: God's Saving Plan of Love**

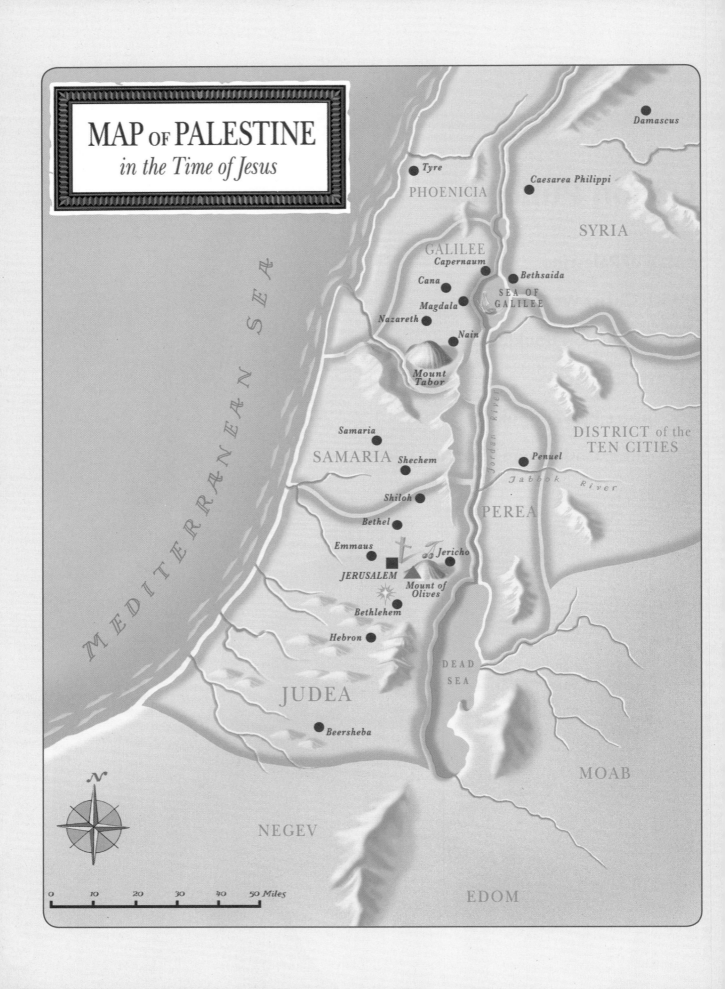

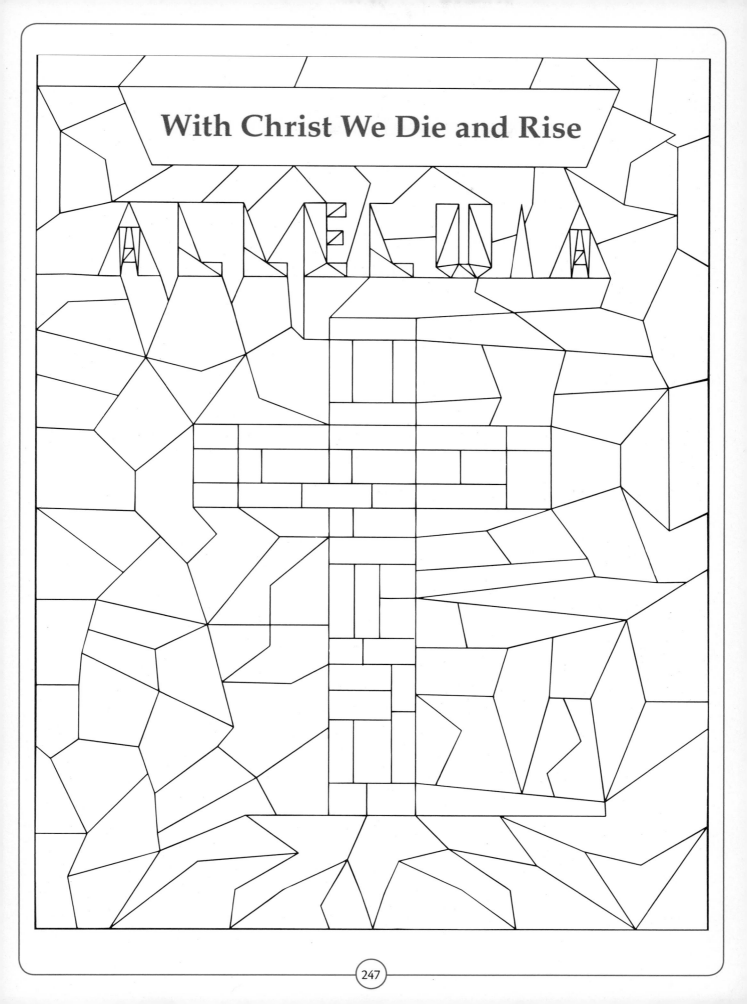

With Christ We Die and Rise

Preparing for Easter

Christ's saving death was completed and made perfect in his Resurrection. Through Baptism, Jesus calls each of us to share in the mystery of his cross. Each year during Lent, we recall Christ's saving love, and we accept the cross in our life. We pray and we fast to prepare ourselves to enter into the fullness of resurrected life with Jesus. We give alms and do kind deeds, sharing the good things God has given to us.

Directions for your Mosaic

1. Spend time in prayer each day. Every day that you do, color a triangle (▲) piece of the mosaic red or orange.

2. Give up something; fast from doing it. Every day you are faithful to your fast and offer it in love to God, color an irregular (⬣) piece of the mosaic green.

3. Each day you have quietly given alms and shared God's love with others, color a rectangular (▬) piece of the mosaic yellow.

On Easter Sunday, place this mosaic where you can see it as a reminder of the joy of the Resurrection.

- Have I taken anything that is not mine? Have I returned things that I borrowed? Have I damaged anything that belongs to someone else?
- Do I speak the truth? Have I been kind in talking about other people? Have I guarded the good reputation of others?
- Am I willing to be friendly to everyone, or do I belong to a closed group of friends?
- Do I do what I can to help those who have less than I do?
- Have I avoided doing good things when I could and should have done them?
- Is something else I did bothering me because it was unloving?

I Read God's Holy Word

[L]et us rid ourselves of every burden and sin that clings to us and persevere in running the race that lies before us while keeping our eyes fixed on Jesus, the leader and perfecter of faith. For the sake of the joy that lay before him he endured the cross, despising its shame, and has taken his seat at the right of the throne of God. Consider how he endured such opposition from sinners, in order that you may not grow weary and lose heart. In your struggle against sin you have not yet resisted to the point of shedding blood.

Hebrews 12:1–4

Some Other Readings:

Mark 2:17
Luke 15:1–10
Matthew 5:13–16

Luke 18:9–14
John 15:9–14
James 2:14–26

How to Go to Confession

- The priest welcomes me, and I greet him.
- I make the Sign of the Cross.
- The priest says a prayer to remind me of God's forgiving love. I say "Amen."
- The priest or I may read about God's forgiving love from the Bible.
- I make my confession. I may begin by saying "Forgive me, Father, I have sinned. My last confession was (number of weeks or months) ago."
- I tell the priest my sins. When I finish, I may say "I am sorry for all my sins."
- The priest talks to me and gives me a penance.
- I pray an act of contrition.
- The priest prays over me and says the words of absolution. I say "Amen."
- The priest may pray a prayer of thanksgiving such as "Give thanks to the Lord, for he is good." I answer "His mercy endures forever."
- Do your penance.

RECONCILIATION BOOKLET

El Greco, *Christ carrying the cross.*

Jesus says, "Take my yoke upon you and learn from me, for I am meek and humble of heart; and you will find rest for yourselves. For my yoke is easy, and my burden light."

Matthew 11:29–30

Name: _____

I Examine My Conscience

Have I loved God?

- Have I spent time praying to God each day? Did I try to give God my full attention when I prayed?
- Have I always used God's name with love and respect?
- Have I celebrated every Sunday and holy day by participating in the Eucharist? Have I really tried to pray and sing at Mass, or was I a distraction to myself and others?
- Have I thanked God for his goodness to me?

Have I loved myself and others?

- Have I been obedient and respectful to my parents and others who care for me? Have I loved and prayed for them?
- Have I shown respect for my life and the lives of others? Have I hurt myself by the use of drugs or alcohol? Have I hurt anyone else through my words or actions? If I became angry or jealous, did I try to handle my feelings in a positive way?

- Have I used the gifts of mind, spirit, and body that God has given me to bring happiness to others?
- Have I shown respect for my body? For others' bodies? Have I used language or viewed images that disrespect the human body?
- Am I grateful for my possessions or am I envious of others' possessions? Do I show respect for God's creation and for the resources of the earth? Do I share with others?

God loves us and asks us to love him, ourselves, and others. When we turn away and fail in love, Jesus invites us to return to him so that he can forgive us. He has given us his Holy Spirit to help us. Let us now prepare to meet Jesus in the Sacrament of Penance and Reconciliation.

I Pray to the Holy Spirit

Come, Holy Spirit, and help me to know how much God loves me and wants to forgive me. Help me to see and to love the goodness God has placed in me and in others. Show me how I have failed to love, and help me to be sorry for my sins.

Come, Holy Spirit,
   fill the hearts
        of your faithful
and kindle in them
   the fire of your love.

I Pray an Act of Contrition

My God,
I am sorry for my sins with all my heart.
In choosing to do wrong
and failing to do good,
I have sinned against you
whom I should love above all things.
I firmly intend, with your help,
to do penance,
to sin no more,
and to avoid whatever leads me to sin.
Our Savior Jesus Christ
suffered and died for us.
In his name, my God, have mercy.

Rite of Reconciliation

I Plan for the Future

I think about how I should change to follow Jesus more closely.
I make a resolution and promise Jesus I will try not to sin again.

Teach us, good Lord,
to serve you as you deserve;
to give and not count the cost;
to fight and not heed the wounds;
to toil and not seek for rest;
to labor and not ask for reward
save that of knowing we do your will
through Jesus Christ our Lord.

Act of Spiritual Communion

My Jesus, I long for you in my soul. Since I cannot receive you sacramentally, come at least spiritually into my soul. As though you have already come, I embrace you. Never permit me to be separated from you.

Morning Offering

As soon as you wake up, make the Sign of the Cross and pray:

O Jesus, through the Immaculate Heart of Mary,
I offer you my prayers, works, joys, and suffering
   of this day
in union with the holy sacrifice of the Mass
   throughout the world.
I offer them for all the intentions of your Sacred
   Heart:
the salvation of souls,
reparation for sin,
the reunion of all Christians.
I offer them for the intentions of our bishops and
   of all members of the Apostleship of Prayer,
and in particular for those recommended by our
   Holy Father this month. Amen.

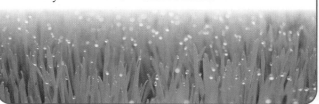

Lord, we beg you to visit this house and banish from it all the deadly power of the enemy. May your holy angels dwell here to keep us in peace, and may your blessing be upon us always. We ask this through Christ our Lord.

Liturgy of the Hours: Night Prayer

Holy God, holy strong One, holy immortal One, have mercy on us.

Byzantine tradition

Salve, Regina

Hail, holy Queen, Mother of mercy,
hail, our life, our sweetness, and our hope.
To you we cry, the children of Eve;
to you we send up our sighs,
mourning and weeping in this land of exile.
Turn, then, most gracious advocate,
your eyes of mercy toward us;
lead us home at last
and show us the blessed fruit of your womb,
   Jesus:
O clement, O loving, O sweet Virgin Mary.

Evening Prayer

Talk to God every night. Tell him how you felt that day and thank him for being with you. Pray any of the following prayers.

My God,
I am sorry for my sins with all my heart.
In choosing to do wrong
and failing to do good,
I have sinned against you
whom I should love above all things.
I firmly intend, with your help
to do penance,
to sin no more,
and to avoid whatever leads me to sin.
Our Savior Jesus Christ
suffered and died for us.
In his name, my God, have mercy.

Talk to God about the things you plan to do today. Ask God to help you do them well and for his glory. Pray any of the following prayers.

The Shema

"Hear, O Israel! The Lord is our God, the Lord alone! Therefore, you shall love the Lord, your God, with all your heart, and with all your soul, and with all your strength."

Deuteronomy 6:4–5

O Lord, I give myself to you, I trust you wholly. You are wiser than I, more loving to me than I am to myself. Fulfill your high purpose in me whatever that be: work in me and through me. I am born to serve you, to be yours, to be your instrument. Let me turn my will over to you. I ask not to see, I ask not to know, I ask simply to be one with you in love.

John Henry Cardinal Newman

2

Psalm 95

Come, let us sing joyfully to the Lord;
　cry out to the rock of our salvation.
Let us greet him with a song of praise,
　joyfully sing out our psalms.
For the Lord is the great God,
　the great king over all gods,
Whose hand holds the depths of the earth;
　who owns the tops of the mountains.
The sea and the dry land belong to God,
　who made them, formed them by hand.

Enter, let us bow down in worship;
　let us kneel before the Lord who made us.
For this is our God,
　whose people we are,
　God's well-tended flock.

3

Psalm 23

The Lord is my shepherd;
　there is nothing I lack.
In green pastures you let me graze;
　to safe waters you lead me;
　you restore my strength.
You guide me along the right path
　for the sake of your name.
Even when I walk through a dark valley,
　I fear no harm for you are at my side;
　your rod and staff give me courage.

You set a table before me
　as my enemies watch;
You anoint my head with oil;
　my cup overflows.
Only goodness and love will
　pursue me
　all the days of my life;
I will dwell in the house
　of the Lord
　for years to come.

2

My Father, I abandon myself to you. Do with me as you will. Whatever you may do with me I thank you. I am prepared for anything. I accept everything, provided your will is fulfilled in me and in all creatures. I ask for nothing more, my God. I place my soul in your hands. I give it to you, my God, with all the love of my heart because I love you. And for me, it is a necessity of love, this gift of myself, this placing of myself in your hands without reserve in boundless confidence, because you are my Father.

Charles de Foucauld

Take and receive, O Lord, all my liberty, my memory, my understanding, all my will. All that I have and possess, you have given to me. I restore it all to you. I surrender it in order that you may dispose of it according to your will. Only give me your love and your grace and I shall be rich enough and shall seek nothing more.

Saint Ignatius of Loyola

3

My Page

For favorite Scripture quotations, personal prayers, and reflections . . .

Scripture Prayer Booklet

God's Word
Is Alive in
Name: ____________________

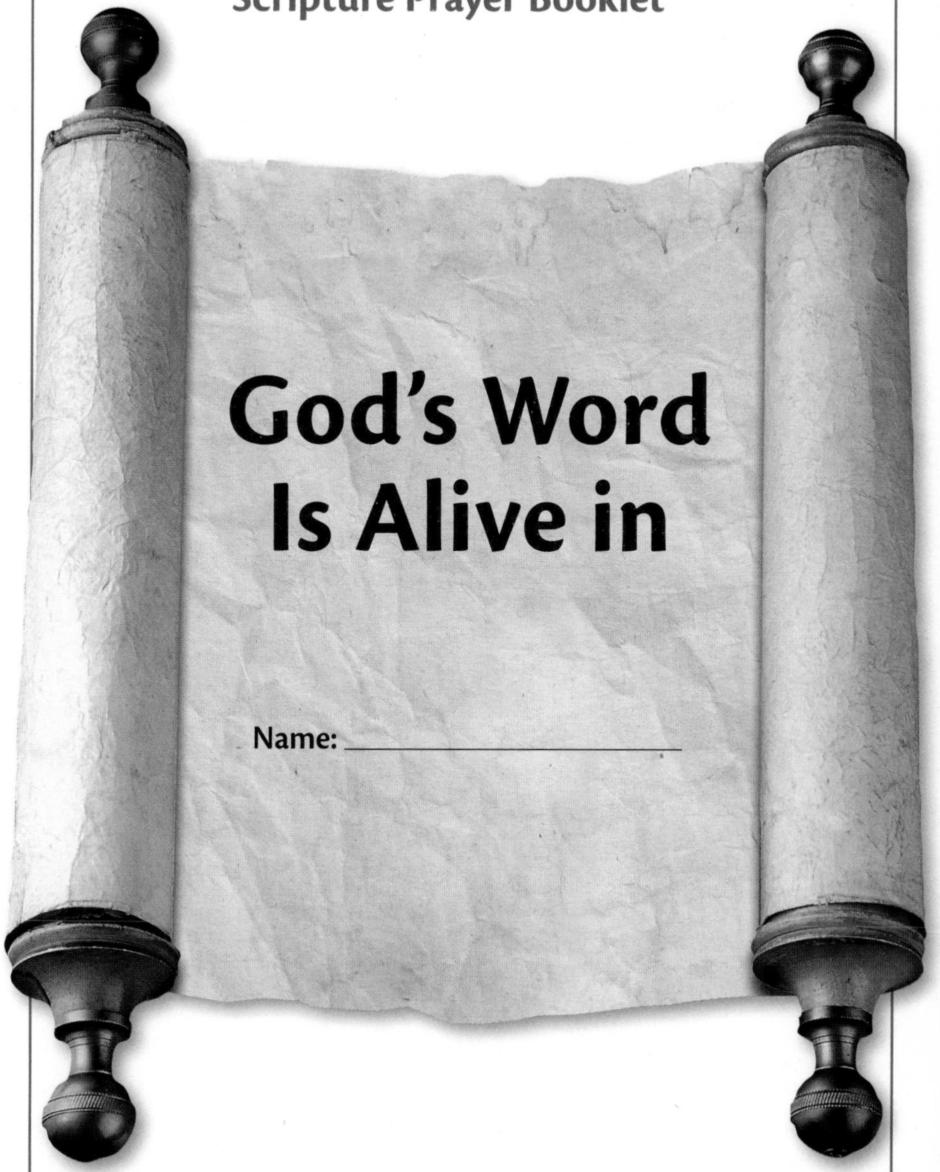

God has gifted us with his holy Word in Sacred Scripture. This Word will guide us wisely through all the events of our lives. We pray that we will really listen and be open as God speaks to us.

Father, we praise and thank you for your holy Word.

We ask you to open our hearts and enlighten our minds as we come to know you better through the inspiration of your Word.

We ask you to give us strength to follow the plan you have for our lives. This plan will bring us closer to you. May we be led by your Son, Jesus, and guided by the truth of your Spirit.

Amen

Read 1 Timothy 4:12. How does this passage make you feel? Write your thoughts below.

Read Psalm 34:1–9 below. Then write words that describe how you felt after reading the psalm.

Psalm 34

I will bless the LORD at all times;
    praise shall always be in my mouth.
My soul will glory in the LORD;
    that the poor may hear and be glad.
Magnify the LORD with me;
    let us exalt his name together.

I sought the LORD, who answered me,
    delivered me from all my fears.
Look to God that you may be radiant with joy
    and your faces may not blush for shame.
In my misfortune I called,
    the LORD heard and saved me from all distress.
The angel of the LORD, who encamps with them,
    delivers all who fear God.
Learn to savor how good the LORD is;
    happy are those who take refuge in him.

List below the things you want to talk to God about.

_____

_____

_____

_____

Let Your Love Shine!

In each candle, write the name of someone for whom you want to pray. Then on that day, make a special effort to keep that person in your thoughts and prayers.

| Sunday | Monday | Tuesday | Wednesday | Thursday | Friday | Saturday |

God's Word Leads to Victory

Read 1 Samuel 17:38–51 to discover how God led David the shepherd boy to triumph.

What special things did David use to help him?

_____

Listed in the crown are Scripture passages that suggest special things or actions that will help you lead a happy life. Read each passage. Then write in the space around the crown words or phrases that will help you remember the message in each passage.

Ephesians 4:32   1 Thessalonians 5:17–18   Acts of the Apostles 2:42

Colossians 4:2

Write on the lines below 1 Corinthians 10:31.

_____

_____

How to Pray God's Holy Word

1. As often as possible, set aside time to be with God.

2. Choose a place to pray—your room, church, outdoors.

3. Ask the Holy Spirit to help you understand. Speak to the Holy Spirit simply, using your own words. For example:

   Please open my heart, Holy Spirit.

   Help me to hear your words to me.

4. Read a short section from Scripture.

5. Think quietly about what you have read.

6. Speak to God from your heart.

How to Remember God's Holy Word

1. Choose only one or two lines from Scripture at first. Read the selection slowly and carefully.

2. Pause and think prayerfully about the passage.

3. Summarize the selection in your own words.

4. Read aloud the selection several times.

5. Write the selection in a Scripture log or journal.

6. Learn the selection by heart.

7. Check—repeat—check again!

Jeremiah was the first prophet chosen to tell the people about the New Covenant God would make with them.

Read prayerfully the two readings from Jeremiah. Then write your own prayer response to God.

Jeremiah 31:3

_____

_____

_____

_____

_____

Jeremiah 31:33

_____

_____

_____

_____

_____

Letting Go of Grudges

We all want to be a friend and to have friends. One of the easiest ways to lose a friend is to carry a grudge. It is much better to forgive and forget, because forgiveness helps build friendships. What does Scripture tell us about forgiveness? Fill in the chart and answer the questions.

Scripture	Lesson Taught
Matthew 5:43–48	
Romans 12:17–21	
2 Corinthians 5:17–20	
Matthew 18:21–22	
Colossians 3:12–14	
1 John 4:19–21	

What must you do to become a forgiving friend? How will you carry out your plan? _____

Where and When to Pray God's Holy Word

Find these passages to learn more about where and when to pray.

	Where to pray . . .	When to pray . . .
Luke 6:12		
Mark 1:35		
Matthew 6:6		
Luke 4:16		
Luke 23:39–42		

Saint Paul gave the Ephesians this advice (Ephesians 5:20): _____

5

Treasure Hunt

Choose a reading from Scripture. In the box, write a word or phrase or draw a symbol to help you remember God's message to you.

When you are thankful, read
◯ Psalm 138
◯ Luke 17:11–19

When you are frightened, read
◯ Luke 12:32
◯ John 14:1–4

When you are discouraged, read
◯ John 16:22,33
◯ Matthew 6:28–34

When you are happy, read
◯ Philippians 4:4–7
◯ Psalm 23

When you need prayer, read
◯ John 14:13–14
◯ Matthew 7:7–11 or 18:19–20

When you need love, read
◯ John 15:15
◯ Philippians 1:7–9

When you need forgiveness, read
◯ Matthew 9:6–13
◯ Mark 11:24–25

When you want to follow Jesus, read
◯ Luke 9:23–26
◯ Mark 6:7–13

History Timelines

In the sixth-grade book, we explore how God has called his people throughout Old Testament history. On the following pages, you will find a timeline of God's Saving Plan of Love, indicating many significant events in Old Testament history. Below are listed some significant events in world history that provide a context for the Old Testament history events on the pages that follow.

4000 B.C. Sumerians settle in the land between the Tigris and Euphrates Rivers.

3500 B.C. Sumerians develop wheels for transportation and a system of writing.

2500 B.C. The city of Ur becomes a prominent urban center.

2000 B.C. **1792–1750 B.C.** Hammurabi establishes the first Babylonian empire and publishes a code of law.

1500 B.C. **1480 B.C.** Pharaoh Tutmose III expands the Egyptian empire through Canaan to the Euphrates River.

1000 B.C. **1200 B.C.** The *Epic of Gilgamesh* is recorded. ❯

900 B.C.

800 B.C. **750 B.C.** The city of Rome is founded.

700 B.C.

604 B.C. The Babylonian king Nebuchadnezzar II conquers the Assyrian empire. ❮

600 B.C. **595 B.C.** King Nebuchadnezzar II rebuilds the city of Babylon.

500 B.C. **539 B.C.** Cyrus the Great of Persia conquers Babylonia. ❯

A.D. 1 **63 B.C.** Roman rule extends to Palestine.

God's Sav[ing]

1900 B.C.

Stories of the Beginning

Creation, Sin and the Promise, Cain and Abel, The Flood, the Tower of Babel

c. 1850 — Abraham Our Father in Faith

1800

Patriarchs

Isaac   Jacob

1700

c. 1650 — Joseph sold into slavery

1100

Kings

Saul

1000 — David Greatest King of Israel

961

900 — Solomon Builder of the Temple

800

Prophe[ts]

Elijah
Isaiah
Amos

Plan of Love

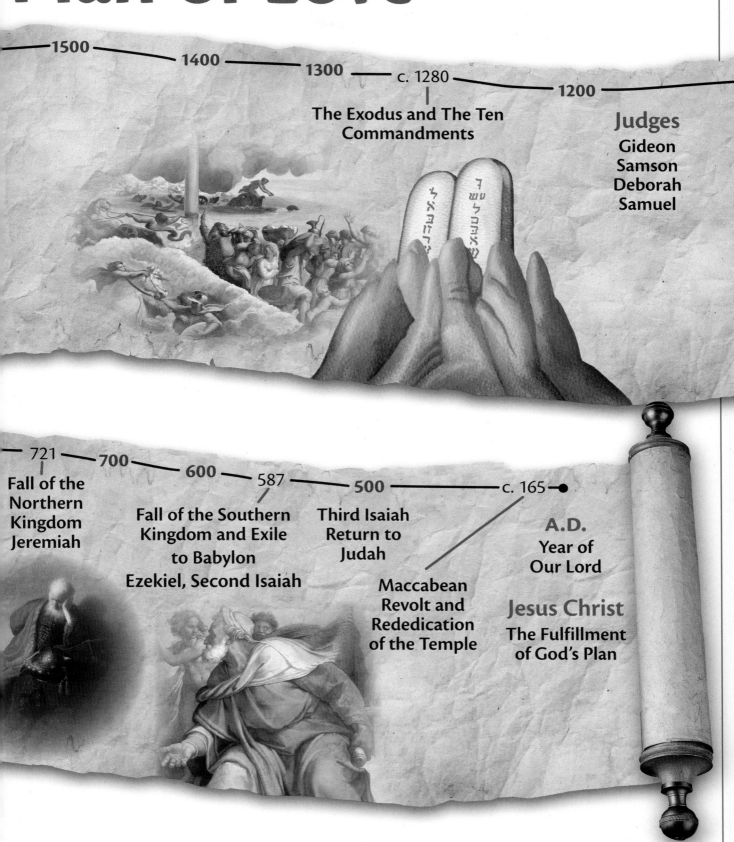

1500 — **1400** — **1300** — **c. 1280** — **1200**

The Exodus and The Ten Commandments

Judges
Gideon
Samson
Deborah
Samuel

721 — **700** — **600** — **587** — **500** — **c. 165** —

Fall of the Northern Kingdom
Jeremiah

Fall of the Southern Kingdom and Exile to Babylon
Ezekiel, Second Isaiah

Third Isaiah Return to Judah

Maccabean Revolt and Rededication of the Temple

A.D.
Year of Our Lord

Jesus Christ
The Fulfillment of God's Plan

Continued from page 244

113(br) The Sermon on the Mount, illustration for 'The Life of Christ', c.1886-96 (gouache on paperboard), Tissot, James Jacques Joseph (1836-1902)/Brooklyn Museum of Art, New York, USA/The Bridgeman Art Library
114(t) The Jewish Museum, NY/Art Resource, NY
115-116(t) Erich Lessing/Art Resource, NY
117-118 Michael Muir
119(t) © The Crosiers/Gene Plaisted OSC
119(b) Michael Muir
120(b) © The Crosiers/Gene Plaisted OSC
121 © Tom Stewart/zefa/Corbis
123(t) Erich Lessing/Art Resource, NY
123(b) © The Crosiers/Gene Plaisted OSC
124(t) Michael Muir
124(b) © The Crosiers/Gene Plaisted OSC
125(b) © William Hart McNichols
126(c) © PIZZOLI ALBERTO/CORBIS SYGMA
126(b) © Images.com/Corbis
127(t) Erich Lessing/Art Resource, NY
128 © The Crosiers/Gene Plaisted OSC
129 Scala/Art Resource, NY
130 Robert Korta
131(t) Erich Lessing/Art Resource, NY
132 Phil Martin Photography
133(t) Erich Lessing/Art Resource, NY
135 Michael Muir
137(tl) © The Crosiers/Gene Plaisted OSC
139 © Medford Taylor/Getty Images
140(t) © The Crosiers/Gene Plaisted OSC
140d(t) © Roger Ressmeyer/Corbis

UNIT 5:
141-142(t) © Sandro Vannini/Corbis
142(b) © The Crosiers/Gene Plaisted OSC
143(t) Alinari/Art Resource, NY
144(t) HIP/Art Resource, NY
146(t) Erich Lessing/Art Resource, NY
146(b) © Leif Skoogfors/Corbis
147(t) © Paul Barton/Corbis
148(tl) Frank Dicksee/Veer
148(t,rc) © The Crosiers/Gene Plaisted OSC
148(cl) © Araldo de Luca/CORBIS
149 Scala/Art Resource, NY
150 © The Crosiers/Gene Plaisted OSC
151(t) Michael Muir
153(t) © The Crosiers/Gene Plaisted OSC
154(t) © The Crosiers/Gene Plaisted OSC
155(t) © The Crosiers/Gene Plaisted OSC
155(b) Bildarchiv Preussischer Kulturbesitz/Art Resource, NY
156 Ray App
158(t) Erich Lessing/Art Resource, NY
159(b,a-b) © The Crosiers/Gene Plaisted OSC
159(b,d) © The Crosiers/Gene Plaisted OSC
159(b,e) © Catholic News Service
159(b,f) © Bettmann/Corbis
160(tl) © The Crosiers/Gene Plaisted OSC
161 Scala/Art Resource, NY
162(c) Ray App
163(t) © Library of Congress, Washington, D.C./Superstock Inc.
163(b) © Tony Freeman/PhotoEdit
164 Scala/Art Resource, NY
165(t) Scala/Art Resource, NY
166(c-e,g) © The Crosiers/Gene Plaisted OSC
167(t) Erich Lessing /Art Resource, NY
168(c,b) © The Crosiers/Gene Plaisted OSC

169 Erich Lessing/Art Resource, NY
170(t) Bill Wood
170(b) Erich Lessing/Art Resource, NY
173 Scala/Art Resource, NY
174a Cameraphoto/Art Resource, NY

SPECIAL SEASONS AND LESSONS:
175(t) © Newberry Library, Chicago/Superstock, Inc.
176 Julie Lonneman/SpiritSource.com
177 Scala/Art Resource, NY
178(t) © P Deliss/Godong/Corbis
178(bl-br) © The Crosiers/Gene Plaisted OSC
179(t) Biblioteca Nazionale Marciano (cod. marc. lat. 1, 77 (=2397), f. 26v ("Albero di Jesse")
179(bf) © The Crosiers/Gene Plaisted OSC
184(bl) © The Crosiers/Gene Plaisted OSC
186 © Scott Dalton/AP/Wide World Photos
187(tc) Kathryn Seckman
187(bl) www.AgnusImages.com
187(cr) © James Shaffer\PhotoEdit, Inc.
189(bc) Scala/Art Resource, NY
190(t) © The Crosiers/Gene Plaisted OSC
190(b) Scala/Art Resource, NY
191(t) Julie Lonneman/SpiritSource.com
194(bl) Queen of the Americas Guild
195(t) © Newberry Library, Chicago/Superstock, Inc.
196(tl) © Fine Art Photographic Library, London / Art Resource
196(b) © Ricco/Maresca Gallery / Art Resource
198 Michael Muir
199 © The Crosiers/Gene Plaisted OSC
200(br) © The Jewish Museum / Art Resource
201-204 Justin Wager

WHAT CATHOLICS SHOULD KNOW:
209(b) © The Crosiers/Gene Plaisted OSC
211 Greg Kuepfer
214 From Fourteen Mosaic Stations of the Cross © Our Lady of the Angels Monastery Inc., Hanceville, Alabama. All Rights Reserved
215(t) vario images GmbH & Co.KG/Alamy
216 Stock Montage, Inc./Alamy
219 Bob Daemmrich/PhotoEdit
222 Myrleen Ferguson Cate/PhotoEdit
224(t) The Jewish Museum NY/Art Resource NY
225(t) © The Crosiers/Gene Plaisted OSC
225(b) Jeff Greenberg/Alamy

LESSON PULLOUTS:
245(br) Bill Wood
246 Bill Wood
249(br) Scala/Art Resource, NY
254(b) © Proof Positive/Farrowlyne Assoc., Inc.
255(t) Kathryn Seckman
259(a) © SEF / Art Resource
259(c) © Corbis. All Rights Reserved.
259(d) © Photograph by Erich Lessing
259(e) © Photograph by Erich Lessing
259(f) © Corbis. All Rights Reserved.

Photos and illustrations not acknowledged above are either owned by Loyola Press or from royalty-free sources including, but not limited to: Agnus, Alamy, Comstock, Corbis, Creatas, Fotosearch, Getty Images, Imagestate, iStock, Jupiter Images, Punchstock, Rubberball, and Veer. Loyola Press has made every effort to locate the copyright holders for the cited works used in this publication and to make full acknowledgment for their use. In the case of any omissions, the Publisher will be pleased to make suitable acknowledgments in future editions.